D0097830

THIS ONE LOOKS LIKE A BOY

My Gender Journey to Life as a Man

THIS ONE LOOKS LIKE A BOY

LORIMER SHENHER

GREYSTONE BOOKS

Vancouver/Berkeley

Greystone Books Ltd.
greystonebooks.com

Cataloguing data available from Library and Archives Canada
ISBN 978-1-77164-448-8 (cloth)
ISBN 978-1-77164-449-5 (epub)

Editing by Jennifer Croll
Copyediting by Alex Kapitan
Proofreading by Stefania Alexandru
Jacket design by Will Brown
Text design by Nayeli Jimenez
Cover photograph courtesy of Lorimer Shenher
Printed and bound in Canada on ancient-forest-friendly paper by Friesens

Some names and identifying details have been changed to protect the
privacy of individuals.

Greystone Books gratefully acknowledges the Musqueam, Squamish, and
Tsleil-Waututh peoples on whose land our office is located.

Greystone Books thanks the Canada Council for the Arts, the British
Columbia Arts Council, the Province of British Columbia through the
Book Publishing Tax Credit, and the Government of Canada for support-
ing our publishing activities.

Canadä

For Dad.

CONTENTS

"I have chosen to change my appearance, something many people do in many ways. From my perspective, my gender has not changed; I have simply made its message clear."

JAMISON GREEN, *Becoming a Visible Man*

INTRODUCTION

THERE IS A line in one of my all-time favorite films, *Moonstruck*, where Ronny Cammareri (Nicolas Cage) tells Loretta Castorini (Cher), "Come upstairs! I don't care why you come!" I feel the same way about you, dear reader. I don't care why you're here, I'm just very glad that you are holding this book, and I thank you.

I am just one transgender man. I don't speak for everyone, nor are my experiences more universal than anyone else's. I can only speak for myself, although I'm sure some stories in this book will resonate for others like me.

Perhaps you've picked this up because you read my last book. You might be the parent of a child questioning their gender and you're looking for guidance. You could be an old fossil like me, wondering if it's too late in the game to find some happiness. Or you might think this gender transition stuff is just so much garbage, the product of an over-indulgent age.

Welcome, everyone. Sincerely. I mean it. We will never show ourselves if we don't talk to each other, even in our difference.

And if you're that kid reading these words underneath the covers with a flashlight, terrified of what you think you might be, this is for you.

There's hope for you.

Your journey won't be easy, but you will never know the heights you can reach if you don't stick around to find out.

I wrote this for you. I was you, once.

No one but you can know your inner world or your sense of self. No one can take that discovery from you. Some may try—out of a misguided notion of love, out of fear for you or themselves, in the name of whatever God they think they know the will of, or in the name of what they like to think is "normal" in this world. Let them try. Give them an honest hearing, but never let them kill your spirit.

Be strong.

If I made it here you can, too. I lived to tell my tale. And so will you.

LORIMER

1

TWO LINEUPS
(1964–1969)

—

MY EARLIEST MEMORY is of the first day of kindergarten. We were told to get into two lines: one for boys and the other for girls. This was the first time in my young life I'd been presented with such a choice, so I walked to the boys' line and quietly took my place. Our teacher, Miss Olson, stepped to the front of our two lines and surveyed us, counting to herself. She rested her kind gaze on me as she instructed all of us to get our coats on for some outside playtime.

As I fumbled with the buttons on my coat, she knelt down beside me and spoke softly, her words burning into my memory.

"Lorraine, is there a reason you didn't stand in the girls' line?" she asked, her eyes warm and caring. I knew it was safe for me to speak honestly.

"I'm supposed to be a boy," I answered. "I don't belong with the girls." She stayed like that, crouched down beside me for a few moments, her comforting hand on my shoulder.

"I understand," she said. "Do you think that could be something private you only share with really good friends?" She nodded encouragingly. "I am very happy to be your friend and I think it would be best for you to line up in the girls' line, but know in your heart how you feel." She smiled warmly. "Okay?"

I nodded and forced a small smile. In that moment, a few months' shy of five years old, I understood how it was. She was so kind to me. She knew I'd be pushed in a ditch if the other kids knew what was up with me.

MY PARENTS HAD braved a blizzard early one December morning to drive to the hospital for my birth. The evening before, as she'd sat in her sewing class, labor pains had gripped my mother. She and our next-door neighbor Sarah—her intrepid companion on various self-improvement courses such as Chinese cooking and knitting—had cut the night short and ventured home through the Calgary snowstorm, Mom wiping the fogged glass as Sarah drove, peering through the windshield. The sewing lessons never translated into any inherited stitching or mending expertise, but tales of Mom drinking copious amounts of stout while she was pregnant— thanks to a Dr. Spock recommendation for anemic expectant mothers— left me convinced I came by my love of beer and later alcohol troubles honestly.

I also credit my ability to fit in anywhere to Mom. Whether it was cooking or sewing classes with Sarah, annual summer family camping trips when my brother, my sister, and I were kids, or tolerating the eight-hour semiannual drives to spend a week with Dad's mother and many siblings in rural Saskatchewan, Mom did it with aplomb, even if her apparent enjoyment may have lacked sincerity. Had she participated in these activities grudgingly or as if they were beneath her, I might have defined her as a snob. But she dove in, if not quite with gusto, then at least with a good college try at merriment.

She'd been born into the role of outsider—she grew up in a rural Alberta town among farmers as the daughter of the bank manager, accustomed to "visiting" without pretension among the locals in her formative years. Perhaps it was her generation's awareness of manners, rendering her loath to rock the boat or draw undue attention to herself, but I believe she carried a comprehension of how unique she was and accepted that her differences would be more difficult to bear if she bemoaned her pedestrian life.

Occasionally, she'd lament a life unlived, telling me that she'd given up a lot for me, for us, without providing any specifics other than regret that she hadn't pursued her own journalism ambitions and sadness that the only career options widely available for women of her era were nursing and education. She had chosen education. She'd taught for four and a half years—one of them at the school where she met Dad—and decided it wasn't for her. Whatever dreams she may have had, she kept them to herself. The truth was, while we shared many traits, my mother loomed over me, a larger-than-life enigma. Much like a mysterious painting whose profundity I only superficially understood, I would spend my lifetime observing her, puzzling over her—sometimes squinting, other times with eyes wide open.

She was not warm, nor was she stone cold; my mother could best be characterized as English. She was born in Alberta to a sensitive, artistic Englishman and a genteel French woman who each were averse to overt displays of affection and self-disclosure. Mom towered in relief above the surrounding terrain, educated and well-read. A swan among hens, she settled right in at whatever farmhouse we were visiting, elegant even in shorts and a cotton blouse, sipping her rye and Coke with Dad's sisters and the wives of his many brothers, making lunch or dinner for the men while chatting about the kids, who played outside in the late summer heat. If my Saskatchewan aunts were Tom Sawyer's Aunt Polly, my mother was a hybrid of Peggy and Joan, pure *Mad Men* in style and bearing, as steely and smooth as they come.

Dad was the only one of his siblings to leave Saskatchewan. He was achingly shy, a quiet, sensitive man. As a youngster, he had stayed home to listen to the radio on Saturday afternoons while the rest of his family went out, tuning in to the Metropolitan Opera's weekly broadcast. When he met Mom, she couldn't get over his deep love and knowledge of the opera, or the fact that he'd developed it in his south Saskatchewan farmhouse kitchen. A moustache adorned his upper lip for almost his entire life, and I'd often get the impression it served as a curtain to hide the rare mischievous smirk he would allow himself. Thick glasses completed his look; his students were known to don joke shop Groucho glasses (complete with nose and moustache) en masse on the last day of school as a good-natured joke that never failed to crack him up. Our Calgary life stood in sharp contrast to the world of Dad's farming relatives. He worked as a junior high principal in the Catholic school system and Mom worked at home caring for Jake and me—and three years later, our little sister Katherine.

My parents worked hard to help our young family make it to each payday, like so many others did in bustling 1960s Calgary. Many of our friends and neighbors worked in education, medicine, and the trades, while others formed the foundation of Alberta's growing oil economy as company executives, lawyers, petroleum engineers, financiers, and rig workers. While we worked, played, studied, and lived alongside one another, families like ours never attained the kind of wealth our oil industry friends came to enjoy.

The blizzard long over, the four of us had driven home from the hospital that cold December to our recently purchased bungalow, tucked into the red Volkswagen bug that was soon replaced with a more family-sensible four-door Plymouth Valiant. Our neighborhood, Lakeview, was a new community perched atop the Glenmore Reservoir, a large lake on the city's western edge. Our house had a postcard-perfect view of the Rocky Mountains to the west out of our front room picture window, from which we could predict the day's weather by the state of the sky over the foothills.

The same year I began kindergarten, my father flooded our backyard to make an ice rink where my older brother Jake and I, age six and five, could play hockey. The surface looked huge to my tiny self, framed by two-by-sixes and lined with heavy plastic. I couldn't imagine it ever filling completely. I stood out there beside my dad in the freezing starlit night, bundled in our puffy down jackets, his gloved hands gently waving the hose back and forth across the ice, which was forming layer by layer. We'd take breaks to go inside and warm up every twenty minutes or half an hour. Sometimes, if we were lucky, there would be hot chocolate waiting for us. After several evenings and a weekend, the rink was full, and the ice solid.

Two nights before Christmas, the late-afternoon winter sky was pregnant with the promise of snow, the grey-white glow not quite cloud cover but definitely not clear. Anticipation hung in the air. Jake and I wobbled around the rink on the soft ankles of secondhand leather skates, leaning on our hockey sticks for support, squealing excitedly at the prospect of Santa's arrival. We jockeyed for the puck, tapping and wedging our sticks together playfully. Our parents watched us through the windows as they tended to Katherine. Jake and I played sports constantly and though each of us wanted to win, we were never rough or aggressive. But somehow, our skates became tangled and I felt myself falling backward, seemingly in slow motion, as the trees became the sky above me an instant before the back of my head struck the ice with a sickening *thud*.

No one wore helmets to skate back in those days. My woolen hat probably cushioned the blow to my head, but I don't remember anything. I don't know how many minutes passed before I opened my eyes, blinking at the sky spinning over me. Jake's blurry form hovered off to one side. I couldn't hear a thing. I lay there for some time, woozy, as a dreamlike revelation overtook me. *I'm turning into a boy*, I thought.

As I lay on the ice, oblivious to the cold and pain, I was gripped by a sudden realization that this was what I'd been waiting for, and I was awash with relief. Until then, I hadn't known it was something I longed for.

I wanted to squeeze my various bits to confirm that they had indeed morphed into boy parts, but I couldn't make my arms move. Nothing was moving. But I wasn't alarmed, and I wasn't afraid that I might be paralyzed or injured. I must have been semiconscious, but I vividly recall seeing my parents' faces come into view beside Jake's, their mouths moving, their hands gripping my shoulders. They must have been shaking me because my view of them jiggled back and forth. Still, I felt nothing.

Please let me look like a boy now, I begged whoever was responsible for this dream.

"Lorraine!" Dad's voice was like a canon, breaking the stillness of the fog encasing me. "Lorraine! Can you hear me?" He looked worried. I hoped it was because he could see I'd changed. I could feel him touching the back of my head gently.

"Ow!"

"Does that hurt?" Mom asked.

I nodded, wincing.

"Is your neck sore?" Dad asked, feeling around my neck and upper back. I shook my head vigorously for no. "Well, I guess that answers that," he smiled—a small, relieved smile. "How do you feel?"

"Dizzy."

"What happened?" Dad asked.

"We were just playing hockey and we got mixed up and she fell and hit her head on the ice," Jake spoke in a panicked rush. "It was an accident."

"I'm sure it was," Mom reassured him.

"Can you get up?" Dad asked. I desperately wanted to ask them if I looked any different, maybe even more like a boy,

9

but I worried that this wasn't a great idea. They didn't seem to have noticed. My spirits began to flag. "Are you still dizzy?"

"Uh-huh." Sadness enveloped me again. My head throbbed, but it didn't seem too bad. I realized that nothing visible had changed. I was still a girl on the outside. Dad gathered me up in his arms and carried me inside, easing me down on the couch. He removed my skates and snow clothes.

"You okay?" he asked. I nodded. "I'm just going to talk with your mom—it might be a good idea to have a doctor see you." I heard whispered discussions in the kitchen; they bustled around, spoke on the phone to someone. I stared out the living room picture window at the snow beginning to fall, the light fading from the short winter's day. My disappointment deepened, and I remembered our plan to watch *A Charlie Brown Christmas* that night on TV. I thought about Lucy pulling the football out from under Charlie Brown every time he prepared to kick it.

I am Charlie Brown.

An hour later I sat high on a doctor's table, dangling my legs over the side as Mom and a doctor talked in hushed tones near the door. I couldn't recall ever being in a hospital and wondered if this might be a place where they could help me turn my body into a boy's. It seemed like something that could get me in trouble if I asked. Something told me it was a big deal. Mom and the doctor finished their conversation and walked over to me.

"Sweetie, I'm just going to call your dad and let him know you're being looked at now. The doctor's going to check your head. I'll be right back," she said, giving my shoulder a squeeze.

"Okay." She was often at her best in real crises.

"Hi, Lorraine. I'm going to feel your head and neck a bit," the doctor said. "Okay?"

"Lori. I like Lori better," I told him.

"Oh, okay. Sure. Lori it is." He smiled as he palpated the back of my skull gently. "Hmm, there's a good bump here. Does that hurt?"

"A bit. Not too bad."

"Do you know if you sort of went to sleep a bit when it happened?"

"I dreamed I turned into a boy." He paused, looking at me as if for the first time.

"Oh," he said, feeling along the back of my neck. "That's quite an adventure!"

"I'm supposed to be a boy, but I'm not. Not on the outside."

"Okay." He held up a finger in front of my face. "Try to follow my finger with your eyes." I tracked his finger as it moved. "Do you feel sick in your tummy at all? Pukey?" I shook my head no. "That's good news." He reached for a light and shined it into each of my eyes. "Just follow the light for me, kiddo. That's it, good." I sat quietly as he wrote on my chart. "Alrighty, let's find your mom and tell her the good news."

Just then, Mom walked in, and I wondered if the good news could possibly be about getting my boy body. The doctor finished writing on my chart and smiled at my mom.

"Well, she's had a good bump, that's for sure," he said, patting me on the shoulder. "She's got a mild concussion."

"Okay," Mom said. She sounded businesslike and ready for directions. "What should we do?"

"Well, keep her up for a few hours tonight, maybe until you and your husband go to bed. Then wake her every two hours, check that she isn't nauseous or dizzy, maybe walk her to the bathroom."

"That sounds serious." Mom frowned.

"She'll be fine—it's just a precaution because very occasionally these bumps on the noggin can cause bleeding inside the brain. It's very unusual for such a light bump, but we like parents to keep an eye on them the first twenty-four hours. After that, if all looks normal, you can rest assured she's in the clear. If anything seems amiss, bring her back in right away."

All I heard was *A Miss*.

DAD DOGGEDLY DOCUMENTED each Christmas with his SONY Super 8 video camera. Grainy images of the annual nativity play Jake, Katherine, and I earnestly performed in the living room—transformed into a theater on Christmas Eve—are forever preserved in their handheld jerkiness. Katherine and Jake never failed to strike devout, pious postures, Katherine's face beatific and serene as she imagined Mary to be, and Jake serious and solemn playing the role I really wanted, a Joseph of few words.

Always the odd man out, I chose to inject comic relief into the nativity play, creating new, uproarious spin-offs of the Christmas story each year. In a zany frenzy, I'd trip and skip through each year's performance as some combination of Falstaff, Puck, Red Skelton, Tim Conway, and Sammy Davis Jr., doing my best to jazz up the age-old narrative. Jake and Katherine patiently allowed it, tenuously grasping my inability to take the play—or anything else—seriously.

One year, taking advantage of one of the few perks of being a principal, Dad borrowed several huge floodlights and three microphones from school for us to play with over the holidays and we used them to enhance our performance. That year, instead of the usual recreation of Mary and Joseph's journey to Bethlehem, we performed a concert as Peter, Paul, and Mary—the singers, not the Biblical figures—where we belted out an unforgettable version of "Leaving on a Jet Plane," along with several other of the trio's songs, bathed by the bright, hot stage lights as our parents shouted "Encore!"

Another Christmas, when we were temporarily living in Indiana while Dad was pursuing a graduate degree, we drove to Florida. Dad bought a Starcraft tent trailer, and he was eager to test it out over the holidays while traveling the US Southeast. Our ceramic farm animals and crèche remained back home in storage in Calgary, so Dad fashioned a nativity stable out of palm fronds, weaving them expertly as he sat at our picnic table. Katherine, who was four at the time, contributed her Gumby, Pokey, and accompanying rubber friends to fill out the nativity players—Gumby as Joseph; Pokey as the pregnant Mary.

Somehow during that Christmas in our tent trailer in Key West, Katherine became very ill. She lay on the bed that converted into the kitchen table, sweating and shivering with a fever of a hundred and four. Jake and I could feel our parents' fear as they hovered over her, Dad snapping his fingers in front of Katherine's dull, vacant eyes as she stared into space, unresponsive. I don't recall how she recovered, but she did, and that was the first time I feared someone in my family might die.

Katherine was a sweet, eager-to-please, sensitive little girl who loved to sing to herself and dance, with or without music. The idea that she might not live seemed horribly unfair and wrong to me. I looked back with guilt and shame on all the times I'd thought of her as a burden because she was younger and unable to keep up with the rest of the family. I struck a deal with God that humid Florida night, swearing to treat her better if only she would survive.

I made many such bargains with God over the years—it seemed greedy to ask for help without offering something of myself, like improved behavior. After my first confession, I understood the quid pro quo nature of the arrangement: I traded my sins in for acts of penance—at worst a few Hail Marys or Our Fathers—and all was forgiven. Surely, God could sort out some of my problems in exchange for a promise to be a better kid. I took to speaking to God directly each night in bed as I said my prayers, more out of habit than true belief.

I crafted a two-part nightly prayer. The first half was stock—a quick synopsis of all the people I loved and wanted Him to watch over for me, a list that rarely changed unless I added someone after careful consideration. Then, I'd move into the freelance portion of the prayer program. That part included whatever had come up on that given day that required specific attention. *God, please let me pass my science test* or *God, please let me have a good race on Saturday.* After Katherine's Key West fever, my requests changed because it occurred to me that I could leverage my good wishes and behavior into rewards. *God, please let me be a boy and I'll be nice to Katherine forever. God, please let me be a boy and I'll let Katherine play with my Hot Wheels.*

God, please let me be a boy and I'll do anything you ask me to.

2

THIS ONE
LOOKS LIKE A BOY
(1969–1974)

MY PATERNAL GRANDMOTHER—a stout, first-generation German Canadian woman, mother of seven, and the widow of Grandpa Shenher—would gesture at me and say to whoever was in earshot, "This one! Look at this one!" as if I were some strange two-headed fish she'd pulled off the line. "This one looks like a boy." She always said it as if I were a museum piece, a questionable stone sculpture, unable to hear, and I would think to myself, *See? Even she can see it! What the hell is wrong with this world? She has about thirty grandchildren; she knows a thing or two.*

My parents, brother, sister, aunts, uncles, and cousins uniformly ignored my Grandma's outbursts, as they would a loud

15

THIS ONE LOOKS LIKE A BOY

fart in a church service. She was lucid and alert in those days, but no one validated her words or the truth I knew she spoke, skipping past them like a flat stone on a still lake, moving on to other topics. Everyone heard. No one stopped what they were doing or saying and I have no memory of anyone meeting my eyes when she said these things. We all just moved on, pressed the lid back down over the boiling pot. That she saw something in me—this thing I sensed about myself—both validated and infuriated me. Since that moment back in kindergarten, I had sought out ways to distract myself from my secret struggle—knowing I was a boy, but living as a girl. The constant stress was a chronic condition, my "cross to bear," as my sixth-grade teacher Mrs. Brassard used to say about every challenge my peers and I encountered in class. As crosses went, this one was a doozy.

What made me like this? I often asked myself. While my gender journey likely began while I grew in the womb, my birth was otherwise unremarkable, according to my parents. Growing up, I had no idea that psychologists were debating how to classify and treat people like me. It would be years before the diagnosis "gender identity disorder" was added to the *Diagnostic and Statistical Manual of Mental Disorders* and decades before the 2013 *DSM-5* changed this diagnosis to "gender dysphoria," defined as the "marked incongruence between one's experienced/expressed gender and assigned gender." Both incongruence and distress must be present. People continue to debate whether a diagnosis of mental illness should be required in order to receive medically necessary health care, not to mention legal and human rights protections.

What I did know was that I'd emerged at birth looking like

an average female infant. I'm sure everyone assumed I would grow up without giving my gender a second thought, let alone entertaining the mental gymnastics of nature versus nurture to try to explain how or why I was *like this*.

I'll leave the debate over why people like me feel that our birth-assigned gender is incorrect to the geneticists, endocrinologists, psychiatrists, and developmental psychologists and say only this: there has not been one waking moment since that day in kindergarten that I haven't felt an all-encompassing, deep, intrinsic sense that I am male. I also would have given anything, *anything*, for this not to have been so—until I finally gave in and transitioned.

WHEN I WAS six, Dad took a paid sabbatical to attend the University of Notre Dame in South Bend, Indiana, and pursue a master's degree in Religious Studies. We rented our Calgary house out to a group of young teachers, packed up the car, and drove south across the United States to our temporary new home: a large old three-story house with an expansive yard filled with huge trees. Beyond the long backyard was a steep embankment, on top of which ran a train track. Early in the morning and late at night every single day, a train rumbled past our home, waking poor Mom each time. On the other side of the tracks, quite literally, was the area of town where less fortunate whites and a sizeable black population lived. We were strictly forbidden to go there and were never told why.

Home to the famed Notre Dame Fighting Irish football team, coached by the legendary Ara Parseghian, South Bend was a football-mad town and Dad—a sports fan who'd taken us to Calgary Stampeders games all through our youth—had a line on tickets. He took Jake and me, then aged seven and six, to several games that autumn, including the much-anticipated match against perennial rival Michigan State.

The game began with a successful touchdown drive by the Irish that sent the capacity crowd into paroxysms of glee. As Jake and I jumped up and down in celebration, I felt hands wrap my waist and lift me high into the air, across the tops of heads, over the crowd. Long before crowd-surfing or mosh pits became common, the fans of Notre Dame Stadium had a tradition of lifting people into the air and passing them hand-over-hand above the crowd. Just as I was losing sight of my family and beginning to feel afraid, I felt a hand firmly grasp my ankle, pulling me back. Without a word, Dad gripped my waist and placed me back down beside him in the stands, but I caught him nod and cross himself in the direction of Touch-down Jesus, the larger-than-life mural painted on the side of the campus's main library building visible beyond one end of the field.

Every morning during the 1971–72 school year, I paused to take in the imposing facade of Thomas Jefferson Elementary in South Bend before walking up the steps and entering my second-grade classroom, unaware that my school was embroiled in a desegregation battle between the US Department of Justice and public schools in Indiana. That August, Indiana Public Schools had been found guilty in federal court of practicing racial segregation. My school was desegregated for the first time that school year, and many opposed it vehemently. I was only aware of its effect on my friendships with Cedric and Ramona, two black kids in my class, because no one seemed to want us to spend time together.

Our teacher, Mrs. Gruber, worked diligently to separate us, even when we tried to team up for group work in the classroom. She repeatedly concocted reasons for why this wasn't acceptable—the three of us weren't close enough in height, we needed to be all girls or all boys, we needed to make friends with other kids "like us," we needed to be at the same reading level. It went on and on. None of the groups Mrs. Gruber formed mixed black kids with white kids. I sensed she didn't like me; more than once she had referred to me as a "troublemaker."

One morning after recess, Cedric, Ramona, and I ran into the classroom laughing, talking about the basketball game we'd just played. A few days earlier, Mrs. Gruber had placed our desks in side-by-side rows instead of traditional columns, and the novelty hadn't worn off yet. I ran in front of the desks, then vaulted over mine to sit down instead of taking the few extra steps to circle around the row. She descended on me like a lion on a hyena, wooden yardstick in hand. She wrenched me by the collar to the front of the row, bent me over, and shoved my face into my desk. She screamed out to everyone, "Class! This is what will happen if you don't obey instructions, if you don't stay in your places!" She swung the yardstick like a baseball bat, hitting me on the backside with her full weight behind it. *Whack! Whack! Whack! Whack!* I lost track of the number of hits. I heard gasps from my classmates. I fought not to cry out or show her how much it hurt. I distracted myself by wondering how a woman so old and spindly could move so fast.

"That!" *Whack!* "Was!" *Whack!* "The!" *Whack!* "Most!" *Whack!* "Unladylike!" *Whack!* "Display!" *Whack!* "I!" *Whack!* "Have!" *Whack!* "Ever!" *Whack!* "Seen!" *Whack!* "In!" *Whack!*

"All!" *Whack!* "My!" *Whack!* "Years!" *Whack!* "Of!" I braced for the next strike, but she paused. I waited for a *Whack!* "Teaching!" or *Whack!* "Beating Children!" The tension mounted.

"What are you doing?!" she finally screamed. I assumed she was talking to me and I dared not move or talk. The answer seemed obvious. *I'm letting you beat the poop out of me, Mrs. Gruber.* But then, a small voice spoke up. I recognized it as Ramona's.

"Nothing, Mrs. Gruber." I peeked up and saw Ramona standing at the door.

"Where do you think you're going?! You get back in your seat! NOW!" As Mrs. Gruber banged the yardstick down hard on the desk beside me and I jumped, I saw Ramona disappear out the door. Splinters of wood flew around us, which only angered her more. She yanked me up by my collar and addressed me. "You! Get back in your seat! If you *ever* do anything like that again, you will see much worse than this! I don't know how they do things in Canada, but your behavior is unacceptable!" I bit my lip and limped to my desk, tears leaking from the corners of my eyes. Jolts of electricity shot down my legs and up my back as I sat down on my bruised rear end and upper legs.

At home that night, I told my parents that Mrs. Gruber had hit me with a yardstick, but I didn't mention how hard or how many times, or show my welts and bruises.

"What did you do?" Dad asked.

"I jumped over my desk."

"Had she told you not to do that?"

"I guess so," I said, uncertain.

"Well, then, I guess you had it coming, didn't you?"

Dad hated the corporal punishment required by his job as a school principal, but in an era where hitting was condoned as necessary for proper discipline, he was expected to mete it out to students who disobeyed. His school board used a heavy rubber strap, about twice as wide as a typical ruler. At home, my siblings and I were spanked with a bare hand occasionally, and my parents trusted our teachers to dole out whatever punishment they deemed appropriate.

We never saw Ramona at school again after that day. We were all too terrified to ask why.

BACK IN CALGARY the following summer, our neighbors and friends eagerly waited for us as we pulled up in front of our house after our American adventure. Barbecues lit and beer cases in hand, they greeted us with a block party, welcoming us back home. We settled back into our relationships with friends; we were a year older, but little else had changed.

"You *have* to be Mary!" Corrine insisted to me. "Katherine's Laura, I'm Ma, and Melanie's always Nellie." The other girls stood around her, nodding in reluctant agreement to her casting for our version of *Little House on the Prairie*. Corrine was bossy and always organized our basement play. Disagreeing with her never went well for anyone. I felt she miscast herself as Ma. She was definitely a busybody Nellie Oleson.

"I'm Almanzo or I'm not playing," I demanded, arms folded, determined to play Laura's husband.

"Fine." Corrine threw up her hands. "We do need an Almanzo, but it'd be better with a real boy."

Melanie spoke up. "Lori's a good boy—she's good at it," she offered.

"Fine." Corrine moved to the blackboard and handed "Laura" some chalk. "Let's start with a lesson. Laura can be teaching us."

"This is dumb," I said. "Laura doesn't teach *us*, she teaches younger kids." I took off the brown vest and Dad's oversized work boots. "I'm going outside." I escaped up the stairs to find Jake—I felt more like I belonged when I played with him and our boy friends.

Since our return from South Bend, I'd begun to notice the group dynamics between the girls and the boys on our block. My neighbors Corrine and Melanie formed a tight group along with Katherine, each of them being no more than two years apart. Melanie was my age and we sometimes played together one-on-one, but if Corrine, Melanie, and I played together it seemed to spark conflict. I suspected Corrine was the cause, because when Jake and I got together with Corrine's older brother Jason, who was Jake's age, we spent hours together and no one ever fought, argued, or ran home crying.

I didn't understand it. I wished the girls would play sports recreationally, outside of the organized girls' leagues that existed for soccer, softball, and hockey. I didn't think deeply on the reasons behind it in those days; it simply seemed like the girls wanted something else, and I didn't know what it was or grasp that anyone could find play centered around sports lacking in any way.

Sports beckoned to me, and Jake was my willing partner. I was the Bernie Parent to his Bobby Clarke, the Jerry Rice to his Joe Montana, the pilot to his brakeman on our tobogganing adventures. We built our own skateboard decks, experimenting with different designs for a skiing-inspired course of skateboard slalom, an alternative to the half-pipe and freestyle events most skaters were doing. We took the bus across the city weekly with the boys from our street to ride the new skate park in an industrial warehouse run by a bunch of Dogtown wannabes.

As teens, we skied the notorious vertical drop of Mount Norquay's North American run until our legs turned to rubber and our woolens hung on us, soaked in sweat. We took over Dad's basement workshop each winter to tape our hockey sticks, sharpen our ski edges, drip PTEX into the gouges in their bases, and read *Ski Magazine* together as we glanced at the sky for any signs of snow. Ours was an easy partnership, free of the bickering and fights common among siblings. Jake was a gentle kid, much like our father; I was the feisty one, prone to more outward expressions of anger and frustration from which he would often talk me down. He never laid a hand on me aggressively or angrily.

The only physical confrontation I can remember between us as kids was when I punched him in the stomach, for reasons I can't recall. What I do remember was the ease with which his thin belly absorbed my fist and the mixture of shock, disappointment, and sadness on his face. I recall wondering at how he conveyed all those emotions to me in that briefest of instants. The idea that I could cause another person pain or hurt seemed unfathomable to me, yet here was my best friend—my brother—and I had hurt him. Years later, when I was twenty-five and trying to convey my gender struggle to my parents and siblings, he would tell me, "You're ruining our family." Only then would I understand how he must have felt that day years before when I punched him for no good reason.

We lived across the street from Clem Gardner Elementary School but attended St. Leo's, a Catholic school a few blocks away. Occasionally, we had days off that the Clem Gardner kids didn't share. On one such sunny, winter afternoon, Jake and I—no older than eight and seven—took to the front yard for a little tobogganing. We raced up and down the twenty-five-foot slope leading down to the sidewalk. To call it a hill was way beyond generous, but we piloted our thirty-inch-round red Super Saucers—disc-shaped plastic sleds—down the slight grade like it was the Matterhorn. Mom was inside with Katherine, now four.

On one successful ride, Jake slid onto the sidewalk just as a boy about his age was walking past on his way home from school, forcing him off the sidewalk to avoid getting hit. Jake stood up beside his saucer.

"Sorry," he said as he made his way back to our yard.

"Don't be such an egghead, stupid!" the boy shouted, spitting on the snow near Jake's boot. "Ya stupidhead!" Jake considered him briefly before passively continuing back to the top of the slope. I had watched the scene unfold from a few yards away, outrage growing in me like a tidal wave. Without any thought, I flipped my saucer upside down, drew my arm back in a Frisbee-tossing motion, and flung the disc with all my might. It dipped and weaved like a surface-to-air missile, the saucer's edge catching the boy right on the side of the head above the ear, taking his wool hat with it. He dropped like a shot moose, silent for several tense moments. Jake and I looked at each other in horror, then back at the boy. Suddenly, he bounced back to his feet, staring wild-eyed at me in stunned silence before tipping his head back and opening his mouth to emit a loud, cartoonish wail. I half-expected to see *WAAAAAAAAAAAH!* trailing behind him in the air. He turned on his heel, hat still in the gutter, broke into a sprint, and ran away up the street, shouting, "MOMMMMMMMMMMM!" which we heard long after he'd vanished from our sight. Jake set his saucer down, climbed aboard, and slid down the slope. I did the same, neither of us mentioning what had happened.

WE HARDLY SAW Dad during the week, except very early in the morning and late at the end of the day, when he'd walk in the door, still nattily dressed in a dark suit and tie after a long day of school or school board meetings.

His weekend clothes in those years were work wear, suited to a construction site, not any office or golf course. The scent of campfire, fermented grapes, and freshly cut lumber emanated from my father's ubiquitous green sweater; an olfactory roadmap of weekends and summers past. I don't remember my mother ever washing it, but it never smelled of sweat or anything foul—just Dad, his projects, and maybe a hint of Old Spice. On Sunday afternoons, to help him morph back into his Clark Kent persona as a school principal, I polished his dress shoes—several black pairs and one brown—for which I was rewarded twenty-five cents a pair. The feeling of the small silver toggle between my index finger and thumb remains with me, juggling the circular metal cap bearing the kiwi logo to just the right position for snapping the can closed, preserving the moisture for the next week. Shoe polish and that sweater; the building blocks of my dad. Hard work intertwined with and fueled by a love of detail, whether it be building a home, teaching high school calculus, or making wine.

As a youngster, I followed him around on weekends and during summers to auctions, lumber yards, his out-of-town garden plot, paint stores—whatever grand project he undertook beckoned my preteen self along to simply bask in his seemingly boundless knowledge and patience. At lunch, I would marvel at his hand, where there would have appeared a fresh cut that had been absent at breakfast. His hands mesmerized me: large, strong, and callused, but with the delicate fingers of a surgeon. Sometimes I would ask him how he got injured. He'd glance at the wound, noticing it for the first time.

"Oh, look at that. I must've caught it on something," he'd say, putting the cut to his mouth to clean the blood before returning to his sandwich. Whenever the wounds were mine, he'd have a look, find me a Band-Aid if necessary, then ruffle my hair or chuck me on the chin, telling me, "It'll be all gone by the time you get married." In early years, I'd laugh along with him at the absurdity of a kid my age ever getting hitched. As I grew older, he'd say the same thing when we'd roof together and I'd wince from the blisters on my shoulders, made by carrying loads of shingles up the ladder. His words about recovering before my wedding—intended to comfort me—would burden me with a sadness I couldn't understand the source of, a sense that I wouldn't be worthy of marrying, despite Dad speaking as though I was the most eligible girl in the world. In his eyes, why wouldn't I be? In his eyes, all of my injuries could be fixed by a kiss and a Band-Aid.

He'd begun studying at the University of Saskatchewan after high school with the goal of becoming a doctor. It wasn't until his funeral, many decades later, that I would learn that his father and mother disagreed about him continuing his studies; Grandpa Shenher wanted him to remain on the family farm, but my grandmother put her foot down and insisted Dad be permitted to pursue an education. Dad had three older brothers and Grandma Shenher argued they were more than capable—well, two of them were, and the eldest, a dedicated drinker and layabout, could be whipped into shape—and so it was that my dad became the only one in his family to obtain a university degree.

He'd hoped, after completing his undergraduate studies, to work for a few years as a teacher and save the money necessary to return to medical school, but he never did. While he did become a fine math teacher and school administrator, his talented hands never graced the medical profession, though he did put them to good use in woodworking and carpentry projects. I have no memory of him expressing regret about this or anything else in his life.

In Dad's world, you did what you needed to do without complaint and without thinking of yourself. A man did what was necessary to make a living, to feed his family, to support his kids, to serve his God. The idea of Dad having a midlife crisis or leaving us to pursue a life unlived seemed as ludicrous as him becoming an exotic dancer. He was quietly dutiful, never resentful, always generous, and happiest among family, students, and friends.

I'd watch his hands grip a metal razor and twist the handle, until—like magic—the top would open like a flower blooming, exposing the flat, double-edged blade inside. Deftly, he'd reach in and remove the old blade, replacing it with a new one without ever cutting his fingers. His face was another story, however.

Before the days when shaving cream came in aerosol cans, he would add some hot water to a little bowl, then whisk his shaving brush around it until a thick lather formed. Dunking the brush in, he'd reach over and dab it liberally on both of my cheeks. I knew what to do next. With three fingers together, I'd rub it around my face and neck, upper lip, and chin, sneaking peeks at him beside me doing the same, making sure I was getting it right. He would always take the last bit on the end of his brush and dab it onto the tip of my nose.

I'd try my best to mimic the upside-down U shape his mouth would make as he shaved his upper lip under his nose. I would use a wooden Popsicle stick as my razor, so I never had to dampen little scraps of toilet paper and dab them onto nicks the way he would when he cut himself, which was frequently. Even so, I'd imitate that, too, wanting to mirror the entire ritual as closely as possible. I'd scrape down on my face and up on my neck, just as he did, then take a washcloth and wet it thoroughly with warm water, rubbing it all over my face to remove the excess cream. My favorite step came last: clapping a splash of Hai Karate aftershave together in my hands before slapping both cheeks gently with it and emitting a satisfied "Ah," just as Dad did when he finished.

As I grew, I tried to copy everything he did—subtle mannerisms, how he held a hammer, the way he bit his lip when measuring a piece of wood—careful not to appear obvious. He possessed one habit I couldn't bear: smoking. His smoking was the one thing we could complain about that would get a rise out of him, as though it represented the only harmless indulgence he allowed himself that wouldn't interfere with being a good husband and father.

I can't think of anything else he did that we complained about, except his bad jokes. But on summer vacations, bombing down the highway in our '65 Valiant, his cigarette ashes blowing into the back seat from the driver's window, I found the one trait of his I never wanted to emulate. As a kid with allergies likely caused by the "cancer sticks," I hated it.

I imagined myself as a man who would not smoke.

3

RENÉE
(1975–1979)

THE HEADLINE SCREAMED: "WOMEN'S WINNER WAS A MAN!"

I huddled over the evening sports section as I read, afraid someone in my family would notice my keen interest. Devouring the sports section wasn't unusual for any athletics-minded twelve-year-old and no one in my family batted an eye, but I was so scared of being discovered that I grabbed the paper and ran with it into the bathroom, locking the door. Eyes wide, I absorbed the details of the story: A successful middle-aged New York doctor had voluntarily gone through sex reassignment surgery from male to female and then competed in the 1976 La Jolla Tennis Tournament Championships as a woman. *There are other people like me.*

My breath came in short gasps. I needed to know everything about what Renée Richards had done. That night and the next, I did not sleep. Determined to learn more, I decided to search the library for information. Our junior high school library contained a substantial and varied collection of books; maybe I could find something there. I searched, using the Dewey Decimal System card catalog as I'd been taught, but information on Renée Richards eluded me. I had no idea what words to use in my search other than her name. Shame dogged my every step, and with it a misguided worry that Melvil Dewey—the man my peers and I had learned created the system—would be disturbed that I was using his book classification system to find writings on such a sordid topic. My familiar sense of myself as unlovable and downright wrong hovered nearby, accompanying me whenever I allowed myself to think too much about pursuing a *sex change*.

The librarian, an older woman I'd always found to be helpful in the past, approached me in the stacks.

"Can I help you find something, dear?" she asked.

"No, thank you," I answered, thinking, *Would you call me dear if you knew about me?*

"Is it about sports?" she persisted gently, as we stood in front of a shelf of sports books.

"Yes! Hockey!" I exclaimed. "I'm looking for a book about Bobby Orr."

"Hmm. Let's see." She picked through several books before pulling out *Bobby Orr and the Big Bad Bruins.* "Here's one." She handed it to me. I pretended to study it carefully, although I'd read it before.

"Perfect. Thank you." I followed her back to the circulation desk.

"I think there's a newer one about him out, but we don't have it. Check the bookmobile, though. It comes tomorrow."

I slept fitfully that night, reliving my failure over and over in my mind. I knew I should have asked her if she had anything on sex changes, but felt certain she'd know it was because I wanted one. I formed a plan and slept for a couple of hours.

The bell rang and I ran out to the bookmobile, which came to our school once a month with its ever-changing variety of books. The converted yellow school bus repurposed as a library on wheels was jammed full, with little space for browsing. I summoned my courage and approached the librarian, a younger man of about thirty. I blurted out my prepared statement.

"Um, I'm doing a project in school about discrimination in sports and I saw this story about a man who changed into a woman and how they let him—her, I guess—play in a tennis tournament. I'm wondering if her life story is here?" I allowed my eyes to meet his. "Her name is Renée Richards."

"That's a toughie," he answered, walking down the aisle, looking up and down. He stopped and thumbed through a section of books. "These are the sports biographies, and I don't see anything here on a Renée Richards, but..." he walked to another section and pulled out a hardcover book. "This might give you some good information," he said, passing it to me. I read the title: *Christine Jorgensen: A Personal Autobiography*. I frowned, looking at the cover, which featured a photo of a woman's face, framed by the remnants of a torn piece of paper. It felt as though he were passing me a message in code. I thought he might tap the side of his nose like I'd seen in a spy movie once. He didn't.

"Okay, I'll take this one."

Huddled underneath the covers in bed that night, flashlight in hand, I read the story of Christine Jorgensen, a Danish

American former US Army serviceman and one of the first people to undergo gender reassignment surgery, in the early 1950s. I don't know what shocked me more: that such liberation was possible or that it had happened over twenty years before I read about it.

I closed the book. I lay there, a Catholic kid in mid-1970s Calgary, tears streaming down my face. *I can never do it. This will never happen for me.* I berated myself silently for opening this can of worms, for picking this scab, for allowing myself to hope—even for the briefest of moments—that my life could be set right. It felt like I'd opened a gift meant for someone else. I couldn't figure out which hurt more: enduring the jolts of disappointment after glimpses of happiness or burying my dream of living the life I wanted.

MADAME DUBOIS COUNTED out rectangular name plates made of card stock and handed them out to the rows of students in my French class. I sometimes imagined Madame Dubois being the same person as my maternal grandmother, Marie Antoinette Royal, or "Toni," as she was known to those closest to her, who had died of cancer when I was six. I vaguely remembered her kindness toward me, her teaching me French words. Still, I didn't pick up much French before she passed away. Most of us in this class were beginners, but we had learned the basics, such as colors and numbers, quickly. Soon, the paper cards made their way down the rows, and I took mine.

"*Alors*, students," she began, "we will now make ourselves name plates to announce our French names." Murmurs of excitement and uncertainty filled the room.

"Ah, *bon*," she smiled. "It is exciting, *non*? You will address each other in this class using only the first name you choose for yourself today. This is your French name. *Votre prénom Français*." She walked to the overhead projector and turned it on to reveal a slide of French names—one list of boys' and another of girls'. Immediately, the name "Sebastian" drew my attention. Just as quickly, I realized I couldn't choose it. Resignedly, I focused on the girls' list, hoping for a neutral name like Kelly or Lindsay, but there were none to be found. My friend Lynn leaned over and whispered in my ear.

"Hey, you can use 'Lorraine.' You're lucky." I shook my head, indicating I disagreed. "How come?" she frowned.

"I'm gonna go for something different," I said casually. Internally, I recoiled the way I always did at the mere sound of my first name, which I'd informally shortened to Lori years before. My parents had often told the story of how they'd been certain throughout Mom's pregnancy that I would be a boy and had already chosen *Peter* for my name. When I was born, they'd briefly considered Joanne—Dad's name was Joseph and Mom's was Suzanne—or Josephine, after Dad's twin sister. But, in one of those name-your-baby parenting fails, they inexplicably settled on Lorraine, despite neither of them knowing anyone named Lorraine.

I wrote "Renée" on a scrap of paper and passed it to Lynn. She raised her eyebrows and nodded approval. She wrote on the paper and passed it back to me. I opened it to read "Brigitte." I gave her a thumbs-up.

Our family friends, the Smiths, had a daughter named Renée far younger than me. A shy, quiet blonde, she struck me as a girl I should model myself after—except for the blonde part, since my hair was sandy-colored. My plan also didn't work in another key way: Renée Smith wasn't into sports.

I made an executive decision that my Renée would be a sporty girl. In the '70s of my youth, it was clear to me there were very rigid definitions of girl and boy; female and male, but I didn't fit into either of them. I observed others working hard to fit into them, and I saw a few examples of boys in my class who were brutally treated because they were "soft" or "weak" in comparison to the rough and tumble "normal" boys. There was no space to be a sporty girl or a sensitive boy in those days. Gender roles were etched so deeply into my peers and me from birth that I still carry many of those attitudes with me today and have to work to confront them.

While I knew that hobbies and activities didn't make a person a boy or a girl, as a boy going through life as a girl I felt I had to pick my spots. Making my Renée sporty was a political move, my stab at a world I thought should exist for me to test out, even if ultimately it might not end up a fit for me. Negative attention made me intensely uncomfortable and aware of my thin skin, and I feared that if I acted like myself, I'd be discovered as the imposter I was. On the other hand, I had a sense that I needed to act bravely so I could feel less miserable in those days of severe gender rigidity, and sports were my salvation. Such was the balancing act of my young life.

"Renée" would be my alter ego; I would become Renée. She would represent the girl I wished I could be, the girl comfortable in her gender—comfortable as a tomboy or as androgynous—who would make all the female puzzle pieces fit and take away my longing. I wrote "Renée" on the card and added a small drawing of a horse, the way I'd seen other girls in class do. As Renée, I would fake it until I made it.

THE DESMONDS WERE my parents' good friends and went to our church. Mr. Desmond worked as a school principal in the Calgary Catholic School District along with my father. The two eldest of their five children—Kerry, a close friend and classmate of my brother Jake, and their only daughter Laura, a year behind me—went to our school. I didn't know any of them well, but what I did know was that they were always kind, circling the periphery of my community and family. I'd never had reason to give them much thought until one Sunday at church.

The midcentury modern architecture of St. James Church appealed to me. I imagined the smooth, white vaulted ceilings, skylights, and few ornate furnishings to be the result of the mysterious Second Vatican Council I'd heard my parents discussing at various times—an apparently tectonic shift in papal ideology that I didn't grasp, nor care to have anyone explain to me. I did know that it had loosened some of the rules we were supposed to live by—we seemed to have fish less frequently for Friday dinner, for one. The Church remained a puzzle to me and older, dank, traditional cathedrals only reinforced the feeling of darkness and mystery surrounding the religion I was born into.

I thought religion was supposed to be a comfort in people's lives, but ours didn't feel like that to me. Shadows and dark corners lurked everywhere, literally and figuratively, a powerful energy I sensed whenever I entered those "holy" confines. The musty smell and the slight chill in the air gave the impression that these interior spaces were not for exploration by outsiders. Even as a very young child, I knew I was an outsider.

The Desmonds sat in their usual pew one section to the left of where my family regularly sat. While some parishioners never strayed from their preferred places, we drifted around a general area about a third of the way back from the front, with no strong preference for either side—squatters among the permanent pew residents.

I felt a small pang of annoyance as I watched the altar boys, some of them friends of mine, lighting candles. I found church excruciatingly boring. I hated figuring out what to wear and thought perhaps wearing the cassock of the altar boys would get rid of that hassle, as well as saving me from boredom during Mass. Our church didn't allow altar girls, which I thought was stupid, because other Catholic churches in Calgary did. But what I really wanted was to be an altar *boy*.

"Did you see Laura's new haircut?" Mom whispered to me during the opening hymn. I located the Desmonds and saw Laura sporting a short, stylish cut—the sassy wedge many young girls and women had recently begun to wear, popularized by figure skater Dorothy Hamill. My stomach tightened. Sitting there with my shoulder-length, quasi-shag mop, reminiscent of mid-1970s David Cassidy, I knew exactly where this would go. For the rest of the service, I stole glances at Laura, my newly-appointed nemesis. It took exactly four seconds into our drive home for my mother to mention it.

"That is a really smart haircut Laura has there," she said. Faint, distracted murmurs of affirmation came from the others.

"Mm-hmm."

"You see a lot of girls with that sexy, short pixie these days," she went on. I cringed. My mom had used the words *sexy* and *pixie*—horrifying in and of themselves. *Pixie* reminded me of some fairy or sprite and *sexy* sounded plain yucky referring to a girl my age. I waited for what I knew had to be coming.

She turned in her front passenger's seat to look at me in the back.

"You should get your hair cut like that," she said with authority. "It would draw attention away from your chin."

"I like mine how it is," I replied. *And what's wrong with my chin?* I refused to give her an opportunity to tell me. The truth was, I didn't love my hairstyle; I wished it were shorter, but people already frequently called me *him* and *he*. This frustrated and upset me, not because they were wrong, but because I knew they were right. If I cut my hair short, I'd look so much like a boy that the shame I felt over the universe's big screwup would kill me. *Renée wouldn't cut her hair that short.*

Shame and embarrassment burned on my face enough as it was. *I don't want to be seen as a girl who looks like a boy, I want to be seen as the boy I am.* When others acknowledged that boy in me, a split second of euphoria gave way to a crushing weight of disappointment and injustice. It seemed easier to avoid being put in that position and try my best to look like a girl, since my parts seemed to dictate that that's what I was.

"It's smart and sporty; you'd find it much easier to take care of," Mom pressed.

"Yeah, no thanks." She turned back to face the road.

"I think a pixie cut would really suit you," she continued. I stared out the window, a giraffe in a world of barnyard animals.

Over the next year, I saw Laura Desmond and her haircut everywhere. Her hairdo bore the hallmark of my failings, looming large as the symbol of my gender dysphoria. If I saw her in the school hallway, I'd duck into the washroom or linger in the gym to avoid her. Her hair became the token of all that I feared because I knew that cutting my hair the same way would reveal my hidden shame to the world. It seemed so pointless. *There's nothing I can do to fix this.*

"Do you want to go to Mass tonight with me or tomorrow morning with Dad?" Mom asked a few weeks later. Saturday evening Mass was a welcome recent development, giving me a fifty-fifty chance of avoiding Laura Desmond each week. I began my mental calculations. *Were the Desmonds likely to be there? How often have I seen Laura at Saturday Mass? Is it better to go with Dad because he never mentions Laura's hair?*

"I think I'll go tomorrow," I replied.

"I thought you liked going on Saturday."

"I do, it's just that . . ." I glanced at the dog lying in his usual spot on the floor. "Riley hasn't had a walk today and I thought I'd take him before dinner." Mom frowned slightly at the dog.

"Fine, as long as you go to church." She grabbed her purse and walked down the stairs and out to the garage.

THE ANNUAL BACK-TO-SCHOOL shopping trip with my mom to Calgary's Chinook Centre Mall filled me with anxiety and despair, and featured more than a few shouting matches in the clothing aisles over what clothing was appropriate for me to wear. We both agreed that this year, the summer before tenth grade, would be the last time she would take me shopping. Next year, I could go on my own and choose what I wanted.

Secure in the knowledge that I only had to get through this one last trip, I endured Mom's snide remarks and sarcastic comments about the wrongness of the clothes I preferred, focusing on my pending freedom. Mom patrolled one side of the aisle separating boys' and girls' wear, me the other, each defending our chosen theater of war. As I picked out boys'

Levi's and sweaters, Mom spoke up, her tone overly practiced and a little shrill in an attempt to sound casual. "We should probably get you a little training bra, something with some support," she said, eyes avoiding mine as she fingered some lace blouses.

"Uh, I don't have any breasts," I answered truthfully. "I don't need one." My body had been very slow to develop and I hadn't even had a menstrual period yet. I wouldn't until I was eighteen. *This one. This one looks like a boy.*

For the last several weeks I'd cursed myself daily after asking her why my chest hurt. I'd been climbing over a fence during a hide-and-seek game on our street—an intensely competitive nightly battle involving at least ten kids, spanning more than five summers—when my chest pressed against the wood as it always did and I felt some tenderness, a bit like sore muscles. Her excitement had shocked me. "Oh, that means you're getting breasts," she practically sang.

That same joyful, celebratory propaganda had dripped from a thinly veiled ad they showed us in school called "Now You're a Woman" or something like that, made by Kimberly-Clark. All of the sixth-grade girls had been herded into a room to watch it, separated from the boys, who watched their own film. We were strictly warned not to talk to the boys about our film and they weren't to discuss theirs with us. We were given sample packs of menstrual pads at the session's end. Watching the film, I'd felt as grossly out of place as I now did in the women's foundations department.

"Don't be silly," Mom scoffed. "You go pick one out—try it on first, you can't tell by looking—and I'll meet you over by the leotards." She pressed twenty-five dollars into my hand and hustled off before I could protest. I stood there, frozen, certain her request was as ludicrous as sending my little sister off to buy a jock strap. It felt that foreign. Finally, I convinced myself that if I just sucked it up and grabbed a bra, I'd be out of there and she would be appeased, and I would never actually have to wear it.

I crept into the women's foundations department like a ninja on an assassination mission, certain someone would stop me and demand credentials proving I was female. I imagined a salesperson calling the police, who would haul me, the creepy boy in women's foundations, off in handcuffs. If I could have belly-crawled to avoid drawing attention, I would have. *Women's foundations? What the hell is a foundation other than a concrete structure holding up a building, or a charitable organization?* I whispered under my breath. *It's underwear. It's just frigging underwear.*

I skulked around the bras—big ones, padded ones, flowered ones—and tried to find something intended for someone who didn't need or want a bra. Glancing around me, I saw women— many at least sixty years old—with huge breasts to restrain, sifting through bins and boxes of undergarments. I imagined within this secret society there existed some mother/daughter bra-shopping ritual, and I swore I would never participate in this with a friend, let alone my own mother. *Get me outta here.*

Deciding the buxom grandmas were not going to lead me to training bras, I struck out for another wing of women's foundations. With fewer mushroom colors and more bright tones, this seemed like a better place to find something my mom would approve of. Within minutes, I found myself in line waiting to pay for a tiny piece of white cotton sporting one microscopic flower between two minute triangles that were intended to cover breasts—thirty-two inches, no cups to speak of. I held it tucked under one armpit, dreading the moment I would have to speak to the cashier. I felt sorry for the aged woman in front of me as she struggled with her purse; hands shaking, back stooped, blue veins visible. *Why can't we hire people to do this?* I was next up.

I heard two voices whispering behind me in line. Until now, I had deliberately avoided eye contact with anyone, but I glanced surreptitiously behind me to see who was speaking. As I strained my peripheral vision in ways I previously hadn't known possible, I heard one of them say to the other, "What does *he* need with a bra, anyway?"

"I don't know," her friend—or more likely daughter—answered with a sniff. My cheeks burned from the fire of embarrassment and misunderstanding. I stepped up to the clerk, who eyed me with suspicion. *Note to self: women's foundations is a snake pit.*

"Yes?" she raised her eyebrows at me, not looking at the mini Maidenform number in my sweaty hand.

"I'll take this one," I choked out.

"Is this a gift?" she asked with a smirk, pretending to be helpful.

"No."

"Because if it is, I can give you a receipt so she can return or exchange it if it isn't right," she persisted, seeming to delight in my growing discomfort.

"It's fine," I said, handing her the scrunched-up twenty-dollar bill, avoiding her eyes and trying not to give her the satisfaction of knowing she got to me, although I'm sure I was unsuccessful. I grabbed my change and walked away quickly, shame boring a hole in my breastless chest as I prepared to meet my mother and endure her delight over my purchase.

Bonding over traditionally female activities—the "sisterhood," as I thought of it—soon claimed most of my girlfriends. Backyard adventures and tennis matches with Melanie and Lynn changed to "talks" in their bedrooms, despite my unsuccessful efforts to steer the activities outside and toward sports. They preferred lounging around, sampling the newest Lip Smacker flavors, dabbing Love's Baby Soft behind their ears, while thumbing through the latest *TigerBeat* magazine with its full, glossy, poster-sized inserts of the Bay City Rollers and Donny Osmond. Gone were the days when my friends wanted to sing like Laurie Partridge or shake a tambourine like Tracy; now everyone wanted to be Keith's girlfriend. This sea change left me strategizing to maintain my cover.

Writing those words now, I'm struck by how conscious, how calculating my actions sound in hindsight. The tug of war between being my true self and fitting in with the group of girls to which I belonged—unfathomably, it seemed to me—raged constantly in my head. The effort to suppress my male self burbled like molten lava under the surface of my consciousness, consuming an enormous amount of my energy, but I had never known anything else.

"Have you got yours, yet?" Lynn asked me one day as we luxuriated in her room.

"My what?" I asked, lazily tossing one playing card after another at her garbage can.

"Your period—or, as Jolene likes to call it, 'the curse.'" She nodded in the direction of her sister's bedroom.

"Uh-uh, you?"

"Not yet." Lynn sat up on the bed, pulling her legs in close to her chest. "I don't really get the girls who act all excited about it, you know?" She frowned, shaking her head. "Like, you bleed all over the place once a month for the funnest years of your life. How is that exciting?"

"I dunno," I mumbled. "It doesn't seem too great to me, either." I thought of my mother's promise to get me "a little belt" when the time came, referring to the uncomfortable belts that had been used to hold the sanitary pads of her era. Mom was suspicious of tampons, which were new to the market. She expressed vague concerns about infections and protecting a girl's virginity, both of which I discouraged her from elaborating on. *How would I run or play in a belt?* I had never summoned the courage to ask her, instead hoping I would magically be spared my period when the great cosmic error of my gender was discovered. I envisioned medieval buckles and locks, metal clanging against me as I skateboarded.

"Do you think other girls don't want it?" Lynn asked earnestly.

"For sure," I said, but the only person I was sure of was me. "I'd rather not get it at all." But Lynn had made me aware of something I'd never considered: If regular girls like her didn't want their periods, could there be more people like me than I realized? "Do you ever wish you didn't get boobs?" I ventured.

"No way!" Lynn shouted, bounding off the bed to stand in front of her large mirror. She eyed her chest—already a 36c— appreciatively. "I'll be able to nurse a whole family with these suckers!" Lynn often spoke of her wide hips and large breasts as perfect for childbearing—an unfathomable act I couldn't

imagine myself ever doing. I slumped deeper into the bean-
bag chair I sat in. She glanced at me, an afterthought. "Do you
not want to get boobs?"

"I don't really care either way," I lied, trying to sound casual.
"At this rate, it's looking like I won't, anyway."

"Oh, you'll get them," she said reassuringly. "Every girl
does, eventually."

I sought solace with my boy friends, feeling secure in the
way I belonged with them. Where other girls didn't seem interested in playing with them, the boys continued to include me
and never spoke badly of girls in front of me or made me feel
like they didn't want me there. I felt very protective of girls,
knowing how it felt to go through life treated as one, even if I
secretly wasn't one. Some of the other boys in our neighborhood didn't treat girls as kindly.

One year, Melanie and I shared a paper route. Every weekday after school and on Saturdays, we'd gather around our
route manager's garage awaiting the delivery of the *Calgary
Herald* before loading our bags with papers and walking our
routes under their heavy weight. All of the other paper carriers
were boys, while Melanie and I were a team of two. I noticed
how different these boys were from my friends when several
of them dominated the conversation, spoke poorly of girls, and
stuck to other off-color topics.

When I hung out with my friends who were boys, we'd ride
Sidney's backyard half-pipe for hours, hanging around talking
skateboarding and trying new tricks. But as my middle school
years drew to a close, so, too, did my place with the boys. One
Sunday afternoon, I walked out of Sidney's house after using
the washroom and right into the middle of a conversation.

"*Then* she just..." Donald stopped mid-sentence when he saw me. Donald and I were neighbors, school peers, and church-mates and had played together since we were babies. Our siblings were friends and our parents close. He shuffled awkwardly, glancing at Rob, another lifelong friend and schoolmate. Sidney skateboarded rhythmically up and down the sides of the half-pipe, staring fixedly at his feet.

"What?" I asked, grabbing my board and standing on it. I knew he hadn't been talking about me because there'd been something a little lurid in his tone, a gleam in his eye I knew I could not be responsible for.

"So, anyways," Donald stammered, "there was a—well, so that's what I'm gonna do my project on." Rob nodded enthusiastically, playing along.

"Cool. That sounds rad!" he said.

"You think his school project is *rad*?" I asked. They nodded, too vigorously. I knew they hadn't been talking about school. This was a weekend, and these were thirteen-year-old boys. My throat clenched a little and I felt like I might cry if I thought any more about what they could possibly be excluding me from. And so I got on the half-pipe. Sidney stepped off to watch me as I rode as if possessed, climbing higher and higher up the plywood, moving from fakies to rock-to-fakies to rail grabs and stalls. I pulled off moves I'd never nailed before.

"Whoo! Give 'er, Lor!" Rob yelled. I heard the others hooting their approval. *They're such good guys. They didn't mean to exclude me; they have no idea I'm really one of them.* My board thundered up and down the ramp, and I grabbed the top rail so often my hands became sore, my thighs burning. Still, I rode higher and harder. *This is it*, I thought. *Nothing's the same, everything's changing.* Finally, I began to slow, no longer fighting for height, resigned to gravity and my own physical limitations. Accepting what was.

"Holy, that was wicked," Donald marveled as I stepped off the ramp. "You're sweating like crazy!"

"You shredded," declared the usually laconic Sidney.

"Yeah," I shrugged sheepishly, grateful I was no longer on the verge of tears. "I should probably get going."

"Me, too," Donald said, kicking up his board. We said our goodbyes to the others and walked the several blocks back to our street, our conversation easy and uneventful. Almost like normal—but I knew it would never be this easy again.

That summer, the hormonal magma of my loosely associated group of boy and girl friends collided, creating new bonds and solidifying others. The games we played morphed from Easy-Bake Oven and football to truth or dare and a kissing game we dubbed "Races" where a pair of one boy and one girl would run around the yard we were gathered at and kiss when out of sight of the group. The pair would run off for a minute or two—from the backyard to the front and then back again—while the remainder of us sat around and talked, arousing no suspicion if a parent were to come outside for any reason.

No one forced anyone to participate, although, looking back on it, the game was rife with teenage peer pressure and performance anxiety. I may have been the only one who cared about running fast in between the make-out portions of the game. I once suggested we time the racing couple, but the others laughed it off, not believing I was serious. Lynn raced with Rob, Melanie with Donald, and I was paired with Alvin, a nice—albeit quirky—lifelong member of our gang with poor handwriting but surprising kissing prowess.

Until then, I had felt neutral and resigned about my own sexuality. Kissing Alvin produced a strange throbbing between my legs, but still, nothing about the experience made me want to be his girlfriend. I noticed boys and found them attractive, but much of my admiration lay in wanting to look like them. I really liked Donald, but this was based far more on mutual interests than attraction. When the time came, though, it seemed to me that he would be the logical boyfriend choice.

I was so sexually repressed and convinced that my attraction to girls was really admiration of their femininity that it never occurred to me that I might be a lesbian—I didn't even realize that was a life option. I understood enough to know that lesbians were women who liked women, but I felt sure I was destined to become a man and a husband to a woman one day. My sexual longings were all focused on an imaginary future where I existed in a male body.

At that age, my friends and I were inhibited, sheltered Catholic kids. Sex rarely came up in conversation, even among my closest friends. We had no language to describe sexual orientation, that there might be options in terms of who we were attracted to, gender-wise; nor did we have any way of describing gender identity, one's internal understanding of one's own gender. Gender was never questioned; it was seemingly immutable for everyone but me. *Lezzie* and *fag* were slurs I occasionally heard in the schoolyard, but more as general insults than loaded put-downs.

I had never paused to consider what the life of a lezzie or fag looked like or meant for such people romantically. My imagination held them fixed in the schoolyard into infinity, stuck in a kind of purgatory of junior high taunting. In the Catholic, conservative Alberta of my 1970s youth, nobody talked about gay people, let alone any LGBTQ role models.

Meanwhile, transgender people were strictly the stuff of circus acts.

4

THE POLISH STUFF
(1979)

I **GLANCED AT** the large Dairy Queen clock: 6:45 PM. Fifteen more minutes until the next phase of my Friday night plan. I was fourteen years old and working my first real part-time job. As I cleaned the deep fryer and bleached the counters, Lynn exited the men's washroom, bucket in hand.

"Men are so gross," she lamented, as she did every shift we worked together. Our boss's creepy son leered at Lynn's breasts whenever he could and always assigned washrooms to her before leaving for the day. "You almost done?"

"Yeah," I answered, spraying the fry area with degreaser and wiping it down. "What time should we come over?"

"After eight," she replied. "When do your parents go out?"

"Their concert starts at eight, so they'll be gone by seven thirty."

"Perfect. James bought a ton of beer. I've already snagged some and put it in the basement fridge for us. Is Melanie coming?" She slipped off her DQ uniform and replaced it with a snug sweater. I changed too, eyes resolutely down, as always.

"She has to come—the only way I can go is if I sleep over at her house so my parents won't know. They'd never let me go to a party without the parents home."

"No, that's fine. I like her." Lynn set the alarm, locked the back door, and we exited into the cool, crisp October evening.

Melanie's family was out that night when I came to call for her. She gestured for me to come in.

"Let's hang out a bit here first," she suggested.

"Okay," I shrugged.

"Do you want a little drink?"

"Sure. What have you got?" I asked, trying to sound like my dad. I hovered over Melanie while she peered into her parents' liquor cabinet.

"Wanna try this?" She pulled out a forty-ounce bottle of clear liquid with an incomprehensible label. "It's the Polish stuff." Rumored to be over 170 proof, revered and spoken of in hushed tones by the adults on our street, "the Polish stuff" was a potent vodka served on the most special of occasions and even then only in thimble-sized glasses, sipped with excruciating slowness.

Melanie pulled out two scotch tumblers and filled them with three fingers of the Polish stuff. "I usually add some water to mine," she advised matter-of-factly as I followed her to the kitchen sink. We each added a splash of water and slammed it back, eyes watering, throats aflame.

"Gahhhhhhh," I gasped. Melanie smiled.

"Good, huh?" I nodded. Since I was a small child I'd been given sips—and more recently full glasses—of beer and wine, and every time I had a first hit of alcohol, relief flooded through me almost instantly. I reached for the bottle and poured us both another. We tossed it back. I poured myself a third glass, but Melanie stopped me before I could pour hers. "I'm good. We still have a party to go to," she reminded me.

"Right." I slammed mine back, already well into my first experience of being drunk. "Let's go!" I have no memory after that and only learned the remainder of that night's story from Melanie, who shared her recollection with me over the next few days.

We reached Lynn's house to find the high school party in full swing, mainly populated by her sister and brother's eleventh- and twelfth-grade friends. Their parents were in Hawaii and mine were safely ensconced at a Calgary Philharmonic Orchestra concert.

Apparently none of my friends could tell I was blind drunk, and my intoxication didn't stop me from drinking several beers while there. From what Melanie said, I was fun, funny, and relaxed at the crowded house party. After a few hours, Melanie and I walked back to her house and crept inside, her family now home and in bed. I was making noise and goofing around, ignoring her repeated requests to speak more quietly. She led me down to their unfinished basement in an attempt to keep me from waking her parents and three older brothers on the top floor.

Once downstairs, I tried to recreate our childhood play-acting games, beginning with Aquaman, my favorite, where I played the lead and Melanie played Aquagirl. But Melanie wasn't playing along.

"C'mon, Mel, be Aquagirl," I implored. Melanie shook her head.

"I think we should go to bed; I'm tired." Ignoring her growing frustration, I began to set up the ironing board. "What are you doing?" she asked.

"It's an underwater rock—I'm gonna swim over it," I announced, backing up to the far wall. "Watch out!"

"Lori! No!"

I ran and leaped, hurdling the ironing board. I ran back and forth, jumping over it several times before catching a toe and crashing, ripping my elbow open on the rough concrete wall and smashing the iron into pieces. I crumpled to the floor, then bounced back to my feet, oblivious to the pain.

"You're bleeding, Lor," she said resignedly. "Don't move, you're getting it all over. Here." She pressed a rag from a nearby laundry basket to the large gash. "Hold this on it, press hard."

Still drunk herself, Melanie somehow controlled the bleeding, while steering me, loudly babbling about Aquaman, up two flights of stairs to her bedroom and into my sleeping bag.

I remember the morning. I woke up in Melanie's bright bedroom, unsure of who or where I was for several long moments, my mind completely devoid of memory, my head pulsating painfully. I moved my arm to rub my face and a sharp pain seized my elbow. The smell of vomit and blood hit my nostrils in a rush and I gagged, but my stomach was empty. Inspecting my elbow, I felt encrusted blood and puke all over my arm, neck, and the side of my face. With my good arm, I touched my head, where dried vomit clumped in my hair. Just then, Melanie entered the room.

"Your mom's on the phone," she said, squatting beside me. "How're you feeling?" Her nose wrinkled at the harsh smell.

"Terrible. I am so sorry."

"It's okay," she smiled. "You were pretty funny."

"Does your mom know?"

"Yeah, but she's just worried about you. She won't tell your parents."

"I know she wouldn't. I feel so crappy, I don't even care," I moaned as I tried to get up. We walked slowly down the stairs, Melanie assisting me, my head spinning, stomach cramping. I reached for the phone with bloodied fingers and took a deep breath, summoning my most normal-sounding voice.

"Hi Mom."

"What time did you get up?" I tried to gauge her tone.

"Just now, we stayed up late talking," I lied.

"Uh-huh. Time to get home, we have things for you to do," she said icily. *She knows.* I'd later discover she and my dad saw the party from the street as they drove home from their concert.

I showered, scrubbing hard in an effort to wash off my embarrassment and shame along with the filth. I ate a piece of dry toast and gathered my things. Mrs. Solesky had washed and dried my clothes while I'd slept, and I apologized and thanked her for everything. She smiled sympathetically and gave me a warm hug. I promised her I'd be back to take the sleeping bag to the dry cleaners and replace the iron.

Filled with shame and dread, I shuffled the full 120 feet from the Soleskys' house to ours slowly, like a death row inmate on his last day. I found my parents sitting quietly in their recliners in the living room, unusual for a Saturday morning.

"Were you at the party at the Rowans' house?" my mom asked before I'd even taken a seat.

"Yeah." So intense was my hangover, I didn't even consider lying.

"Were you drinking?"

"Yeah."

"Where?"

"Melanie's. And at Lynn's."

"The Soleskys were out? You said they'd be home."

"Yeah."

"What were you drinking?" Dad finally joined in.

"The Polish stuff. And then some Crown Royal. And beer."

"You drank *the Polish stuff*?!" they exclaimed in unison, eyebrows raised. I nodded. My head ached more from the movement. I thought I detected a smirk on Dad's face. His moustache turned down slightly when he was amused.

"Well," Mom said. I waited several moments for more. She appeared uncharacteristically at a loss for words. "You've probably suffered more than you would from any punishment we could give you. Go help your dad clean the garage." She banished me with a wave of her hand.

That was the last time either of them spoke to me about drinking. Socially, I was incapable of having just one drink. I didn't drink daily and often went several weeks between drinks. Where some binge drinkers aim to get blind drunk, my goals were less clear: I simply couldn't stop once I started, even knowing the result could be a blackout.

Drinking eased my social anxiety. When I drank, I didn't worry about not fitting into my gender, or my skin. I was popular, and I enjoyed it, but I lived in constant fear of someone learning the truth about me. I had the high social standing that came with being an athlete and a good student. No one teased me, bullied me, or made me feel like the outsider I knew myself to be. I was keenly aware of the privilege I enjoyed as a white, middle-class, non-marginalized person, and I was terrified of losing it. Drinking helped me maintain my facade.

After graduation, many of my classmates came out as gay, lesbian, or bisexual, but I'm not aware of any other transgender people who attended school with me. I have tried for years to explain the dynamic around LGBTQ awareness at Bishop Carroll High School in the early 1980s, but I've never been able to. While the student population had its fair share of entitled frat-boy types, I don't remember witnessing or hearing of anyone being called out or teased by any of the masters of the universe for being different or queer.

As an androgynous-looking teen, perceived by others as a tomboy, I certainly could have been targeted, but I never was, perhaps due to my popularity. My high school was an extremely classist place where it was very easy to determine where kids fell on the social and economic spectrum. As long as they fit in economically and didn't challenge the status quo in any other ways, even the most effeminate boys and butch girls studied with, interacted with, socialized with, or were themselves members of the popular crowd.

Still, I tiptoed carefully, walking a tightrope between finding some comfort in my skin and maintaining a school wardrobe that wouldn't attract negative attention. Working after-school and summer jobs at various places from Dairy Queen to an athletic shoe store gave me the means to keep up with the trends touted in *The Official Preppy Handbook*, a satirical 1980 paperback most kids in my high school were desperate to emulate. Calgary was the new Connecticut, and boat shoes, chinos, and polo shirts were all the rage for anyone who was anyone.

Formans Menswear occupied a busy corner in our local mall. Tasteful lighting and dark wood paneling gave the store a piano-bar vibe. Navy-suited and black-tuxedoed mannequins posed in the window displays, classy and Bond-like. Breathless, I drew myself up to my full height whenever I stepped inside that magical world of menswear, glancing shyly at the dapper salesmen gliding through the tasteful displays with confidence and efficiency.

I desperately wanted a Lacoste shirt, one of those pretentious little French alligator-emblem golf shirts that all the cool kids in school wore, but I feared a dark or neutral color would play up my masculinity and spotlight me as a gender outlaw. I chose a pink version, loose and unassuming, killing two birds with one crocodile—vaulting me into the realm of the cool and cloaking me in faux femininity. I wore that shirt two or three times a week for the next two years, convinced it was my protective cape.

The fact that today I can sit back and remember several schoolmates who I later learned were gay, lesbian, or bisexual and say, "Duh, of course they are," only reminds me that I never considered any of us as "other" during my school years. So earnest were my own efforts—conscious and predominantly unconscious—to cloak my transgender self and adhere to mainstream behaviors, that I failed to consider that others might possibly fall outside the mainstream, too. Many of the queer kids I knew came from very affluent Calgary families whose fathers owned or held executive positions in large oil companies or law firms. While wealth and social standing brought these kids popularity at school, I can only imagine that the pressure to remain closeted as children of prominent people in a conservative city was a burden. The refusal to believe that anyone in the ranks of this elite Catholic high school could be anything other than straight and cisgender (the term for those whose sense of self and birth-assigned sex align, according to society's norms) was so deep that bullying as we now know it did not exist, as far as I was aware.

One of my school friends was Attila Richard Lukacs, known then as Rick Lukacs. Today, Lukacs is a world-renowned painter and visual artist. He's also an out gay man whose early career featured bold, homoerotic depictions of gay skinheads with a militaristic theme. While he wasn't openly gay in high school, he was the only LGBTQ person I knew at that time who I suspect knew exactly who and what he was in those days. He didn't seem to try very hard to hide it and had the confidence, carriage, and physical size to discourage any potential bullies.

Bishop Carroll High wasn't a typical high school. It followed a unique independent study model, which drew many elite athletes. My initial plan was to continue my downhill ski racing training that first winter of high school, but the sad fact was, I wasn't all that elite myself. Some of my friends went on to Olympic and World Cup success, but I remained a steadfast middle-of-the-pack finisher through my last racing season in the International Ski Federation system. Skiing six times a week throughout the winter—shivering in spandex racing suits awaiting my turn to launch myself down Rocky Mountain courses—plus rigorous dry land training spring and fall left me burned out.

That fall, I discovered the gym at school was frequently open during the day, and I soon joined regular coed pickup games of basketball. Basketball had called to me even back in junior high. It has a creative, spontaneous quality unique in competitive team sports; you can potentially make something amazing out of every touch of the ball, every defensive stop, every shot. If ski racing—beating the clock in the fastest run down the mountain—represents pure science, basketball displays athletic performance art. But I'd always been cut from the school teams, told by coaches that if they could carry fourteen players on a squad I would be one of them, but there was only room for twelve.

On a rare afternoon off from dry land ski training, I found myself taking an old orange rubber basketball to the schoolyard across the street, where I shot basket after basket and worked on my fledgling game. The only coaching I'd received was in junior high gym class, but the game came to me intuitively. I couldn't jump very high, wasn't particularly fast, and still hadn't reached my full height, but I possessed good hand-eye coordination and quick reflexes. *I love this game.* After an hour and a half, I walked back across the street in the fading light and informed my parents I was quitting ski racing. Not even the iconic blue and black leather Skimeisters team ski jacket was enough to keep me racing.

"Are you sure?" Dad asked. "You love skiing."

"We can certainly find other things to do with that money," Mom chimed in.

"I think we should make sure it's really what you want," Dad said to me, eyebrows raised.

"I like the dry land training the most, but it's so much time skiing every night and weekend," I said. "I kind of want to try some other stuff."

"Like what?" Mom demanded.

"Basketball," I blurted. "I want to try out for the basketball team." Dad tugged his moustache, as he always did when deep in thought.

"Are you sure?" he asked. "How long have you been thinking this way?"

"Since school started. I'm tired of being cold all the time. Plus, I'm never gonna make the national team," I reasoned.

"True," Mom agreed. I wasn't sure if it was the being cold part or my lack of talent she concurred with. I drooped as I stood before them, suspecting it was the latter.

"Well, if you're sure, it's fine with us," Dad said. "I'll miss watching you race."

"You can come to my games," I smiled at him.

"There you go—I will do that," he replied.

"If you make the team," Mom interjected.

"I'm gonna make the team."

Six weeks later, I made the junior varsity team.

The morning of my first early practice, I walked into the kitchen to find Dad making oatmeal. He made it for Jake and me every weekday morning before six, but I was usually asleep.

"What time do you want to leave?" he asked me.

"For practice?" I replied, surprised. "I was going to take the bus."

"You don't need to. I'll drive you."

"Great. Thanks." We sat down and ate our oatmeal in silence, each reading the paper. From that day forward, he drove me to every morning practice for three seasons. Sometimes we spent our time together in easy silence, other times we talked about all kinds of things, from his job to the performance of the Calgary Flames to chemistry basics to the *Farmers' Almanac*.

After a few short weeks of practice, the regular season began. Our first game was against Henry Wisewood High. I came off the bench late in the first half and took a position on the foul lane as one of my teammates shot free throws. The first shot swished through the net, but the second rolled around, hit the backboard softly and fell off the left side of the rim. I jumped into the lane and grabbed the rebound. One pump fake, then I gently laid the ball up toward the glass with my left hand. I watched, wide-eyed, as it kissed the backboard and fell perfectly into the basket. I pumped my fist in the air and shouted, "Yeah!" as I ran back on defense. I hollered joyfully, my fist still raised, all the way to the opposing team's key. The coach nodded to me to start the second half, and I played the rest of the game.

Later, in the locker room, my friend Talia, a friendly eleventh-grader I'd played with in open gym throughout the fall and who'd warmed the bench the entire game, congratulated me.

"You did really great," she said. "But I'm a little sad you played so much."

"Really? How come?" I felt guilty, expecting that she'd lament her own lack of playing time.

"Because you would have been so fun on the bench with us. We gave each other hairdos."

"Did you really?" I couldn't imagine not watching the game, prepared in case the coach subbed me in.

"Yeah. It's one of the best parts of being on the team!"

5

SHIRLEY
(1980–1982)

―――――

THE FOLLOWING SUMMER, I lied about being sixteen and landed a ten-day job at Calgary's summer rodeo fair, the Stampede, calling numbers and collecting money in the midway bingo tent. My friend Megan and I stood out from the traveling carneys as the polo shirt–wearing, scrubbed, naïve schoolkids we were. We reported to a person named Shirley, whose name and gender didn't seem to match.

Shirley stood six feet, two inches tall; a broad-backed, tough, and—though it sounds cliché—extremely-kind-underneath-a-gruff-exterior person who owned the bingo tent and traveled across North America making a living. Shirley wore men's clothing and never told us what pronouns to use (because people didn't specify that in those days), but as I came to know him, I learned that he identified as male. He dressed like a motorcycle gang member: plaid shirt, Wrangler pro rodeo jeans, heavy black Dayton boots, wallet chain, black leather bracelet, and a men's chunky gold ring. His voice was low-pitched, his face leathery.

Megan and I reported to Shirley each morning at 10:30 to open the tent and clean the surrounding area, which included a large concrete water fountain—a permanent feature of the Stampede grounds. The first day Shirley instructed us to "go wake up the folks sleeping rough." Megan and I just stared at each other, uncomprehending, frozen in place at the tent's entrance. We noticed these people each morning and generally gave the fountain area a wide berth before entering the bingo tent, sensing we ought to be afraid of the motionless lumps but seeing no threat.

Shaking his head in disappointment, Shirley walked past us out into the midway sun toward the fountain. Ten or twelve sleeping (we hoped) people lay on the ground—a microcosm of downtown Calgary, where people would use words like *hobo* and *bum* to refer to what we would later call the homeless community. I couldn't imagine the discomfort of sleeping as they did, on damp and uneven ground, limbs askew, in various positions covered by assorted blankets and jackets on the grass surrounding the fountain. Tugging on the large, retractable janitor's key ring permanently chained to his thick black leather belt, Shirley selected a moderately sized key and employed it to gently tickle the ear of the sleeping man nearest to him.

"Rise and shine, partner," he said softly. "Time for bingo." He tickled until the man groaned and stirred. "Atta boy." Shirley stood and turned to us. "Like that—just be nice and get 'em all sitting up." And with that, he turned and walked back into the tent, leaving Megan and me to wake everyone.

A few days later, as Megan and I collected money from the tables on a break between bingo games, Shirley stepped away from the calling mic and beckoned me to his office, a small table behind a plastic curtain at one side of the tent. I worried I was in trouble somehow, but my concerns were unfounded.

"You wanna call numbers, ace?" He always called me *ace*, which I kind of liked. "You've got a good, strong voice."

"Sure," I said uncertainly. "It is hard?"

"Nah, you'll be a natural; just pull out the ball and say 'under the B,' then pause a sec, and then call 'nine' or whatever the ball is. Easy." He took a wooden toothpick from a drawer and placed it in the side of his mouth.

"Right now?"

"No time like the present," he said, and looked at me intently. I didn't feel like he'd dismissed me yet. After a pause, he said, "You and me, we're kind of the same, you know."

"In what way?" I asked, although I felt like I knew.

"I see you watchin' me, tryin' to figure me out," he said, gesturing for me to sit down on the rickety wooden chair in front of his desk. I hesitated. "It's okay." I felt reassured and sat down. He took his seat behind the desk. "Do you have any questions you want to ask me?"

My mind reeled. *Does he mean about bingo calling? About why I watch him?* I felt afraid to somehow unintentionally offend him. He was still my boss, if only for another six days.

"You're a woman, right?" I ventured cautiously. He smiled slightly. The toothpick moved a little.

"Well, that's a complicated question." He rubbed his chin thoughtfully, then found the toothpick and rolled it between his finger and thumb. "I was born with woman parts; my folks named me Shirley. But I never felt like a Shirley, never felt like a girl." I listened, transfixed, trying not to appear too interested. "I rebelled. They hit me, tried to whack me into shape, into being a proper girl." He paused, looking off into the midway through the open side of the tent. "It wasn't good. I think they were scared of me. So, I ran away."

"How old were you?" I asked, wide-eyed.

"Thirteen." I couldn't imagine being on my own at fifteen, let alone two years ago.

"Wow."

"Yeah. Wow."

"What did you do?"

"Not much to do. No education. No one lookin' out for me. I joined a circus—funny, huh?" I nodded. "But, I got to be me. I wore my boy clothes, got to be myself. Got myself a bingo business." He gestured toward the tent. "Even had a lady friend, for a while." This last piece of news floored me. I wanted to ask him more, but felt it would be too much. For me, not for him. I retreated to safer ground.

"Why did you keep calling yourself Shirley?" He winced slightly and took a deep breath.

"That was a tough one. It seemed like the only thing I had that was mine. The only thing that tied me to my roots. But, no one messes with me—I mean, look at me." He gestured to his broad shoulders and black leather fiddler cap, the type I'd seen bikers wearing downtown. "No one messes with me, no one asks me why my name's Shirley."

"Yeah." I sat there imagining leaving my family behind. *This one.*

Suddenly, a torrent of words rushed out from that place I'd always kept locked up tight. "I'm like that, too. I'm a boy inside, and I just, I just—" I stammered. I felt tears coming. I swallowed. "Forget it." I rose. "I gotta go call the numbers." I turned to leave.

"Ace?" Shirley called after me. I turned and stopped.

"Yeah?"

"Figure out what you need to do to survive. Wear what you can get away with to make you happy, listen to your parents, but remember: soon you'll be on your own, free to live your life." I nodded vigorously. "You're gonna be okay." He winked at me, then waved me back to work

Over the years, in times of darkness and uncertainty, Shirley's words would come back to me often. *You're gonna be okay.*

Megan frowned at me from the tables as I exited the office, squinting with concern. I gave her the okay signal, smiled weakly, and made my way to the bingo mic. I hit the button, releasing a floating ping-pong ball into my hand. Leaning into the mic, I called, "Under the I, nineteen. I-nineteen."

I HELPED DAD roof houses the rest of that summer. It was just the two of us, because Jake wasn't interested and painted houses instead. Dad and I worked well together, and when the next summer approached, I looked forward to helping him again. He was building a home for his best friend Ken's family and I assumed he would include me. My parents had brought my older cousin Kevin in from Ottawa to help, even though Kevin was not a keen carpenter. His parents were worried he had fallen in with a bad crowd and thought he needed to get away for the summer. Dad enlisted Jake and Kevin for his paid crew, but he didn't extend the invitation to me. Thinking it an oversight, I assumed I was still included and mentioned it one morning in the spring.

"When are we starting on the Fitzsimmons' house?" I asked as the two of us ate breakfast. He didn't look up from his paper.

"Well, I think Kevin and Jake are going to be helping me," he said, taking a bite of oatmeal. Crushed by disappointment, I couldn't speak. "Your mom has a lot for you to do around here this summer. She'll need you for the apples," he added, referring to the annual two-week harvest and pie-making enterprise our one apple tree generated. "I don't think I'll have enough work for three of you." I heard regret in his voice, but he wouldn't meet my gaze.

My construction apprenticeship under my father ended unceremoniously in that moment, without another word. As was my habit, I retreated to the rec room downstairs to listen to music in the dark. Bruce Springsteen, the Ramones, the Sex Pistols, the Clash, Joy Division, the Cure, Tom Petty and the Heartbreakers, and so many other artists spoke to my teen-aged anger, angst, and upset. But it was Bruce Springsteen I most closely related to; his early lyrics of disconnection and hopelessness, trying to find his place in a world he didn't fit into, resonated strongly with me.

Realizing I couldn't stay downstairs forever, I enrolled myself in the University of Calgary basketball summer league and camps, taking the bus to campus several times a week to play with top high school- and university-level players. I threw myself fully into basketball, first out of desperation—but this quickly grew into love. For the first time in my life, I felt almost comfortable in my body.

I grew to love the impromptu pickup games I played in more than camp and league play, mainly because the players in those games included me readily. We played for hours without referees and with no organization. Few women players at that time would join pickup games with men. In those days, sports other than figure skating, swimming, soccer, or gymnastics were considered "unladylike" and masculine by some. More than a few times in the '80s and '90s, I saw female players pack up and go home without playing rather than join an impromptu pickup game if there weren't enough players for a women-only game.

I would work the phone to get players together and scour the city for open gym times for pickup games. There were three or four venues where the best local players played, depending on the day of the week or the time of year, and I figured out where to go to get the best competition, often playing against top national team–level players and former American college players who became local playground stars.

I loved basketball's every single nuance. That quintessential gym smell of sweat and varnish, the squeaking sound basketball shoe soles make on the hardwood, the pounding of the ball, the shrill echo of a whistle followed by the silence of halted play. I loved walking into the gym. I loved the warm-up. I loved practice. I loved the drills. I loved playing alone. I loved playing with others. I loved hanging around the gym. I loved basketball shoes. I loved my sweat-soaked T-shirts. First one in the gym, last one off the court. That was me. And I loved it all.

WHEN I WASN'T playing basketball, I behaved typically for a teen in the early '80s: I was self-absorbed and focused on my friends, and spent my time drinking outside of home without my parents' knowledge, working part time, and performing well enough in school. I wasn't home a lot, and when I was, I kept to myself, listening to music or watching basketball on TV. My parents were busy with their lives and I with mine.

"We'll be back in a week," Mom announced as she passed Dad her suitcase. The summer before twelfth grade, my brother, sister, and I all held jobs. Every evening after work I played basketball, and family vacations were a thing of the past. Mom stepped into their bathroom and applied a coat of lipstick, leaving me standing outside the open door. "Want some?" she gestured with the tube, a little giddy, unable to hide her excitement at getting away from us for a few days alone with Dad. She blotted with a tissue.

"Uh, no thanks," I muttered, wondering why she always asked despite my never agreeing to try it. She brushed past me out of the bedroom, waving at Katherine as she slipped on shoes and breezed out the front door of the house, calling out as she went.

"See you in a week!"

Jake drove them downtown to the station, where they boarded a VIA Rail train that would take them through the Rocky Mountains to Vancouver on what I assumed was a routine vacation.

They returned a week later as promised, grinning happily, laden with souvenirs. The following day, both of my parents entered our large basement rec room while I was watching a football game. Mom walked to the TV and turned it off.

"Hey!" I protested, before it dawned on me how unusual it was for them to come down there. "What's going on?"

They each took a seat while I lounged on the couch. Dad seemed somber and kept his gaze down, while Mom was all business and efficiency. I felt dread in the pit of my stomach.

"Well, you know your dad and I went to Vancouver," she began.

"Yeah."

"But what you don't know is that we also went to Vancouver Island." She took a breath. "To check out private schools."

"For what?" I asked, completely clueless as to what was coming next.

"For you."

"What?!" *Surely, this is a mistake.* I looked from one of them to the other and back again, incredulous that they would think of sending me away for this last year of high school when it was so important for me to obtain the basketball scholarships I was pursuing. "I don't need to go to a private school."

"These are private girls' schools, very highly regarded, where you can reach your potential—" I cut Mom off.

"I don't want to go to a private girls' school, my potential is fine right here," I snapped, my voice rising. Mom glanced over at Dad. *Here we go.*

"Now just listen to what your mother has to say," Dad interjected softly.

"What about what I have to say? Do they have a basketball team at this school?" I looked her hard in the eyes.

"No. The one we like has no basketball team," Mom answered.

"Forget it. I'm not going. I refuse."

"Now just—" Dad sputtered, but Mom cut him off, seething.

"You are *awful* to live with. You come and go like a boarder; you act like we owe you something! I have news for you: we don't owe you anything!"

"I'm not going. You can kick me out, but I'm not going." I tried to process how the people who brought me into this world didn't think they owed me at least a chance to pursue my dream of a basketball scholarship. What I'd always wanted was their help. I strongly suspected that they knew about my being a boy. *How could they not know? How could they not see it?* Time and time again, I'd silently implored them: *Help me! Why won't you help me?*

My parents had never talked to me about my behavior. I didn't have a curfew. I failed to fathom how they could consider me a problem child compared to the kids I knew who were doing drugs and shoplifting. I considered what options were available to me as a sixteen-year-old. "I'll go live at Lynn's."

"You will *not* go live at Lynn's." Mom almost spat the words out.

"Fine. But I'm not going away to school. Why do you want to send me away?" My anger threatened to erupt into full-blown rage. "You have *no right* to do this to me!" My voice rose with each word.

"Oh, we have every right! You are ungrateful and—" Mom began.

"No one wants to send you away, we all just need to stay calm," Dad interjected reassuringly.

"Joe—"

Dad looked me in the eye, finally. "You'll have to help your mom out a little more around here if you're staying," he said quietly. I knew then he didn't want me to go.

"I can do that," I said, with more sincerity than I felt.

"As long as you start to realize living here is a privilege, not a right," Mom snapped, jaw tight. I stood up.

"Are we done?" I asked. Mom sighed loudly.

"Yes," Dad replied. I walked out of the rec room and up the stairs, grabbed my basketball, and ran across the street to shoot. I felt more alone than I ever had. We Shenhers never fought and rarely raised our voices to each other—although anger's sneaky cousin, passive-aggressiveness, always appeared when there were disputes—so this open conflict was unusual. Our way of resolving conflict was to ignore or deny it so that nothing was ever resolved.

The last Saturday night of summer, I met my friends at Rob's house, where we drank beer until after midnight. Since the episode at Melanie's in tenth grade I had tried not to drink more than a six-pack in one night and hadn't blacked out again, but I drank a few more that night. Donald and I walked the four blocks to our street together, staggering a little as we lamented the end of our last summer as high school kids. Somehow, we ended up in the schoolyard across from my house. In typical drunken fashion, one minute we were talking, the next we were kissing, and soon we were rolling around in the dry grass.

After a few minutes of making out, Donald pulled back from kissing me and asked, "Can you give me a blow job?" Impulsively, I laughed out loud. It wasn't that I was a girl who didn't give blow jobs; it was more like I was a straight boy who had never, ever considered it.

"I don't even know how!" I laughed at the ridiculousness of his request. He didn't share my sense of mirth and began

explaining what he wanted me to do. I thought of an old episode of *Saturday Night Live*—Chevy Chase and Jane Curtin on
the "Weekend Update" set, Chase speaking into a phone, saying, "Nooo, you're not supposed to blow on it. That's just an
expression." I felt repulsed at the prospect, but in my drunken
state, I gave it an honest fifteen seconds of dedicated effort
before I pulled away, resigned to my nausea. "I'm going to
puke if we do this. Sorry."

We both fell onto our backs on the grass, staring up at the
starry night. "No, I'm sorry. I shouldn't have asked you. I just
thought maybe we could practice on each other, you know?"
he said.

"Yeah. I've thought of it, too," I lied. "But I don't even know
what I'd want you to do. I think kissing is all I feel like doing."

"No prob." Suddenly, I felt very sober and very tired.
"Wanna call it a night?" he asked.

"Yeah," I said. "Wanna skate at Sid's tomorrow?"

"Yeah, call me."

"Okay." We walked through the field to the street, and he
pecked me on the cheek before I crossed to my house. The
next day, I called him. Donald told me he'd meet me at Sid's,
which was unusual. Once we met up, things between us were
awkward. After that day, the distance between us grew, and
I was confused, resentful, and sad. He only saw me as a girl
to experiment with, and now I had to watch my friend slowly
disappear. I began to imagine a future where those closest to
me couldn't see me, didn't know me.

Twelfth grade passed quickly and graduation loomed. Basketball and partying with my friends consumed most of my
time, but I still managed to complete my coursework a couple

of months early and gain admission to the University of Calgary. Although I was just seventeen, I'd convinced my parents to let me take a full-time groundskeeper job at the private golf club near our house at the beginning of May and I spent my evenings at the university playing basketball.

Very few of my school friends were coupled off, so most of us chose to attend graduation with dates who were friends. Rob was medium-height, dark, exceedingly good-looking, and very much interested in not hurting the feelings of any of the many girls in our school who wanted to go out with him. There was no one I wanted to go with, and so we decided to go together, agreeing that we were free to go wherever we wanted with whomever we wanted throughout the evening with no hurt feelings on either side.

Earlier that spring, Mom had announced that she wanted to make my grad dress. I'd avoided the dress discussion for months, refraining from comment when she'd ask what material, color, or style I wanted. Her vision involved Princess Diana. Mom often told me she thought I bore a striking similarity to the Princess of Wales, a notion I found ludicrous at best, but—in the same way we know dogs can hear sounds humans cannot—I secretly hoped that perhaps her sense was right and I simply couldn't see the resemblance myself. I did allow that we both had a prominent nose. If I had to stay stuck in female form, it took away some of the sting if it was an attractive one.

Mom brought home from the fabric store huge swaths of what she called polished cotton in a bright solid shade of teal green. I don't remember being consulted about any of this, but I also don't recall conflict. I was indifferent and resigned to most rites of passage, and this was no different. I picked up the pattern that fell out of the shopping bag as she removed the material and saw an illustration on the package of what was essentially a monochromatic Snow White dress. High collar, three-quarter-length puffed sleeves—all trimmed with a ruffle—a bow around the waist, the skirt falling just slightly below mid-calf. I thought with desperate longing of Rob's planned grad suit: a white tux jacket, crisp white shirt, black tuxedo pants, black bowtie and cummerbund. *That's what I'm supposed to wear.*

The dress project took over the dining room table for many days. Mom worked on it whenever she could between her job at a bookstore and working to keep our house running. I immersed myself in basketball—my salvation and haven—occasionally standing for Mom to pin sections of the pattern and fabric together around my arms or waist, frozen so I wouldn't get pricked by the many pins. I feigned mild enthusiasm and felt badly that something Mom was so excited about caused me such inward anguish. That she was doing all of this for me made me feel even worse because, as always, I existed completely unknown to anyone but me. *How could she have such a wrong idea about what I would like to wear?*

I threw my basketball shoes and water bottle into my gym bag one evening, preparing to rush out the door to a game, when Mom called out to me, "Come straight home after because I want you to try this on!"

"Okay!" I hollered, halfway to the car. I knew tonight was *the* night. She had reminded me several times over the past couple of days that we were close to having a real fitting, sans pins.

Jackie Popilchuk stood six feet, four inches and outweighed me by at least a hundred pounds. As she received the pass into the low post, I slid over from the help side to double-team, hoping to get in the way of her almost-unstoppable postgame. Back to the basket, she considered her options, faking to one side before pivoting to the other and squaring up to the hoop in one powerful motion; she led with an elbow and, with full force, struck my waiting face. I heard a loud *crack* and staggered backward. My teammates caught me. The ref whistled the play down.

I couldn't see, but I can't say if it was because my eyes were pressed shut or the pain had blinded me. I heard a woman's voice close to my ear say, "Just relax. I'm just gonna touch your nose a little and see what's going on." I gurgled some sort of affirmative response, choking on the blood in my throat. I felt her hands gently feeling the sides of my nose, then suddenly, *whack*—in a lightning-fast motion, she jerked my nose back into place. My friends later told me it had looked like my nose was part of my cheek. After a short burst of pain, normal feeling returned and I felt immeasurably better. The woman looked at me with concern.

"I'm the student trainer here," she said. "Is that better?"

"Yeah, thanks," I said, holding a tissue to my bleeding nose. "Can I go back in?"

By the time I got home after my game, both of my eyes were black and my red, bruised nose had swollen to twice its normal width. I entered through the back door and kicked off my shoes.

"Is that you?" Mom called from the dining room.

"Yup." I started up the steps toward her.

"What's wrong?" she asked, just before I entered the dining room. "What happened to you?"

"I got hit in the nose." Her face fell. She shook her head slowly and sighed deeply. I stood there a few moments, unsure of what was coming next.

"*You* are going to wear *this* dress?" A drop of blood slowly escaped one nostril, rolling onto my upper lip. I wiped at it with the back of my arm. "Well, you can't put this on tonight. You're a mess; you'll get blood all over it." She put her head down and went back to finishing a seam, done with me.

6

GETTING A FLAT
(1982–1983)

THAT FALL, I chose to attend the University of Calgary and try out for the basketball team. I'd also received interest from the University of Lethbridge, where two of my previous high school teammates had gone on to successful playing careers, and though they pushed hard for me to join them, my heart was with the Calgary Dinos. The U of C program represented all I thought I wanted to be: respected, admired, mainstream. Year in and out, the Dinos finished strong in the Canada West conference and were perennial fixtures at the national tournament. Their roster included all-Canadians and all–Canada West conference players. I longed to be a fish in their big pond.

Dinos head coach Donna Roman (later Rudakas) ruled over the gym, an intimidating figure with a steely, withering gaze. She rarely watched the summer league games, but she controlled every aspect of the summer basketball camps each year and did all the teaching. I had first met her when I was a gangly fifteen-year-old basketball camp participant the summer before eleventh grade.

I was immediately struck by the unspoken emphasis Donna placed on her comportment and that of her players. A subtle yet pervasive aura of superiority hung in the air of her gym and shrouded her players. She often referred to us as "ladies," with what I felt was a hint of elitism. Only one player on her team had short hair; the others all wore their long hair in perky ponytails and many showed hints of light makeup. *If they accept me, maybe I can be normal, too.*

The previous season I had watched Donna's team play against other universities and the contrast was marked; the players on the opposition teams were the sort of women my mother would call "mannish"—many were muscled and sported short, utilitarian hairstyles. I possessed no words or experience to make sense of the subtle and not-so-subtle homophobia in sports in those days—no one did. As in high school, the unspoken, unacknowledged fear of *other* hummed like an electrical current underneath the surface of all our interactions.

When the players returned to the gym after showering to watch the featured men's game, I noticed the Dino women had transformed from sweating athletes into runway models, while the opposition's unisex clothing was remarkable only in its drabness and distinct lack of fashion and femininity. The Dino team existed in a higher, classier realm, one that intuitively felt safe to me; a place I could cloak my male self and remain undetected. Basketball Renée—that was who I'd be.

On the last day of camp, Donna strutted over to me as Mom waited for me to change my shoes so we could drive home. Head down, I heard her voice. "Lori, is this your mother?" I clumsily stood up, nodding as I introduced them. Mom looked at her impassively.

"Hello."

"We think your daughter has a great deal of potential," Donna enthused, effortlessly switching from the domineering, not-easily-impressed coach to practiced recruiting agent in seconds. "We see big things for her here."

"Really," Mom said, unmoved. It wasn't a question. I saw a barely perceptible shift in Donna as she recognized that this was not a typical fawning parent begging her to notice her child athlete, but rather a person who viewed her as barely a step above a television evangelist. Mom could not care less, and Donna knew it.

"Were you or your husband athletes? She seems to have a real feel for the game," Donna pressed on.

"No."

Neither of them used to enduring indignities, they regarded each other in silence, these two tough, steely women. I realized with a start who Donna had reminded me of when I first met her. Inside, I was dying. I knew if Donna had been a debate team coach, the interaction would have unfolded much differently.

"Well, I hope you'll consider having her attend the University of Calgary when the time comes," Donna said with a forced smile. "We'll try to get to some of her games this year."

"Uh-huh. Thank you." Mom smiled faintly and led me out of the gym. I waved weakly to Donna.

"Thanks, Donna," I said. She nodded.

Over the next two years, as I found myself developing friendships with other Dino prospects and current players, I felt a slight chill from Donna, but I suspected it had nothing to do with my mother. I'd catch her watching me when I hadn't been looking, her lips pursed while her cold, disapproving gaze rested on me for a moment. Then she'd look away instead of smiling at having been caught, as though I wasn't worthy of further scrutiny and she'd been watching me to confirm her judgment. There was nothing creepy or lecherous in her watching; Donna seemed obviously heterosexual, if her choices of friends and favorite players were any indication, and she eventually married a man and had children. I felt her eyes boring into me at times, trying to figure out what my deal was, leaving me feeling naked and exposed instead of known, seen, and accepted.

I'd injured myself somehow over the summer leading up to team tryouts, but it didn't seem serious to me. Pain radiated deep from within my left hip and hamstring after one hard day working on the golf course and it lingered, persisting for several weeks, but it hadn't yet affected my game or movement. I felt fit and ready to give it my all. The moment I'd prepared for and agonized over for three years had arrived. My chance to belong to something, to craft an identity as a student athlete and basketball player, presented itself.

I finished the first week of tryouts feeling strong and confident about my chances of making the team. But the stress of the week had accumulated: adding two hours of basketball practice—plus taping and warm-up—to an already-packed schedule of attending classes, buying books, and never-ending reading left me ready to blow off some steam. A large group of us from the team, along with some members of the men's team, planned to go see an intimate fifteen-hundred-capacity concert with a college band out of Athens, Georgia, called R.E.M.

The band played tracks from their first EP, which I'd been listening to for weeks. I wasn't the only one affected by the free-flowing beer. Lead singer Michael Stipe stopped a few bars into "Gardening at Night" to announce, "Man, I gotta take a piss," before walking off stage, only to reemerge thirty seconds later and start from the top. It wasn't until I heard him interviewed many years later that I learned they'd written that song after a road trip experience where Stipe had to urinate and asked Bill Berry to pull over so he could do some "night gardening."

By that point, I was drunk. Several of us headed over to a local pizza place after the concert for a late bite. As I climbed out of the back seat of the car and stepped over the large decorative rocks bordering the parking lot, disaster struck. My left ankle rolled violently in both directions, tearing all the ligaments around the joint. At the emergency room, they confirmed my worst fears: I had a severe sprain that would put me on crutches for two to three weeks, with no likelihood of basketball for at least four.

Donna looked less than impressed when I hobbled into practice on Monday. Several of the team's seniors had been with us and likely reported my drunkenness to her. I hoped she thought enough of my playing ability to keep me as the eleventh or twelfth person on the roster, but when she posted the list on the dressing room door that Friday, my name was nowhere to be seen. I'd been cut. It was barely mid-September of what would have been my rookie year, I was only seventeen years old, and my basketball dreams had been shattered due to my own stupidity. I drove home in a mess of tears and snot, so distraught that I left my backpack on a couch in the phys ed building. I didn't retrieve it for four days.

It was a huge blow. But somehow, it felt even bigger than it should have, as though my insides had disappeared and I was just a hollow shell, rattling and empty. No one in my family knew what to say beyond, "Oh, that's too bad." I buried my head in my dog Riley's soft fur and sobbed. *Who am I, if not a basketball player?*

I didn't know it then, but what I did next would be the first of many distraction techniques, unconsciously designed to create upheaval in my life and push my real troubles into the background. Over the next thirty years, I would repeatedly change clothing, hairstyles, cars, homes, jobs, careers, cities, boyfriends, and girlfriends in an effort to rewrite my script. These small infusions of drama gave me a high in those early days. Over time, however, I needed more and more self-imposed stimulation to mask my pain, and the effects wore off much faster.

Word reached my friends on the University of Lethbridge team that I'd been cut. They told their coach, who had just that week watched a player leave the team for academic reasons. They soon hatched plans to bring me there to fill the void. Changing school partway through the semester was unheard of in Canadian university athletics, but less than a week later I stood in my parents' bedroom begging them to let me go to U of L after the basketball coach, Eliza Burns, paved the way.

Later, the Canadian Interuniversity Athletic Union would implement a rule forbidding such midsemester transfers.

Dad wanted to please both me, who desperately wanted to go, and Mom, who worried about the cost of on-campus housing. But playing on the team ensured I would receive a scholarship thanks to Alberta's Heritage Fund, and Mom acquiesced. On Thanksgiving Monday in 1982, I moved into a four-room suite in residence with my two former high school teammates who played for U of L and suited up for my first practice as a Pronghorn, the University of Lethbridge's mascot, a reindeer-like animal previously unfamiliar to me.

I came to Eliza's team damaged in more ways than one. While my injured ankle healed well, the pain in my left hip and hamstring lingered without explanation. I ran slower and moved with less agility than I used to and my play suffered. Before, I had consistently been in the middle of the pack during full-court sprints—"suicides," as they are known in basketball—but I now finished near the back. Even the larger, slower post players gave me a run for my money, and Eliza suggested I was dogging the conditioning drills.

Basketball and drinking became my two primary activities, with school finishing a very distant third. My teammates and I didn't drink during the week because of practice, but we made up for it on Saturday nights. Dance parties in the U of L main foyer were plentiful and when they weren't, residence never closed down.

The University of Lethbridge is an Arthur Erickson-designed architectural masterpiece, expertly cut into the side of a river valley, with academic classrooms and offices on the top several floors and residence on the bottom. I was shocked by the contrast between the fresh, gleaming, bright, open academic spaces and the cellar-like feel and stench of student housing the first time I rode the elevator from the main level down to residence. As the doors opened, the overpowering blast of stale beer and liquor—the smell of small-town bars and dirty, beer-soaked, terry tablecloths—nearly knocked me back into the elevator. Residence was party central.

Residence also exuded a very straight, cisgender, and conservative vibe, though I wouldn't have been able to articulate it as such in those days. Most of U of L's students hailed from small-town Alberta and many came from Mormon communities to the south. The undercurrent of pressure to conform to traditional gender norms and behavior permeated every interaction, but excessive drinking was widely encouraged, even among the Mormon kids. As in high school, other options didn't occur to any of us.

My roommates were three very attractive, seemingly straight women—two had long-term boyfriends and the third dated someone for most of that year. Conversation often centered on boys, who was seeing whom, and our plans for the future. I assumed they would all want to marry men and have children, while that prospect seemed alien to me. Several of my teammates would later come out as lesbian, but every single one of us had boyfriends that year. I had several—all very nice and patient young men who never complained or asked me to go beyond our very vanilla making out.

In my abbreviated first semester, I neglected my studies. High school hadn't challenged me and I had no real concept of how to study or how much effort I needed to put in to pass my courses. One evening, as my roommates and I walked through the school on our way to residence from practice, I noticed many students in a large room, sitting at tables, all deep in thought, reading and writing. I turned to my friends and asked, "What are those guys doing? It's too late for class, isn't it?" They chuckled a little until they realized I was serious.

"Shen, that's the library."

"What?"

"The library. You go there to study and write your papers?"

"Oh."

By the end of first semester, my GPA was below the 2.0 needed to stave off academic probation. My hip injury showed no signs of improving, and my resulting poor play planted me firmly on the bench for most of our games. The training staff had no idea what was wrong with me and the team doctor, at a loss, suggested treatment for a torn hamstring. My reduced activity due to injury, increased drinking, and poor late-night, drunken food choices—far from Mom's nutritious meals—left me nearly twenty pounds heavier by Christmas break and unknowingly battling depression.

My slim, athletic frame morphed into a doughy, pear-shaped form I could not recognize in the mirror. Suddenly, heavy breasts hung from my chest where before there had been barely-noticeable bumps. My hips, which I'd been proud of for their boyishness, curved and filled out my jeans. My previously neutral body declared its unwelcome femaleness loudly and boldly. Until then, I hadn't realized how much my lack of noticeable hips and breasts allowed me to tolerate my female body. While I loved and admired female bodies in general, mine felt foreign to me. My injury and weight gain combined to slow me down on the court and I could feel my grasp on the game slipping away.

Eighteen was the legal drinking age in Alberta and although I'd been drinking since fourteen, celebration was mandatory on my birthday that December in Lethbridge. My roommates planned a large party for me in residence, presenting me with a gigantic, forty-ounce glass beer stein, which they continually filled with Black Russians throughout the night. After leaping all over the furniture in the party room, I blacked out. My friends put me to bed, no one thought anything of it, and we all laughed at my debilitating hangover the next day.

The celebration continued when I returned home to Calgary for Christmas break. My old friend Lynn invited me for a birthday drink at the University of Calgary campus pub, and I drove the two of us there. It was a freezing winter night, snowy and twenty degrees below zero, and our breath hung in the air as ice crystals glittered around us. I planned for a quiet evening—one drink, two at the most—and home to bed. Making a good plan had never been my problem; following through after my first drink was. My lapses in judgment after consuming alcohol—even half a drink, let alone eight or ten—were the most dangerous and shameful effect of my drinking. On most occasions, as soon as I started to drink, my resolve vanished and my thirst for more became insatiable.

We each finished our first glass of red wine and I suggested we have another.

"I don't know, we probably shouldn't," Lynn said.

"C'mon, it's my birthday. It's Christmas. One more glass," I urged.

"All right."

I don't remember much after that, but that second glass led to a bottle and I don't imagine Lynn drank much of it. I recall us rattling home in Dad's cold-as-an-icebox little blue Honda Civic, driving south on Crowchild Trail, Lynn scraping the windows from the inside, me piloting in a stupor. Lynn alerted me to a noise.

"What's that?"

"It's nothing, let's just keep going," I said.

"I think we have a flat tire," she insisted.

"Nah, it's just icy—chunks of ice on the road," I reassured her as we continued past the Currie Army barracks. "It'll be fine."

"We should stop," Lynn stressed.

"I'm just gonna drive us home. We need to get home, it's too cold." I drove the remaining two miles to Lynn's house and parked the car, our teeth chattering more from the bumpy ride than the cold. We got out and examined the front passenger tire and saw that all that remained was a few ribbons of rubber and a very badly damaged rim.

"Oh," I said. "I'll leave it here. I shouldn't drive anymore."

"Good idea." We said good night. I staggered home and fell into bed.

Mom knocked on my door the next morning and stuck her head inside. "Where's the Honda?" she asked.

Honda ... Honda.

Eyes closed, I saw my mind as a white blank, the *tabula rasa* I'd learned of in English class. No thought existed for several seconds.

Out of nowhere, I blurted out, "Lynn's! It's at Lynn's."

"Well, your dad needs it. You'll have to get up and go get it."

"Okay, but I got a flat, so I left it there instead of driving it." I lay there wondering how I knew this.

"Alright, talk to your dad about it," she said, and left the doorway.

Dad and I walked up to Lynn's through the frosty, clear December morning. He said nothing as he squatted to survey the destroyed tire and rim, tugging absently at his moustache as I stood by in the throes of an excruciating hangover. He rose with a sigh and said, "Well, let's change this and take it in for repair." That was all. No lecture, no anger, no demand that I pay for it, no grounding or loss of car privileges. "You may as well learn how to change a tire, right?" I nodded my aching head as he began patiently describing the tire change procedure and showed me how to do it myself. I tightened all the bolts and we drove it home.

I returned to Lethbridge for Boxing Day practice before the team drove to Montana for a tournament. The mysterious, ever-present hip/butt pain plagued my every move, severely limiting my playing ability and relegating me to the bench in all but the least competitive games we played. Our team doctor failed to diagnose the injury, instead suggesting I stop playing sports if it hurt. The school placed me on academic probation, which meant I had to pull my 1.8 GPA up over a 2.0 that term if I wanted to remain on the team and at the university.

My formerly loose clothes still fit tight; what little confidence I once had in my appearance languished in the tank. My mid-December birthday bender long forgotten, I embraced new opportunities to medicate my depression, pounding back the beers with my teammates in a Montana country bar that New Year's Eve without any consequences other than winning a silver Coors Light baseball jacket in a chugging contest—and a hangover.

Several weeks passed with my injury showing no signs of healing and my play worsening. During practice before a regular season home game against the University of Calgary, our Canada West rival, Eliza advised me I wouldn't be dressing, citing my injury and resulting poor play as the reason. I knew Eliza had been considering this move for a while, but missing the chance to prove how wrong Donna had been for cutting me was devastating. My game was wrong, my academic life was wrong, my body was wrong, my love life was a crazy mess as I juggled two boyfriends—and I didn't know how to fix any of it.

My roommates and I stepped into the long tunnel that joined the athletic complex to the university's main building for the five-minute walk back to residence. The brown, concrete walls of the windowless tunnel closed in on me like a tightening straitjacket, imaginary straps pulling, crushing my desperation closer to me. I clenched my fists and shut my eyes, stopping as my roommates kept walking. I let out a piercing, long, primal scream, unlike anything that had ever come out of my mouth.

And I didn't stop.

I raged and thrashed and screamed at the top of my lungs, fighting my roommates as they tried to hold me and calm me down. They must have been shocked, to say the least, but I don't remember them in that moment, only the darkness inside my head and body and my unending screaming.

They half-carried me, kicking and hollering, back to the athletic complex and into the women's locker room. Practice had run late, so the building would have been relatively empty. I don't know if anyone saw us or asked my roommates what the matter was with me. I do recall they seemed a little dazed, likely because my behavior was both stunning and completely out of character. From within, I observed the chaos with detached amusement and curiosity.

What the hell, Shenher? This is a little extreme, don't you think? They're gonna think you're nuts.

They held me, soothing me until I finally settled down, mostly out of exhaustion. We all walked back to residence several minutes later and never talked about it.

The following Monday after practice, Eliza instructed me to come to her office. Rumor had it she was a closeted lesbian, living with a partner she referred to as her "roommate," a quiet, unassuming teacher and high school basketball coach named Violet. A few members on both the women's and men's teams often made jokes about Eliza; they would suggest we make deals with her by offering to exchange sex for playing time, or issue tongue-in-cheek "warnings" about not letting her come too close. Homophobia ran rampant, and while the jokes and comments remained sophomoric and rarely, if ever, became cruel, I filed away these real-life examples of how others spoke of queer people—or anyone different—behind their backs.

I enjoyed my player-coach relationship with Eliza and learned a lot from her in the gym. I liked her, though I wasn't sexually attracted to her. I often lamented to myself that if my problem were as simple as being a lesbian, I wouldn't be afraid to come out and embrace my identity, imagining that relief would come swiftly. Because I knew I wasn't a lesbian, I found it amusing when I'd get the sense that Eliza was trying to figure me out, perhaps making guesses about my sexual orientation, asking herself, *is she or isn't she?* We talked a lot on road trips and I knew she had no clue about the real me.

"Hey Coach," I said, as I tapped on her office door.

"Lori, come on in." She gestured to a chair.

"Thanks." I felt nervous, thinking one of my roommates— who were both on the team—must have said something.

"How are you doing?" she asked. I wasn't sure of how to respond.

"Um, pretty good, you?"

"I'm doing well, thanks." I remembered she had a degree in psychology. She sat there quietly regarding me for a few beats. "So, I heard you had a rough time the other night after practice. Do you want to talk about it?"

"Hmm, not really." I shrugged.

"Okay." She paused. "Well, I'll start. You were apparently very upset about something. Was it about basketball?"

"Kinda." She nodded. "Yeah, I guess it's stupid, really."

"Try me," she offered. I sighed, wishing I was anywhere but there.

"It's okay. I'm good now," I said, rising to leave. She gestured for me to sit back down. I sat, sighing again. My chest felt tight. "I just really wanted to play against Calgary."

"That's understandable." Clearly, she wanted more.

"So, I just want to be good, you know? *Really good.* I'm playing like crap, my leg is stopping me, no one knows what's wrong with it. And now I'm getting fat and I'm freaking out."

"You are a good player."

"I know, but I'm not improving with this thing. I want to be really good, like National Team good."

"That might not be realistic right now with an injury."

"I know," I said, despair creeping in. "But I *want* to be good. I *have* to be good."

Eliza eyed me with concern. I felt my cheeks burning with shame. *God, I sound pathetic.*

"Get that leg better and you'll be back at it. Then, you can put in the work, okay?" I nodded. "Good. And Lori?"

"Yeah?"

"No more screaming. You worried your teammates."

"Yes, Coach." I choked the words out and practically ran out of her office, suffocating with embarrassment.

7

UNEVEN
(1984–1987)

FORTUNE CAME TO me in the form of my great-aunt Mary
Helen, whom I had never met, who passed away in England
the summer after my first year of university. Great-Aunt Mary
Helen, who had never married, named my sister Katherine
and me two of seven "young ladies" designated as beneficia-
ries of a mid-five-figure sum from her estate. My left leg injury
had deteriorated further. I was in pain no matter what I did,
and my improved financial circumstances didn't make me
much happier.

I felt ashamed imagining that if Great-Aunt Mary Helen
had known me, she would have realized her mistake in including me with this group of young women. She thought highly
of my mother, which was the reason she had given my sister
and me this gift. My fraud felt complete as I looked helplessly

at our excluded brother Jake, who felt slighted by someone he now privately considered a man-hating old maid. What he didn't know was I would have traded places with him in a heartbeat.

I regained my academic mojo but remained injured, unable to play basketball at a high level. Convinced that Lethbridge was responsible for my depressed state, I left its winds and tumbleweeds behind, spending the next two years studying in Calgary and Victoria, respectively. My roommate in Victoria was wonderful: a loyal friend, future Olympian, and former high school basketball rival. A mesh basketball net hung from her bedroom's ceiling fixture; her teammates had cut it down and presented it to her to celebrate her star performance when her high school beat mine 40-37 in the Calgary City Championships. That net represented all she possessed that I did not: physical wellness, talent, comfort in her skin, success, *normalcy*. Despite my hip injury, I tried out for the UVic team and was among the last cut—regretfully, it seemed, and with sympathy—by legendary coach Kathy Shields, who was no stranger to injuries herself. I made the JV team, but my injury prevented me from playing that year.

The pain became part of my every waking moment, forcing me to select forty-five-minute classes because I couldn't endure the pain and numbness for an hour and fifteen. Somehow I'd gotten ahold of Tylenol 3 with codeine and popped the pills like candy all through the winter semester, enabling me to walk to school and sit in class without pain. Drinking every weekend didn't touch the pain, but it enabled me to laugh, dance, and forget how different I felt from everyone else for a few blissful hours. It's a miracle I didn't die in my sleep.

Victoria was different. Although I'd had several boyfriends in Lethbridge and Calgary, I remained completely single at UVic, while my roommate and our friends dated several young men during the year. None of the boys I met that year expressed any interest in me. My injury took so much of my energy that I had little left to maintain a female presence and I stopped trying. I enjoyed friendships with men and women, but nothing more. It felt as though I'd finally been revealed as the fraudulent girl I'd always known I was, and in an odd way this made me feel both resigned and relieved. I was able to stop pretending, at least to myself.

Still, I didn't share my predicament with anyone, and I wouldn't acknowledge my attraction to women for several more years. My sexual orientation was mixed up in societal expectations, and I continued to confuse my admiration and jealousy with attraction to both genders. I couldn't figure out how to be with either women or men because I wasn't living life as the man I knew I was. I was too afraid to try to connect with anyone in an authentic way.

Mom's cousin was a Calgary nurse who pulled some strings to get me in to see the Calgary Flames' orthopedic surgeon to examine my injury as soon as I returned from Victoria in the spring. After a couple of tests, he sent me for same-day imaging of my back. The scan showed I had a prominent disc protrusion and the surgeon scheduled surgery for the following morning.

After surgery, the surgeon told me that my sciatic nerve—the largest in the human body, as thick as a thumb, running down each leg from the lower spine through the buttocks all the way to the feet—was pressed almost flat by the weight of the bulging, ruptured lumbosacral disc. The nerve's location explained why my pain was in my hip and hamstring rather than in my back.

I awoke from the general anesthesia in tears and my parents feared that the surgery had failed.

"What is it? Does it hurt?" Mom asked. I shook my head.

"No," I answered. "It's *gone*. It's finally gone." After nearly four years of constant pain, it was gone. I could feel where the operation had separated my lower back muscles, bruising them as the surgeon held them aside for hours with clamps, but the pain, that indescribably deep nerve pain, had miraculously disappeared. The surgeon told me it was the worst disc protrusion he had ever seen, and I didn't doubt him.

I spent the summer recovering, unable to believe that I might again enjoy an active, pain-free life. Three months later I returned to playing basketball, and three months after that I ran my first marathon, feeling like a modern-day Lazarus. I was just twenty years old, and I vowed I would never take my health or the ability to play basketball for granted again.

News that my high school friend Gareth—on whom I'd had an intense crush throughout grades ten and eleven—was returning home from his Ontario university for a few weeks late that summer threw me into renewed efforts to look and behave like a normal young woman. I set out for Calgary's tony Mount Royal Village shops, where I picked out a new outfit: a light blue Calvin Klein denim miniskirt and a red, white, and blue Ralph Lauren cotton sweater with a nautical theme. As usual, I hoped that dressing myself up in designer labels would somehow validate my female appearance. I headed for the dressing rooms and waited for the saleswoman to notice me.

"Can I help you, miss?"

"Um, I'd like to try these on, please," I answered. Despite the goal of buying clothes that would make myself look more feminine, it didn't feel affirming to be seen as a young woman and I felt stung by being called "miss"—another reminder that if people could only see me as the man I knew I was, all this effort would be unnecessary.

"Of course, right this way," she smiled, and led me into a cubicle.

I pulled my heavy sweatshirt and loose basketball shorts off and tried the items on. I scowled at my figure in the sweater; with my weight gain, my right breast had grown at least one cup size larger than my left, to the extent that it pulled on my neck a little when I ran, causing muscle imbalances and aches. The skirt fit perfectly and matched the sweater well. I decided to ignore my asymmetrical chest and not let it affect my confidence, unaware that many women had some size difference between breasts. I turned my thoughts to Gareth and our past high school fun.

I recalled warm summer afternoons when my group of friends and I used to sail Megan's dad's sailboat around Glenmore Reservoir, known for its changeable conditions and challenging waters. On calm days, we would plunge a twenty-six-ounce bottle of vodka into a dehydrated watermelon and float around, eating large pieces that kept us buzzed for hours.

I bought makeup for the first and only time in my life that afternoon, grimacing in the drug store as I grudgingly selected mascara, blush, and eyeliner, the entire premise ridiculous to me. *If I'm doing this, I have to do it right.* I pulled my shoulder-length hair—grown out over my months of recovery that had stipulated no sitting, so no haircuts—into a high ponytail, a new style for me after years of my David Cassidy shag. I applied a splash of women's Polo perfume, a gift from the previous Christmas. Then, I left for Gareth's.

I pulled up in front of Gareth's upscale home, heart pounding in my lopsided chest. He was smart, funny, kind, good-looking, athletic, a good friend; there was no good reason for my apprehension. He had been excited to call me when he got home a few days earlier and suggested I come over.

Gareth's colonial home looked just as I remembered it from a couple of years before. I stepped out of the car in my new stylish flats, which accentuated my shaved, suntanned legs, confirming I'd made the right call to forego nylons. I gently banged the door knocker. The door opened and Gareth's mother stood there. For a split second she seemed not to recognize me, then her eyes bulged a little and she exclaimed, "Lori! It's so good to see you! I didn't recognize you for a second—come in!"

"Hi, Mrs. Jordan," I said, smiling. "How are you?" I'd always liked her immensely. She was warm, intelligent, and the first divorced person I'd ever known. She seemed happy, upbeat, and busy in her life as a business owner and mother. In our house, the mere mention of anyone divorcing came with hushed tones, clucking tongues, and the somber shaking of heads.

"I'm fine, Lori. Let me go get Gareth, he was just showering after a run."

I lingered patiently in their cozy kitchen. I heard Gareth's feet thump down the stairs and watched him bounce into the kitchen. "*Bonjour, ici* Radio Canada!" he said, a throwback to a school French exchange trip to Montréal and Quebec City we'd taken in tenth grade. I saw something flicker across his face as he took me in.

"*Bonjour!*" I replied, each of us facing the other awkwardly, not hugging, not shaking hands. After a moment, Gareth patted me twice on the upper arm, the way a boss does with a just-fired employee. *It'll be okay, you'll find something else, I'm sure.*

"You look very... summery!" He laughed. I was certain that wasn't what he really meant. "I mean, this is a very different look for you."

"I could go back and get something more wintery," I replied, frowning slightly.

"No, no, that's not what I mean," he stammered politely. "I'm such a goof. I'm just not used to seeing you look so... so *fancy.*" My heart broke in that moment, knowing I'd failed to achieve whatever look I'd hoped for. Knowing he didn't care for me that way. Knowing deep down I didn't even want him to, but not knowing what that meant or what I did want. I didn't know what I was trying to achieve. "I've just never seen you in a dress. Are you okay?" he asked.

"Yeah, I'm fine, really good," I said with a sunniness I didn't feel. "What do you wanna do?"

"How about a walk?" he suggested eagerly.

We set off down the hill into River Park, which wound along Calgary's Elbow River. Our conversation fell back into the easy friendliness we had always enjoyed and I was reminded of how witty and intelligent he was, and how very platonic our relationship had always been.

"Do you remember how we used to wrestle sometimes?" he asked.

"Totally," I said. "I could never quite beat you."

"I'll have to remain undefeated, I guess," he teased.

"We could always schedule a rematch," I countered, aiming for a flirty repartee.

"Well," he said, drawing the word out. "We're probably getting a little old for that, you know?"

"Yeah, you're right. We are." Another stab of disappointment pierced my chest. *Can you not even give me the wrestling?* I thought of Jake and the hurt of slowly losing him and my other boy friends at puberty.

Later, I drove home, too deflated to cry. I slipped quietly into the house and ran to the bathroom, where I scrubbed the makeup from my face. *I don't want to be with him, I want to be him.* I stepped out of my name-brand clothes, disappointed again by the false prestige and acceptance they offered.

My inheritance provided me with more than enough to buy a car and pay for my education, and I chose to return to the University of Calgary and live with my parents. Jake and Katherine had left the nest and Mom and Dad considered me less offensive company than I'd been in high school and a decent contributor to interesting dinner conversation.

More and more, my breasts were creating conflict between my cognitive and physical identities. Looking at myself in the mirror, I found it increasingly difficult to reconcile the body I saw with the brain in my head. I consulted a plastic surgeon—whose daughter had been my high school classmate—to talk about reducing the larger breast that was not only plaguing my thoughts but also causing me significant discomfort during exercise. I went to the consultation alone, without telling any-one my plans.

I explained my concerns to the doctor and surprised him by lifting my shirt unsolicited, without shyness or shame, to show him the problem. He asked me to wait a moment and called in his nurse, explaining that this was his procedure with female patients. She joined us and I doffed my shirt again. How could I tell them these breasts felt rented to me? That I forgot I was female until I looked in the mirror? That I felt no shame or desire to shield them from view because *they didn't belong to me, they were given to me in error.*

They made some calculations and notes and advised me I could put my shirt back on. The nurse passed me a photo album and told me to have a look and see what I would like done. Page after page of women with their faces blurred, all naked from the waist up showing their surgically altered breasts. *What I want done is to take them off completely. I don't want them, they aren't mine, and I don't need them because I'm a young man. Could I please return them?* Until that moment, I had never acknowledged any specific wishes for what I wanted my body to be.

"I'd like the right one made smaller, to be the same size as the left one," I said, familiar with the disappointment I felt at having to compromise.

"Your left one is barely an A cup," the doctor said. "We could enlarge the left one to match the right and you'd be a solid B cup on both sides."

"God, no!" I blurted. "I mean, thanks, but I run marathons and play basketball; I need them smaller so they don't hurt my neck when I do sports." *I need them gone.*

"I understand," he said, nodding. *No, you don't. You have no clue, but no one does.*

"The good news is health care will pay for it. Because you're having pain and other symptoms, it's not considered elective surgery."

"That is good news."

I scheduled the surgery for the end of the semester and went home to tell my parents. Dad blushed with embarrassment and offered little input other than saying he was glad I wouldn't have a sore neck anymore. Mom enlightened me on a whole myriad of plastic surgery dreams she had for me.

"You should also get your ears pinned, and maybe get a chin implant, too," she—never having had plastic surgery—enthused.

"A chin implant?" I frowned. "What do I need that for? And what's wrong with my ears?"

"Well, your chin, it's a little ... weak." She shrugged. "And your ears stick out. Remember Kurt got his done? They're much better now." Kurt was my cousin and, in fairness, the kid had looked like a human Dumbo before his surgery.

"My ears aren't anything like Kurt's." I wondered silently what else she thought was wrong with me. *Everything.* "Anyhow, I'm only doing this breast thing. That's it." I frowned at her again, puzzled by this sudden and previously unspoken interest in my having multiple surgical procedures. *Maximal surgeries for a minimal chin.*

The surgery proceeded without any complications. I felt a strange pride in the scarred breast—it was a glancing but significant blow against my mistakenly assigned femaleness. It wasn't that I wanted to mutilate myself or that I felt hatred toward my body or my breasts; they just weren't *right*. Although I had no idea in those days that transgender men often underwent "top surgery"—a full mastectomy with chest contouring—I saw my breasts as accessories, never meant to be a permanent part of my body.

My early twenties held little promise for me accepting or improving upon my female experience. My renewed ability to exercise helped me regain my slim, boyish shape, but depression fell on me like a heavy fog, relieved only briefly by basketball and nights drinking and dancing in the clubs or at parties. I was frequently ill with head colds, sore throats, and felt a general malaise and fatigue all the time, which led me to see my family doctor. She spoke to me for several minutes, took some blood, and gently asked if I could be depressed. I assured her there was no way I was depressed, that I was certain I suffered from some serious illness. She explained that she found that unlikely and would call me if my blood work showed anything unusual, and I left.

A few months passed and my energy level and health didn't improve, so I went to a Calgary clinic where a well-known sports medicine doctor named Ralph Strother worked. My colleagues at the specialized running shoe store where I worked part time spoke well of him, so I booked an appointment. Again, I shared my concerns as he listened with obvious empathy. He asked to check my vitals and as he did, he asked me about my life.

"You have a very strong heart—you're obviously a runner," he observed, moving to look in my ears. "What else do you do for training?"

"Basketball, weight lifting, cycling—but mainly running and basketball," I answered.

"Hmm," he murmured, checking my reflexes several times. "And you had recent blood work, right?"

"Yup, all clear."

"Hop off the table and have a seat here." He motioned to a chair and sat across from me. "Everything else okay? School going well?" I nodded. "Okay. My suspicion is you may be suffering from depression."

"Really?" I asked, disbelieving.

"Quite possibly. It can feel and look a lot like a physical illness. It is an illness, all the same. You feel lethargic, get little niggly colds and things that don't heal up, mainly because your whole system is down, you know?"

"Uh-huh."

"Is there anything you've been upset about? Anything troubling you deep down?" I shrugged, not wanting to have this conversation. "If you aren't comfortable telling me, it's okay. You might find it helpful to talk to a friend, or maybe see a psychologist or therapist. They can be terrific people to share problems with and help you figure out a solution so you can feel better."

"I don't know," I said, doubtful anyone could help. "I think I just have trouble with my, you know... femininity, that's all." He nodded patiently.

"I had a young man in here the other day who was having a tough time, working through whether he could be homosexual—gay, I guess." He looked at me meaningfully. "He decided to find a therapist to talk with, and I told him if he continued to feel lousy after talking about it, there are medications for depression that are proving very effective for many people struggling with different life issues." His eyes felt like an X-ray, scanning me, knowing exactly what was going on inside my head. *He doesn't know. How could he possibly know about this? No one talks about it, no one knows about it. I'm the only person I know like this in Calgary, in Canada.*

"I don't want to take medication."

"I understand. You don't have to do anything you don't want to, but just remember it's an option. You don't have to feel bad forever." *Actually, I'm pretty sure I do, Doc.*

"Thanks, Doctor. I'll think about it."

"Okay. Take care. And pop back and see me in three months' time and we'll see how you're feeling, okay?"

"I will. Thanks." It would be far longer than three months before I returned to see him, not because I didn't like Dr. Strother, but because I liked him so much, I didn't want to disappoint him.

8

A GUY CAN DREAM
(1988–1989)

SIX YEARS, FOUR schools, four changes of major, and a degree-and-a-half-worth of coursework later, I was about to graduate from the University of Calgary with a BA in English. I carried a reduced course load in my final year, which enabled me to work part time at the Tech Shop, the running store I'd had a job with all throughout high school and summers.

On a cool, grey March day the previous spring, I'd been working alone in the store when two athletes entered wearing flashy, thigh-length ski jackets pronouncing them as members of the Monaco Bobsled Team. In the year leading up to the 1988 Calgary Olympic Winter Games, many athletes trained in town and shopped in our store, but I'd never seen these two before.

The shorter of the two was a handsome dark-haired man who seemed to speak only Parisian French. His taller, fair-haired companion spoke French as well, but when he spoke with me, he switched to English with ease, displaying the accent of a Canadian news anchor.

"Is this you?" he asked me, pointing to a framed photo on the wall, a group shot of several staff members after we ran the Calgary Marathon.

"Yeah, that's me," I answered, feeling a little unworthy to be in the same photo as several of Canada's top distance runners when I was a three-and-three-quarter-hour marathoner at best.

"Wow, a marathon—that's big time," he said without sarcasm. I shrugged, trying to appear nonchalant. He held up a large black ballet slipper. We were the only non–dance shop in town that sold ballet slippers for men and women.

"Do these jocks come with straps?" he asked with a boyish smirk. I couldn't help but find him amusing. The thing was probably a size ten or eleven.

"You wish," I replied.

"A guy can dream, can't he?" He moved over to a rack of Adidas Olympic sweatshirts that were all the rage ahead of the Calgary games. I returned to the front register where I'd been working on some pricing and inventory. After a hushed conversation in French between him and his teammate, the fair-haired man picked up six of the sweatshirts—a hundred dollars a pop—and placed them on the front counter.

"Can I keep all my things here until I'm done?" he asked.

"Sure," I replied, adding, "Just let me know if there's anything I can help you with."

"I will." He moved over to a rack of running tights and began selecting several pairs. I wondered what sort of wisecrack he might make about them. He spent the next fifteen or twenty minutes working his way around the store, trying things on and cracking cheesy jokes to make me laugh. Then he became serious. "So, do you work here full time?"

"No, about half time," I said. "I'm just finishing the last couple courses for my degree."

"Cool." He placed a pile of high-tech running clothing on the counter. He and his friend discussed the many items the store had and each added to his respective pile. The French man paid for his items first, speaking no English. Bags in hand, he continued to browse while his friend paid for his stack of things.

"Does your friend speak any English?" I asked.

"Oh, yeah, he's just a snob." He smiled mischievously at me.

"You speak perfect English," I ventured. "Were you born in Canada?" He laughed.

"No, my mother's family is American," he said. "I was born in Monaco, but went to school in Philadelphia. I spent a lot of time in the US growing up."

As I rang things in, I knew it would be a large sale, but I inhaled slightly when the total came to well over three thousand dollars, the largest sale I'd ever had working there. He passed me his nondescript-looking VISA card, which bore the name Albert de Monaco.

"Would you like to have dinner with me tonight?" he asked me as I frowned at the card, racking my brains to figure out why I felt I should know him. I ran the card through the reader and waited for it to respond, half thinking the name was phony and I'd be told to seize the card and call the police. It came back approved and I watched as he signed the slip.

"I'd love to, but it's my mother's birthday," I replied. "My family's taking her out for dinner."

"Too bad," he said, sounding like he meant it. I still wasn't sure if he was kidding, since strange men I'd just met didn't often ask me to dinner. Still, despite the lack of any romantic yearnings on my part, I felt a little disappointed I couldn't make it because he seemed like a very interesting person.

We talked more about his training as a bobsledder for Monaco's national team and he said he'd be back in Calgary later in the year.

"Is this the best place to find you, then?" I wondered what "best" meant—better than my house? Better than my gym? Best for what?

"Yeah, I'm here quite a bit," I answered.

"Thanks again for all the help. You're a good salesperson. Really."

"Thanks. It was my pleasure. Good luck with your training."

"You, too," he winked. "With the marathons, I mean." He and his friend walked out, laden with several bags each.

I told the story to my family at dinner and we all laughed about how hard it must have been for me not to ditch them in favor of a dinner date with a dashing athlete. My mom expressed mock indignation that I would even consider missing an occasion as important as her birthday for a date, and I forgot all about it as the week wore on.

That Saturday at our weekly staff meeting, store manager Ron mentioned the sale. "And Lori, congrats on the de Monaco sale, three thousand bucks!" As the staff oohed and aahed, my colleague Carol jumped up and ran to the back storage area.

"Be right back!" she shouted. As we all exchanged puzzled

looks, she returned clutching one of the *Sports Illustrated* magazines from the staff washroom. She found the "Star Tracks" section near the back of the magazine and pointed to a picture of Prince Albert of Monaco. "Is this him?" She handed it to me.

"Yup." Over the years, I've wondered how much my mom secretly wishes I'd skipped her birthday for a meal with a prince, but I think he and I both lived out our destinies.

My passion for sports intersected with my love of writing when ABC Sports hired me as a researcher for the 1988 Calgary Winter Olympics. My idea of what a researcher did proved to be wrong. I'd imagined myself toiling away in a film library, but instead found myself at a desk on set sixteen hours a day, seven days a week, taking the on-air talent on tours of Calgary and trading pins with the likes of Michael J. Fox and Woody Harrelson.

For the eight weeks surrounding the games, I provided ABC's writers and broadcasters on *Good Morning America*, *Late Night with Frank and Kathie Lee Gifford*, and the prime-time Olympic coverage hosted by Jim McKay and Keith Jackson with local Calgary knowledge and background.

Prince Albert of Monaco came on the show and we laughed and chatted on the set, recalling our first meeting the year before at the Tech Shop. We promised to have a coffee later in the week if our schedules allowed, but with me working sixteen-hour days seven days a week and him competing, it was no surprise that it was the last time we spoke.

The real buzz for me came not in rubbing elbows with celebrities, but in being at what felt like the center of the news, sports, and entertainment universe. No one forced me to work such long days; I never wanted to go home, fearing I might miss something amazing. I was the only person with my particular job as a Calgary expert and all-around gofer; everyone else was either a writer or an on-air host. All of my colleagues normally worked in New York City as writers for magazines such as *Sports Illustrated*, *Newsweek*, and *Time* or as broadcasters covering various US professional or NCAA sports teams nationally and locally.

When I allowed myself to imagine living a normal life, I dreamed of living and working as a writer in New York City. I shared this dream with a couple of my colleagues, including my boss, Draggan Mihailovich, who would go on to become an Emmy-winning producer with CBS's *60 Minutes*. They were supportive and generously offered to help me find a job and use their names as references. The idea both thrilled and terrified me and I saw the opportunity as one that doesn't come around every day. I told them I would be available at the beginning of May and resolved to keep in touch while I finished my last semester.

All of my fears and insecurities roared to the surface, yet again. How could I set out on this professional path knowing I presented myself as someone I wasn't? I saw myself as an imposter, posing as a woman, inauthentic to my very core. Whatever talents and skills I possessed alternatively shone and hid, bobbing above and below the water's surface like a drowning swimmer. *Now you see me, now you don't.* One moment, I thought I held the world by the tail, the next I quaked with self-doubt.

One day I stood in front of the job board in the student union, reading an advertisement for an entry-level pharmaceutical sales job with 3M Canada. Salary, bonuses, company car, benefits. *Security.* A week after finishing with ABC Sports, my mood had darkened and I felt the ache of knowing the high point of my fledgling professional life was fading from sight in the rearview mirror. My dream of New York now seemed impossible and I panicked, wondering what I would do after graduating. I hurriedly submitted an application for the 3M position.

A few weeks later, I handed in my last final exam at U of C and ran to the car, where Dad waited to drive me to the airport for a flight to 3M Canada's headquarters in London, Ontario. I sat through a jam-packed day of exams, personality inventories, and interviews before I was offered the position. I accepted. 3M Canada flew me home to pack some things for the three-week training session and I flew back to London three days later. I would be marketing the cardiac medication Tambocor to cardiologists all over my territory of Alberta and Saskatchewan, and, when not on the road, I'd work from my apartment.

One lunch hour, I broke from our group of fifteen to pick up some new nylons at the local mall. Not knowing my way around, I wound my way past the stores until I turned a corner and stood in front of a massive wall of mirrors, showing me from every angle. I stared at this sharp-dressed *woman*, clad in a burnt orange, brown, and green Jones New York houndstooth blazer, forest green Holt Renfrew wool turtleneck and matching pencil skirt, and dark brown belt and pumps, and realized with a shock that I could not recognize the person looking back at me. *This is not me. What am I doing here?*

I stood like that for several minutes, a conflicted Narcissus, both obsessed with and disdainful of my image in the mirror.

Am I too focused on my physical image? On myself, cloaked in the false security of these designer labels? An older woman walking past me asked if I was okay. I nodded, wordless, and she continued on her way, satisfied. *I always manage to satisfy the onlookers,* was the thought that echoed in my head. *I always play my role. I can fool all the people most of the time. What does that mean?*

Rattled, I checked my watch and realized that I was going to be late getting back to the training if I didn't move. I forced my legs to walk and returned to class, playing my role again. Later on, back in my hotel room, I turned on MTV as I changed into my running clothes. A new video played, a grainy, hand-held camera image shot from a moving car. The singer, who I would later learn was Tracy Chapman, sang the words to "Fast Car." The haunting beauty and loneliness of the music struck me deep inside like a dagger; the lyrics described a hard life and memories of better times riding in a fast car. I broke down completely; those deep, wracking sobs of grief shook me.

As I traveled over and over to western Canadian hospitals, a question plagued me: *Is this all there is? Is this the rest of my life? I am Willy Loman.* Somehow I had chosen sales, a profession steeped in superficiality and first impressions, and I held that job for less than six months before depression and loneliness led me to resign. Still, after leaving 3M, I worked in both advertising and insurance and wouldn't leave the field for another two years, the pay and perks seductive and narcotic at times.

The funny thing is I was good at sales, which only made me feel more conflicted. The closest I got to my New York dream was a short trip in November 1988 to run the New York City Marathon, where I stayed with friends from ABC who again tried to encourage me to come and work there. Draggan took me to lunch and urged me to let him introduce me to some people, but somehow the idea seemed too impossible to entertain, too impractical. I declined. *If they knew the truth about me, they would never help me find a job; they would never be my friends.*

Back home, I volunteered with a group of University of Calgary alumni giving speeches to high school students on the value of a university education. I'd always loved public speaking and welcomed the chance to give back to the community and to my school. I agreed to speak at a local high school and took some time out of my morning schedule with my boss's blessing. I chose to wear a fitted, dark green, wool Balenciaga dress with black leather buttons I'd bought in New York.

Standing in front of the class, I spoke eloquently and passionately about the doors my degree had opened for me, even very shortly after graduation. I found myself exhorting the students to follow their dreams, encouraging them to take risks, confront their fears, pursue fields of study and work that they loved, and not seek jobs strictly based on the security they could provide. Somehow, what I said seemed to inspire them and, to my shock, they rose to their feet in applause when I finished. I felt like the biggest phony, like a giant hypocrite. *You're a fraud. You can sell anything.*

I slid into my brand new Honda sports coupe—another status symbol that failed to satisfy me—and drove, but not to my office and not to my apartment. Instead, I found myself parked in front of my parents' home, staring at the dashboard. Finally, I let myself in the back door, called out a hello, and was met by Mom, who was in the kitchen.

"Hi, Mom." I slipped my pumps off and stepped into the kitchen. She frowned at me.

"What are you doing here? Is everything okay?" Emotion choked my throat and I couldn't speak. I cried few tears, but those deep, wracking sobs of grief that I was becoming all too familiar with overtook me. I reached for her and hugged her, her body stiff with shock and discomfort. "What's the matter? What happened?" It was nearly a minute before I could speak, shuddering and sobbing incomprehensibly.

"I'm—just—so—lonely," I finally gasped. I hadn't wanted to say anything, but it popped out from nowhere. She held me at arm's length to look at my face, confusion written all over hers.

"How can that be? You have so many friends," she said. We sat down at the kitchen table.

"I feel so alone," I lamented. "I don't know why."

"Aren't you supposed to be at work?"

"Yeah, I'll go back in a minute."

"You should probably get back there. Have you been away for long?" I nodded.

"A couple hours. I was giving a speech." She passed me some tissues.

"You don't look too bad; no one will notice," she said, trying to comfort me, but her efficiency and concern about my job only made me feel worse.

"Okay. I better go." I finished dabbing at my eyes and stood up. "Thanks, Mom."

"Have a good day." I walked out the back door, got in the car, and drove back to the office, where I resumed my work.

Depression dogged me the following months until I accepted that my true passion lay in writing, and I finally left sales.

My parents couldn't understand why I would shun stable, lucrative jobs and I had no answer for them. But I immediately landed a job as a copy runner with the *Calgary Herald*, the city's leading daily newspaper in those days.

Adrenaline coursed through my body during every shift. Similar to how I'd felt about ABC Sports, the *Herald* newsroom represented the living, pulsating center of the city to me. In the pre-Internet world of the late 1980s and early 1990s, my copy runner job consisted of physically tearing paper stories off the machines owned by each wire service—Reuters, Associated Press, United Press International, and Canadian Press—in the wire room, a small office in the newsroom. I would scan each news item and determine which editor's desk—World, Canada, City, Sports, Business, Lifestyle—to run it to. Reporting jobs were scarce, but the editors routinely assigned me features and I published several pieces there. I rarely wanted to leave at the end of my shift.

I spent most of my time off playing pickup basketball at various gyms in Calgary and began dating a handsome young African American man I'd met one Saturday afternoon. Marcus was in town from Alabama for several months of sales training, ironically, and we hit it off immediately. My friends all liked him and I found him warm, soft-spoken, and smart. He and his two colleagues were easy to be with and began playing ball and dancing at the clubs with my friends and me. I liked hanging out with him, but I also liked the sense that my friends were more relaxed around me with my first boyfriend in years, as though they were relieved that I was straight and normal. I wanted that so desperately; I worked to maintain their comfort.

I felt shadowed by a sense that something remained missing in my relationships with men until I made a decision to lose my virginity to Marcus a few weeks before he was scheduled to return to the US. In the same way I had tried marijuana to confirm for myself that I wasn't interested in it, I felt I needed to sleep with Marcus to see whether or not I was heterosexual. I'd been working so hard on suppressing my transgender identity that I hadn't thought critically about whether it was more who I was going to bed *as* that was my problem, rather than who I was *with*. Now that I knew a couple of lesbians and gay men, I felt like my life would be so much easier if my only problem was being gay. Homosexuality looked like a walk in the park to me, compared to being transgender.

I booked a room at the Banff Springs Hotel and picked Marcus up after work late one winter evening. All he knew was that I was taking him somewhere nice. We drove west on the Trans-Canada Highway through the bright, clear night, seeing stars and the northern lights, which mesmerized Marcus, since he'd never seen anything like them in the Deep South.

"Are those reindeer?" he asked, pointing to the animals pictured on the large yellow warning signs near Tunnel Mountain.

"Moose. They have huge antlers, like reindeer. I've never seen them near this stretch of highway, but you do see bears quite a bit along here."

"Like *grizzly* bears?" Marcus peered out the window into the starlit night, wide-eyed.

"Sometimes, or black bears. Brown bears, too."

We drove in silence for a few beats as we rounded a long, sweeping curve in the wide highway. Suddenly, a massive bull moose loomed, standing right in our path. I jammed on the brakes as I swerved to the left to avoid hitting him. We then passed the moose very slowly, Marcus watching through the passenger window, the huge beast merely two or three feet away from him with only the car door separating them.

"Whoa . . ." Marcus breathed. "Dang, that's a big one."

"That is a big one."

"Damn." Marcus twisted in his seat, watching out the rear window as we slowly left the moose behind us. It was lucky there was almost no traffic on the road. The moose turned and galloped back into the woods.

Marcus's eyes widened further as we left the car with a valet and a doorman opened the grand old Banff Springs Hotel's main doors for us.

"It's like a castle," he marveled.

"This is my favorite hotel," I told him. We checked in and found our room.

After touring the hotel, we settled on the bed watching TV, both of us tired and a little overwhelmed. I have no idea whether I tended to attract queer-identified men, but looking back, it wouldn't be a surprise. I was very boyish-looking—my hair was very short, my body slim and muscular, my casual clothing androgynous—and, like all of my boyfriends, Marcus seemed in no hurry to get my clothes off or have sex. Making out was our preferred activity, and we did so for a long time. Finally, I asked, "Should we do this thing?"

He smiled at me, lazily stroking my stomach. "Yeah, let's do it."

"Okay. You have condoms, right?"

"Check."

"I just have to use the washroom—be right back." I kissed him and grabbed my overnight bag, closing the bathroom door.

My heart pounded in my chest like a jackhammer. I sat on the lid of the toilet and closed my eyes, trying to figure out what I was feeling. *Terror. Yes.* Not fear of Marcus; I was terrified of getting pregnant. *I seriously doubt I'm capable of getting pregnant, but it would be just my luck that I would and I'm not even a woman.* I fumbled in my overnight kit and pulled out one of two barrier method contraceptives I planned to use in addition to Marcus's condom—a spermicidal sponge and some kind of cervical cap deal I'd seen in the drug store. *Can't be too careful.* "Ha!" I laughed out loud at the utter madness of such obsessive behavior. Marcus tapped gently on the door.

"You okay in there?"

"Yup, be right out," I called, my voice higher than normal. I double-checked the instructions and readied myself for contact. I thought fleetingly of how much happier I'd be if it were my penis we were working with, then just as quickly dismissed that dream, admonishing myself for indulging in fantasy. *Deal with the parts you have, Shenher.*

I returned to the bed and we got down to what I thought was going to be the business. After a few minutes of foreplay, I suddenly pulled back.

"Is the condom on?" I asked.

"I have it all ready to go, don't worry," Marcus reassured me. I felt grateful one of us was calm.

"Okay, because we can't forget it, you know."

"I know, girl." *Girl* clanged in my head like a broken church bell and I felt all kinds of wrong. We resumed where we'd left off, Marcus gentle and me nervous as a priest in a lingerie store, not feeling at all sexy. *So not me. I'm not a girl.* After a few more minutes, we both lay on our backs, nestled together. "Is this working for you?" Marcus asked, genuinely interested. I sighed.

"It's nice," I answered.

"A ringing endorsement," Marcus laughed, hugging me close. "Seriously, we don't have to do this, it's cool with me."

We lay there like that for a long time. I didn't realize I was crying until Marcus noticed his chest was wet. He propped himself up on an elbow to look at me. "Hey, what's wrong? I don't want to make you cry." I shook my head.

"You didn't; it's me," I whispered. "It's not your fault at all."

"You can tell me."

"Telling people doesn't make it better," I said softly. "I've tried a couple of times." He laid his head back down beside mine.

"I might not be able to fix it, but I can listen." I felt his heart beating against my cheek. I felt a crushing sadness to know that he would soon return to the US. I didn't move. Resigned, I inhaled deeply.

"Here's the deal," I began. "And you definitely can't fix it."

We lay there and I told him of my secret self. He listened quietly—so quietly, I feared that at any moment he would stand up, get dressed, and walk out the door. But he listened until I was done.

"I feel so bad for you," he said softly. "What a burden the Lord has given you to carry." He'd told me before of his Southern Baptist upbringing, though he was no longer active in a church. Still, when he uttered phrases like that, I had to smile. "What?" he asked, self-conscious.

"I can't believe you're still here, talking to me."

"Where else would I be?"

"I dunno."

"I can say I've never met anyone like you."

"I've never met anyone like me, either," I laughed. "Hey, I'm sorry tonight didn't quite go how we'd hoped."

"Ah, don't worry about it. I feel pretty special you even tried at all."

"I wanted to close my eyes and pretend it would just be normal, you know?" He wrinkled his face up in distaste.

"Ouch. Thanks," he smiled.

"You know what I mean. It has nothing to do with you. You're great."

"So, what do we do now?"

"Can we hang until you go back home?"

"Sure. Friends?" he raised his eyebrows, waiting for my answer.

"Yeah. Although I will miss the necking."

"Maybe we could do a little of that, just until I leave?"

"I think I could manage that," I laughed, pulling him close.

Marcus left two weeks later and although we exchanged addresses on his last night, we never were in contact again.

My relationship with Marcus remains in my memory as one of those precious gifts of connection that are fleeting, beautiful, and meaningful. At low points, remembering Marcus's understanding and acceptance of me kept me going and gave me a glimmer of hope there might be more people in the world who could see past this curse I lived with.

COWBOY POETRY
(1989–1990)

CATHERINE FORD, THE *Calgary Herald*'s formidable managing editor, encouraged my writing and advised me to look for work as a reporter/photographer in a rural center since there were no openings at the big Alberta dailies. Heeding her words, I struck out for the weekly community papers of Alberta. After working for a brief time in the small town of Hanna, my editor asked me if I would be willing to move to a larger paper he owned and his wife operated, the *Pincher Creek Echo*. I became the *Echo*'s only reporter/photographer, renting a room in the small house of a terrific fishing guide named Vic.

Compared to Hanna's starkly beautiful ranch lands, Pincher Creek was a picturesque dream: luscious green foothills becoming larger and more forested as you drove west and the prairies met the mountains. My job entailed chasing down stories across a large territory and I'd regularly drive west through the Crowsnest Pass and south to Waterton Lakes National Park. One July Fourth, I drove all the way to Babb, Montana, for lunch.

One weekend, my editor assigned me to cover the Best of the West Pincher Creek cowboy poetry festival, a highlight for a lone, small-town reporter. At this annual event, cowboys read poetry without a mic and occasionally played guitar on a small stage under the stars, while an eager audience of local artists and ranchers listened with rapt attention. The first night's reading stirred me deeply; listening to a soft-spoken, proud ranch hand talk of existential loneliness and pain in the midst of his deep appreciation for a life lived outdoors, I felt a kinship with him and the men that followed. I could relate to tales of solitude on the range because they invoked my own powerful sense of loneliness.

Although I had more than enough photos and information to write my story after that first night, I returned the next evening wearing jeans, a plaid shirt, old cowboy boots, and my beloved denim Lee Storm Rider jacket with its corduroy collar and blanket lining—all under the relative cover of darkness.

Until that night the most undeniably male ensemble I'd ever dared to wear, other than basketball or workout gear, was a baseball cap and jeans as I hiked near my house in the dusk. I knew many women who wore caps as casual wear but, just like having short hair back in the days of Laura Desmond, it was far more loaded for me. I usually felt terrified to wear a ball cap because it confused people. But now, an overwhelming compulsion to stop resisting my true gender identity took hold and I felt powerless to stop it.

No one knew me, as I'd only been in town a few weeks. I sat on my blanket under the stars as the poetry and music washed over me. An aproned man of about forty-five walked up, carrying a large roasting pan with tin foil covering the top.

"Wouldja like a burger, son?" he asked, squatting to my level and setting the pan on the grass. He pulled back the foil to reveal several huge, steaming burgers.

"Yes, please," I answered, pulling my wallet from my jeans. "How much?"

"Two dollars, bun included."

"You come here every year?" I asked.

"Yes, sir, I do," he replied proudly. "Wouldn't miss it."

"Are you a rancher? Is this your beef?" My reporter's mind buzzed with questions.

"You bet; I got a cattle ranch up near Longview. This is the only weekend I take off all year. A fella needs to be among people now and then, you know?" I nodded. He passed me a burger and offered condiments. I spooned onions and mustard on top.

"Thank you." I bit into it greedily, realizing how hungry I'd become.

"My pleasure, son—you take care, now." He stood and moved away through the crowd.

"Yes, sir." My face burned with both pride and embarrassment, the incredible high of being seen as a young man battling mightily with the shame of deception. In the past, I'd felt angry and frustrated when people assumed I was male, but today, in my cowboy clothes, it felt right, as though this was meant to be. *Am I deceiving him if this is who I am?* I had never considered this question before.

My work days continued to involve short road trips, and I found myself drinking beer in Crowsnest Pass biker bars and having illuminating afternoon conversations with the intriguing strangers who frequent bars during the day. Because I looked like a bare-faced teenage boy the proprietors invariably demanded identification from me and I gladly complied, breathing through their double-takes and apologies when they saw the *F* on my driver's license.

"What's your story, hon?" Maggie ran a dish towel around the inside of a beer glass before placing it on the shelf with the clean ones. I made a mental note to switch back to bottled beer from draught. I shrugged noncommittally and took another swig from my glass.

"C'mon. Everyone has a story." She leaned in further across the bar and smiled. She was pretty and not much older than me. I'd noticed her since the first time I visited this seedy bar beside an old sawmill on the side of the highway. We often talked about the weather as she worked. The winter sky grew darker as I sat there.

"What would you like to know?"

"Why do you always come in alone?" She stopped cleaning, focusing on me.

"Because I *am* alone," I smirked coyly, watching her blue eyes sparkle. She turned away from me, walking down the bar to a customer who'd caught her eye, to pour him a beer. Eventually, she returned to me.

"That sounds a little sad," she said. "You don't have a boyfriend?" I shook my head. She stood still, watching me. "Girlfriend?" I shook my head again, feeling a flush rising in my cheeks. "I'm sorry, I didn't mean to pry."

"It's okay." I watched her, surprised, realizing my attraction to her. "I've just never thought about it before," I lied.

"The boyfriend part?"

"No, just all of it." She nodded knowingly. I knew she didn't buy it. She leaned in a little closer to me, but not aggressively, and not so much that I felt uncomfortable.

"I'm drawn to people who are a little different," she said. "So are a lot more people than you might think." I watched her as I took a swig of beer.

"I didn't know that," I croaked.

"I get off at six," she said softly. "You want to talk a little? We could go somewhere else."

"Okay." Six was only fifteen minutes away. She smiled and walked into the kitchen area, out of sight. A wave of panic crested inside my chest. I took a twenty from my wallet—far more than covering the two pints I'd had—placed it beside the glass she'd wiped earlier, grabbed my coat, and walked quickly out to my car. I pulled onto the highway, my stomach twisted in knots. I felt like a jerk imagining Maggie when she saw that I'd left. I knew I could either disappoint her then by walking out or disappoint her later when she discovered what I was— more than just a little different. I never returned.

What is the matter with me? Everything. Who could ever love me? No one.

That summer a violent conflict between Indigenous land protestors and Canadian government forces took place in Oka, Quebec, over the threat of traditional Mohawk lands being developed into a golf course. Back home in Pincher Creek, we had our own local crisis. As summer heated up, I began reporting on the opposition to the contested Oldman River Dam project a few miles northwest of the town. Indigenous people opposed the project as one that threatened their traditional ways of life, and environmentalists joined them, warning of irreparable damage to the ecosystem of the area if the project went ahead.

The Peigan Nation's Lonefighters Society, a collection of Indigenous activists from the 75 percent of the Peigan Nation who opposed the dam, welcomed me as an embedded journalist that August. Their camp was located in the crusty, dried-out riverbed just downstream from where excavation work had already begun despite a court order ruling against the dam's construction. I traded in my Honda CRX for an old Suzuki Samurai 4x4 to make the trip over the rugged terrain.

I visited the camp several times, sleeping overnight on the ground under the Lonefighters' tents. They treated me with respect and generosity, sharing their food, passing the pipe to me to smoke with them, and allowing me to smudge—make an offering of burning tobacco—when I came and went from the camp. I brought the *Pincher Creek Echo* to them each week. They eagerly read my stories and allowed me to photograph them and the area around their camp.

As the situation escalated into an armed standoff between the Lonefighters and the Royal Canadian Mounted Police (RCMP), I witnessed firsthand a tiny microcosm of the racism experienced by Indigenous peoples in Canada. My editor demanded that I stop covering the story from the camp because, despite my attempts at balance, she felt our paper's advertisers would object to us questioning the legality of the dam project.

I admired the Lonefighters' struggle; they had no choice other than to fight for what they believed in. I was aware of the protective cloak of white privilege I wore. I understood fundamentally that I could choose whether to show my otherness or hide it, whereas Indigenous people did not enjoy that freedom of choice. I refused to stop covering what I believed was the most important local issue that year, so my editor and I amicably agreed to part ways, forcing me to look for a new job.

I STOOD IN front of the full-length mirror in my newly rented room and surveyed myself, arms folded across my shirtless chest, wearing only a pair of men's boxer briefs. Not only did I need to consider the old adage about making sure one wore clean underwear in case one ended up in the hospital, I had the added worry of making sure I wore underwear corresponding with my assigned sex in preparation for such situations. The boxer briefs seemed too bold a statement—I felt ill-equipped to explain them in a medical setting—so I only wore them when I was alone in my room with mournful Britpop such as the Stone Roses' debut album and the Smiths' *The Queen Is Dead* playing in the background. Most nights, Elvis Costello's "Town Cryer" lulled me to sleep, the aching beauty of the orchestral outro sweeping me away.

Now living just outside of Edmonton, Alberta, I covered sports and crime for the *Morinville Gazette*, a local weekly paper, and lived with a wonderful couple, Ted and Louise Code, who ran an environmental consultancy firm from home. The *Morinville Gazette* employed a second reporter, Sharon Buckley—an Irish Canadian with a delightfully sardonic, razor-sharp wit—and we soon became friends.

Ted, Louise, their dog Max, and Sharon provided me with a family of sorts and I felt welcomed by them. My brother Jake worked as a lawyer in downtown Edmonton and we saw each other as much as our busy schedules would allow. Still, I felt that familiar ache—of loneliness, of not being known, of not allowing myself to be known. Of hiding in plain sight.

The paper assigned me to cover Junior A hockey—a dream in a province whose backbone was ice hockey. I dreamed of returning to the *Calgary Herald* or another daily as a sports reporter, so I welcomed this assignment. I drove an hour through a blizzard and arrived at the arena early one evening to cover my first game. I'd covered lower divisions before, but not Junior A. I carried a new 35mm Canon SLR camera with an automatic winder capable of shooting eight frames per second, exciting new technology vital for taking great action shots.

St. Albert won the game and I made my way through the large crowd to the dressing room to interview the players, thrilled with the photos I'd captured. I stood patiently outside the door as the players walked inside, high-fiving, giving each other elaborate postgame handshakes, and performing stick-tapping rituals. The coach was the last of the staff to enter the room, and I caught his eye as he followed them in.

"Hi, Coach. I'm from the *Gazette*. Can I come in and talk to some of the guys for a minute?"

He eyed me up and down, taking in my big snow boots, heavy down jacket, wool hat, and camera bag.

"What's your name?"

"Lori Shenher."

"Lori."

"Yeah."

"Sorry, Lori. No ladies allowed in the dressing room." I tried not to show how hard "ladies" stung. Even if I had been a lady, that word would have pissed me off.

"Uh, okay. I'm fine with the whole dressing-room thing, they can do what they want."

"Yeah. Right up until you complain about their language or a towel slipping or them asking you out." He paused, looking at me closer again. "Although, that probably won't be an issue for you—you're one of those dykes, I'm guessing."

He walked into the dressing room without another word. I stood there, my jaw clenched tight, furious at being misidentified as a lady and a lesbian. Furious at myself for not saying something. Furious at the world, because what could I say? I waited nearly forty-five minutes until an acne-faced player came out who I recognized as the scorer of two of St. Albert's goals.

"Hey, Dave, I'm Lori Shenher from the *Gazette*. Great game tonight—you got a sec?"

He smiled and stopped. "Sure!"

NOTHING HAD PREPARED me for Edmonton in November. Unlike Calgary, which enjoyed occasional Chinook winds that could melt the ice away and raise temperatures from far below freezing to near room temperature in a span of hours, Edmonton remained cold and dark from October to April. Determined to leave as soon as possible, each Sunday I visited Edmonton's Whyte Avenue—a trendy, bohemian stretch of coffee shops and artsy boutiques—to buy a *Calgary Herald* and a *Vancouver Sun* and scan the job sections over an espresso.

One day, after a disappointing read of the *Herald* that produced no journalism jobs of interest, I opened the *Sun* and began reading. A couple of pages in, a feature story exploring the availability of "sex change" services in Canadian cities leapt off the page at me. I read eagerly about a clinic in Montréal offering surgeries for transgender people before I came to information describing western Canada's only gender dysphoria assessment clinic: a place where people who suspected they might be transgender could be assessed by medical doctors and psychologists. It was in Vancouver, operated by Vancouver General Hospital (VGH). According to the article, a positive assessment was the ticket to allowing a person to physically transition.

I sat there staring at the page. This was the first news story about transgender people I'd seen since learning of Renée Richards as a child. A strange new combination of shame and giddiness swept over me—in the past, I had felt only shame and hopelessness. *Could I actually do this thing? Could there be hope for someone like me? Could this be more than a distant fantasy?* It seemed decadent and childish to dream about such a thing. *Maybe this is real.*

I read further about how some larger public sector employers' medical benefit plans in Canada had begun covering transition treatments—hormones, surgeries, psychological counseling—and I imagined myself finding a workplace with such coverage. That same *Vancouver Sun*'s weekend employment section featured a recruitment ad for the Vancouver Police Department—a large organization that I figured must have a comprehensive health plan—and I decided to submit my application.

I'd considered policing before. I was drawn to the stability of a regular paycheck and the promise of a pension. The seamier side of life intrigued me; I knew I was able to fit in anywhere and imagined detective work to be similar to investigative reporting, where I saw myself as a truth seeker. Policing would provide me with exciting work, benefits, interesting experiences to write about, and a gender-neutral uniform, solving the daily dilemma of dressing myself. I was particularly interested in the good pay, as my rural reporter's salary barely covered my living expenses, and the *Gazette* didn't reimburse the gas I used to get to the hockey games I covered. My youthful impatience made the wait to find a job at a major daily intolerable, and my gender issues eroded my confidence in presenting myself professionally. I began to imagine Vancouver—a place I'd wanted to live since visiting on basketball road trips—as a place I could reinvent myself.

10

THE TRINITY OF MISUNDERSTANDING
(1990–1991)

LATE IN 1990, I flew to Vancouver for a day to be assessed at the VGH Gender Dysphoria Clinic and to visit the Vancouver Police Department (VPD) to pick up an application package. The VPD errand provided me with a more comfortable justification for the trip, but I told no one of either venture, departing and arriving back in Edmonton in the winter darkness. I visited the VPD first, taking a seat as directed in the small waiting room of the recruiting office alongside three stiff, white, young, scrubbed-looking men dressed in suits. A woman with a great mane of black hair called me to the front desk after a few minutes and asked me several questions. Apparently satisfied with my answers, she handed me a thick envelope filled with application documents and I was free to go.

As I walked through Vancouver's horribly neglected Downtown Eastside—a neighborhood filled with people suffering from untreated trauma, addiction, malnutrition, and mental illness—and over the Cambie Street Bridge to the upscale, bustling west side where VGH stood, a surreal incongruity struck me. Here I was—a person of privilege seeking a position of power. I'd just left a part of town full of people living on the fringes to reenter an affluent area where I looked like I belonged—yet I was expecting to receive a diagnosis of a condition that would leave me highly marginalized.

I stood on the street outside the hospital entrance, frozen. I had gone to a lot of trouble to come here, including confiding in Dr. Strother, who'd provided me with much-needed support and the required physician reference. Still, I felt panicked. *I don't need to be here. I can't do this. This is crazy. What if they agree I am transgender? What if they find I'm not? What made me think I could actually do this, that I could change something as seemingly immutable as my sex?* My heart pounded in my ears, throat choked, chest clenched. *Get your ass in that door.*

I took a deep breath and pulled the door open. In the elevator, I fought the urge to keep riding past the floor that the clinic was on, and stepped out into the hallway. Something about the neatly scripted letters of the VGH logo and the words "Gender Dysphoria Clinic" on the frosted glass window comforted me, signaling a level of professionalism and respectability I didn't expect. *What did I expect?* A shady, back-alley doorway, entered only after furtively tapping out a secret knock? The kind of place women were forced to go for abortions before they were legal; dirty, unsafe, and drenched in shame?

I walked in and stepped up to the reception desk.

"Hi, I'm Lori Shenher. I have a nine o'clock appointment."

"Excellent. Is there a name you'd prefer we call you by?" I frowned, confused. "Some people like to use a name that they feel better corresponds to their gender identity."

"Oh. Uh, Lori is fine," I said, remembering settling for Renée when I wanted to choose Sebastian in French class. "Maybe one day," I muttered under my breath as I sat down in the waiting area. A few minutes later, a warm, attractive, middle-aged woman with a neat brown bob greeted me.

"Lori? Hi, I'm Dr. Diane Watson. Come on in," she said, ushering me into her office. I knew her name from the newspaper pieces I'd read. She was a psychiatrist and the head of the clinic. "How are you?"

"Fine, thank you," I answered. Her manner felt welcoming and I began to feel far more at ease. "How are you?"

"I'm fine, thank you for asking." She folded her hands on her desk. "Tell me what brings you here."

I began telling my story, not knowing how much detail to include. She asked if she could take notes, and I agreed. When I'd finished, she reassured me that I could tell her anything that came up or I'd forgotten and explained that the day would consist of a physical examination, several psychological tests with her and her psychiatry resident, Dr. Kaye, and a final meeting with her to discuss their findings.

The only thing I can specifically remember about my test results was that Dr. Watson said they were almost off the chart, although I know those weren't her exact words. I measured as high as anyone she had ever tested for traits common to transgender patients, she told me. She qualified her comments to allow for variability in the findings and in gender identity in general, but she told me she had no doubt I presented as a transgender person in every clinically measurable way. A letter to Dr. Strother in my file reads: "Lori, by both of our opinions, suffers from true transsexualism. She was informed of this and treatment options were discussed with her."

A sort of manic euphoria overtook me when I heard this news. It wasn't as though the findings surprised me in any way; if anything, they validated all I'd been through and knew about myself. But Dr. Watson's words made it *real*, a living rabbit pulled from a hat that before today had held only my thoughts and intuitions, confirmed by no one and nothing empirical.

Dr. Watson explained that scientists studying gender dysphoria believed that the condition affected over 0.6 percent of the population (in North America alone, more than 1.6 million people in 1990)—but that it was difficult to quantify for certain because of the shame and stigma that prevents many from coming forward for assessment. Research in the field at the time of my visit was still in its early stages and Dr. Watson wasn't able to tell me much about any possible biological reasons behind why I was transgender.

Dr. Watson said that given that I had typically functioning anatomy for someone assigned female at birth, there was no way of knowing if I could be intersex—someone born with atypical variations in genetic structure, sexual anatomy, reproductive anatomy, and/or chromosomal makeup—without more extensive testing. We agreed that the end result wouldn't change much in terms of my reality: I felt like a man, despite my female anatomy. I didn't feel a need to pursue further testing to confirm this disconnect I already felt inside of myself.

Leaving the clinic, I peered out at the late-afternoon darkness and heavy rain lit by the harsh glare of street and car lights. I located Cambie Street—the only thoroughfare to the airport I knew of—and walked south, hoping to encounter the Airporter bus and save myself cab fare. Hailing a cab would be pointless anyway, as I was walking faster than the cars stuck in gridlock.

My denim jacket and backpack grew heavy, soaked with rain. I'd walked more than twenty blocks, but still no bus. What little knowledge I had of Vancouver was failing me and I became disoriented in the dark. I saw a brightly lit colonial mansion looming in the darkness down the road. I walked there to dry out and determine where I was in relation to the airport.

At the end of the long driveway I pulled the gigantic door open and stepped inside. The cold air—how was it that it felt colder than outdoors?— and smell of mold assaulted my nostrils and I immediately knew this was not a place to get warm or dry. As I turned to leave, a voice called out.

"Can I help you?" I pivoted to see a middle-aged man in a dark suit and navy raincoat approaching me from a large stairwell. He had the neatly trimmed hair and look of an FBI agent or a clergyman. He eyed me with suspicion. *What is this place?*

"I'm just trying to find the way to the airport; I got a little turned around." He peered at me, unconvinced. Another man—a cookie-cutter duplicate of the first—appeared at the top of the stairwell.

"What's going on, Mike?" he demanded as he descended the steps.

"Hey, Jim. This guy just wandered in off the street and I'm checking him out."

"I don't need checking out—I was just hoping to get directions to the airport. Could you call me a cab?" I said.

"We aren't a hotel, bud," Mike stated.

"Yeah, do we look like concierges?" Jim said, deadpan.

"Well..." I said, before deciding against humor.

"Are you a girl? You got any ID on you?" Mike asked.

"Of course I have ID," I replied, ignoring his first question. "Why wouldn't I?"

"Show it to me," Mike demanded.

"I don't even know who *you* are," I said, making no motion to retrieve my ID.

"We're RCMP officers. You just walked into HQ for E Division, so we want to know who you are," Jim said.

"Fine, I'll find my own cab. Thanks for the chat." I turned, stepped outside and started up the driveway. Mike followed me and called out into the darkness.

"You can probably find a cab at the Oakridge mall. It's just a right on Cambie and a few blocks up." I stuck my arm in the air in a wave without turning around and kept walking. *Do I really want to be a cop?*

The day's excitement slowly melted into all-too-familiar fear as I sat on the plane and thought about coming out to my family. In Dr. Watson's office, the prospect of transitioning had shone bright and manageable, and the matter-of-fact way she'd presented it made it seem as though people did this all the time and could live good lives afterward. But now I remembered her mentioning that I had to live as male for a year—or was it two?—before I'd be allowed to pursue any medical transition treatments. The voice in my head that dutifully reminded me that in this world people like me were unnatural sprinkled a powder of doubt on my plans.

All of the most negative things I'd heard or suspected about transgender people played in a loop in my mind, over and over again. *You'll never be a "real" man. People will think you're a freak. People don't want their children around someone like you. No one wants to marry someone like you. People will think you're weird, flaky, a creep. You can't coach basketball if you're transgender.*

This is why it's easier not to dream.

That evening, alone in my room in Morinville, I stared back at my image in the mirror and asked myself a simple question: *How will you live the rest of your life?*

My thoughts wandered to my parents and I began to think— unrealistically—that they must know who I really was. I began to justify this with examples. My father would often relay conversations back to me that he'd had with friends where they would tell him "what a neat kid" I was. Those exact words always accompanied these stories. He never said "neat girl"— always "kid." Desperate for some sign that others saw me for who I truly was, I interpreted such things the way I most hoped they could be. I remained stuck, that angry and desperate sixteen-year-old boy in the shell of a twenty-five-year-old woman.

I barely slept during the month leading up to Christmas. One minute, I rehearsed my coming-out speech to my parents. The next, I imagined myself wrestling a genie, trying to jam him back into the bottle. But the genie had grown into a giant, like an oversized balloon, and when I squeezed one portion, other even less manageable parts squirted out. Driving from Edmonton to Calgary on December 24, my mental tennis match raged on. I walked into my parents' home to the smell of Dad's cabbage rolls and Mom's baking without having reached a firm decision.

On Christmas night I stayed up late alone and watched *Tootsie* on TV. I'd seen the film many times before; it centered on Dustin Hoffman's character, an actor named Michael Dorsey, deciding to inject life into his floundering career by dressing in drag to win a role as a woman on a daytime drama. But that night, the scene where Jessica Lange's character Julie Nichols and Dustin Hoffman's Dorothy/Michael lie in Julie's childhood bed together talking about men struck a nerve in me. In Julie's view, they were just two good gal pals having a slumber party—but Michael was struggling with whether to come out as his true identity and express his attraction for Julie.

I lay there on the couch—glancing over at my Christmas gifts, which included lacy floral women's pajamas—resigned to my grief. That film scene so perfectly captured the pain I felt of connecting with someone who was growing to care for me but had no idea who I really was. It epitomized the risk inherent in telling the truth about myself, knowing I could quite possibly destroy any feelings someone had for me once they knew the truth. Dorothy is a fictional character, Michael Dorsey in drag, but it is the deception—of others, at the cost to oneself—that brought the subject of the film into the realm of the transgender experience, for me. In that moment, I knew I had to tell my parents about myself. Regardless of what I chose to do about it, I could no longer pretend I was not what I knew myself to be.

The next morning I stared at the walls of the family room, waiting for my parents to join me after a big Boxing Day breakfast. My grandfather had lived with us for many years after my grandmother died, and this had been his TV room, where I'd sit with him for hours, watching shows together and talking. He now lived in a nursing home, requiring more care after several falls, and though I visited him often, I missed him terribly.

Looking at the family photos on the sideboard, I cringed at many of the different incarnations of myself that had sat in that room over the years. A deep sadness permeated what should have been a cocoon of comfort and safety I felt in this house I'd called home for twenty-five years. My heart broke for that little boy in the photos who tried so hard to look and act like a normal girl.

I'd made my invitation to talk something over with them sound casual, and both of my parents eventually drifted into the family room to join me. Now it was my turn to deliver shocking news after a trip to Vancouver.

"So, I have something I need to talk to you about," I ventured. Calmly, I described my visit to the clinic and what Dr. Watson and her team had found. Mom looked at me in shock, shaking her head. Dad sat motionless. My hopes sunk as I saw the angry and confused expressions on their faces. Two sides of a triangle of misunderstanding.

"That's ridiculous—that's not possible," Mom said quickly after I finished telling them of my diagnosis. "Who are these people to tell you that?"

"Mom, they're right. I went there because I already knew what they would say about me," I said, determined to remain calm.

"They don't know the first thing about you. This is totally irresponsible!" Her voice rose.

"Mom, don't blame them. This is about me."

"So, what? Are you going to get a sex change, then? Is that what you're telling us?" Mom demanded.

"I don't know. Maybe." I wanted to say yes, but I was scared of her reaction. Transitioning continued to feel like a pipe dream, too fantastical to be possible.

"Is that what you want? A sex change?" she demanded. I took a deep breath, swallowing hard.

"In a perfect world, yeah, maybe," I replied softly, not meeting her gaze.

"A *maybe* sex change," Mom snorted. "Joe, are you hearing this? This is crazy." Dad looked up. My heart broke as he nodded in agreement.

"I don't understand this," he began. "You aren't intersex, you weren't born a hermaphrodite," he continued, going through his checklist of the only scientific ways this could possibly make sense to him.

"No," I agreed.

"Then this is all in your mind; this is a psychological issue," he said.

"In my mind, I'm male. I'm a man," I said simply.

"That's ridiculous. They have filled your head with nonsense; you need some kind of treatment," Mom said.

Help me.

"Yes, you need to go somewhere they can cure you of this," Dad agreed. "God doesn't make mistakes." Panic gripped me as it dawned on me that they could have me committed to a psychiatric facility.

"No, I'm not going anywhere like that."

"Like what? Where they can help you?" Mom asked angrily.

"They won't help me. They'll try to talk me out of how I feel."

"You don't *feel* your gender," Mom said, exasperated.

"I think people do. Do you feel like a woman?"

"That's ridiculous. Of course I do, but I don't spend my time thinking about it," she scoffed.

"Exactly," I finished, rising from my seat. "I'm gonna go."

"But you don't need to go back until tomorrow," Dad said. "Sit down and think about this."

"Dad, I've done nothing but think about this for twenty-five years," I retorted before walking out. I packed my bag efficiently, suppressing my feelings of panic and loss, then walked to the kitchen to grab some food for the three-hour drive back to Edmonton. Dad joined me and I clung to the hope that he would soften.

"I think we need to talk more about this, get you checked in somewhere for a real assessment," he said quietly. I shook my head.

"No, Dad. I've had a real assessment. I know you're only saying that because you're worried, but there is nothing wrong with me other than I was born like this." I walked past him and put on my boots. "I gotta go."

He came down the steps as I stood up, bag in hand. He hugged me tight. I felt my throat choke up and tears come to my eyes. I swallowed hard, collecting myself before we parted.

"We love you. Call us when you get there."

"I will." Descending the steps to the front yard, I wondered if I would ever set foot in that house again.

More than three months passed before I spoke to my parents. Sharon and I both quit our reporting jobs at the *Gazette* on the same day, a defiant gesture against a mean-spirited editor who had radically altered the copy, angle, and source information in every story we filed. Sharon applied successfully to the University of Alberta law school and I saw this as my chance to move to Vancouver. I felt no fear, only relief at leaving Alberta and starting fresh in a new environment. I'd mailed in my application to the VPD before Christmas and advised them I'd be living in Vancouver by February.

Ted and Louise drove me and all of my belongings—which half-filled their minivan—to Vancouver, where they'd arranged a room for me to rent in a shared house with several of their old friends. They combined a much-needed visit to escape the harsh Edmonton winter with their desire to see me settled in before heading back to Alberta a week later. Their concern touched me deeply. Once in Vancouver, I worked in a running shoe store while awaiting news on my application to the VPD. I planned to touch base with Dr. Watson's team once I got settled.

In addition to the VPD, I also applied for a job as the head coach of the Langara College women's basketball team. They offered me the job, but I turned it down, for complicated reasons.

I loved coaching basketball. In Calgary, I had led a high school team to the city championships and seriously considered working toward coaching at a higher level, including completing what little outstanding education faculty coursework I needed for my teaching degree. All that remained was fulfilling the requirements for a practicum year of teaching, which I'd considered as an alternative to accepting the VPD job.

Although I loved coaching, I'd never felt at home in that community. There were no openly queer basketball coaches in Alberta—or anywhere else I was aware of. There were certainly no openly transgender coaches. I still had no idea how I was going to live my life, going forward. History and pedigree formed the foundation of the basketball coaching world and it seemed impossible for someone to show up somewhere to coach without a great deal of scrutiny into the person's past as a player and coach. Just as in high school, the subtle homophobic undercurrent vibrated so far underground that no one ever spoke of it, at least not around me. This was an era where, in many circles, gay and lesbian coaches and teachers were painted as potential pedophiles. Sadly, there are still many places where that ridiculously misguided stereotype persists, even as cisgender male coaches are the ones most often convicted of sexually assaulting young athletes.

All of the lesbian coaches I knew were closeted, terrified at being discovered, living in fear of the loss of their recruits and their coaching jobs. Mainstream media outed women sports coaches in the '90s with alarming zeal. In a highly competitive recruiting world, university and college administrators feared—and still do to this day—that LGBTQ coaches would deter parents from sending their kids to their school. It became easier for them to hire a cisgender and straight (or at least deeply closeted) coach than to risk prospective athletes' parents meeting queer coaches. Consequently, there are very few out queer coaches.

For a closeted transgender person whose life had been one long battle to keep my identity under wraps, taking this on publicly seemed like too much for me. I detested the idea of pushing myself deeper into the closet, but I also feared losing something that meant so much to me. The VPD offered me a spot in the next police academy class the day after Langara offered me the coaching job. I turned down Langara, removing coaching from my life before anyone could take it from me.

It was the decision that felt safest for me. I wouldn't change my choice—but I do regret the state of that world. The idea of building a life and a reputation, working so hard for the kids under my guidance only to live in constant fear of it being taken away when someone deemed me unworthy because of being transgender, was too much. It might have gone well, but the prospect of humiliation terrified me.

I chose policing.

I chose to wear a uniform every day so that selecting what to wear could be less disheartening. I chose benefits. I chose to work alongside the most conservative group of people in my professional experience. I knew I was settling on many levels, putting aside my dream of sports and investigative journalism in favor of criminal investigation. Perhaps I unconsciously chose power and privilege in a tough profession to discourage anyone from messing with me. I chose to learn the physical skills needed to defend myself and others.

But policing would only magnify my sense of being an imposter. Daily, I would wonder at how *they* let me into their world and accepted me as one of them. Somehow, I passed as a cop, an authoritarian, and an ally.

Training at BC's police academy, known as the Justice Institute of British Columbia (JIBC), poured the cement foundation that solidified my self-image as an outsider in policing. I understood the game and recognized the hoops I was expected to jump through, so I bit my tongue and rarely openly questioned the JIBC's methods or policing's paramilitary structure and culture.

My JIBC instructors' teaching skills, policing experience, and subject matter knowledge varied greatly. Fortunately, in the harder skills such as firearms, driving, physical training, legal studies, and traffic, my peers and I seemed to be in good hands and as my career progressed, I felt fairly confident we had been given a solid grounding in these areas. However, in the softer skills such as investigation, patrol, and human relations, our instruction was somewhat less than inspiring.

Corporal Jack Handler taught us the antiseptically named Human Relations course. A sophomoric, pudgy man, he tried to cover for his apparent lack of communication and social skills by inserting himself into our class conversations during coffee breaks and joining in the generally good-natured—among the recruits—ribbing and insults that would often fly between classmates as we got to know each other's foibles. Handler's attempts to be one of the gang fell flat; he was overly familiar with the women and derogatory and belittling toward the men and whatever respect students normally held for a teacher and senior officer evaporated within a few days. His behavior as a man rankled me. I felt I was a better man moving through life as a woman than I observed him to be as a visible man.

Storytelling forms a large part of police culture and lore. Handler's stories began believably enough, but rapidly devolved into implausible tales detailing his heroics and imagined Lothario-esque abilities, almost always set in the Downtown Eastside's most popular strip club, the Number Five Orange. Despite the class never responding or reacting, he would tell his stories daily—always variations on a tale featuring sundry uses for a stripper pole, gorgeous-but-misunderstood exotic dancers, and burly organized crime thugs hotly pursued by Handler for their criminal activities.

None of us ever lodged a complaint, partly because the stories were such pathetic attempts by Handler to make us think he was cool and partly because our instructors made very clear to us from the first day that they were all-knowing and above reproach. We were know-nothing recruits. Mutiny was not an option. We weren't prepared to die on the first hill we encountered. That didn't stop us from talking privately about what an idiot we thought Handler was, though. I became so annoyed by his lack of maturity that I stopped taking notes and tuned out during his lectures.

As the weeks passed, I became more and more dismayed that someone with such lamentable people skills and the compassion of a panty-raiding keg-tapper was teaching us how to interact with the public—including people with mental health conditions, sex workers, drug users, suspects, witnesses, victims, and other vulnerable community members.

Exams were a regular feature of the JIBC curriculum and we were tested almost daily. Many subjects required rote memorization: traffic laws, powers of arrest, the Police Act, and Criminal Code of Canada definitions all fell into this category. But preparing for our Human Relations midterm exam also turned out to be an exercise in memorization, regurgitating Corporal Handler's personal take on dealing with people in various states of distress and other scenarios—the Gospel according to him, crafted through his ten or so years as a police officer. Outside of class, my classmates and I spoke openly about how ridiculous it was that this "material" constituted our training in Human Relations, but we resigned ourselves to our plight.

I made a plan on my own and did not share it with the others. I didn't study for the exam, did not review what few notes

I had wasted my time taking, and began to look at each topic and imagine how I might handle the situation as a police officer, as a member of the community, and as a human being.

When exam day came, I answered each question truthfully, earnestly, and thoroughly—but not according to Corporal Handler's lectures. Two days after the exam, our class supervisor, Corporal Gil Puder, called me into his office.

"You wanted to see me, Corporal?" I asked, standing at attention in front of his desk. Military formality was mandatory at all times unless ordered otherwise. He nodded and gestured to a chair.

"Yes. At ease—sit down, Shenher." I focused on his eyes because I thought—though I couldn't be sure—I detected his moustache twitching ever so slightly in the way I knew it did when he was amused. He rarely appeared amused or laughed with students; he was a tough, no-nonsense supervisor, but I had seen glimpses of his personality during the noon hour basketball games we both played in and I could tell he respected me as a player at the very least. He held up what I was fairly sure was my exam paper and I wondered if he respected me as a student quite as much.

"We have a problem with your Human Relations exam," he said quietly. "You got a 63. The class average is 87."

There were rules in the academy about how far below the class average you could be, and my score was way outside the acceptable range of 5 percent. I felt anger rising in my throat. I knew my answers were appropriate—more than appropriate. They were entirely reasonable given that the nature of Human Relations was completely subjective and the very notion of testing people on how they would respond in fluid situations involving human beings in crisis and under great stress was ludicrous.

"Corporal, with all due respect, this course is total bullshit," I said. "I find it really hard to believe that a guy like Corporal Handler can teach me anything about human relations and I would never handle anything the way he suggests." I braced myself for what would come next. Expulsion? Discipline? Push-ups? They made us do push-ups for everything from crooked ties to marching badly; what would they do to me for blowing an exam in protest? I pictured Richard Gere struggling in the mud in *An Officer and a Gentleman. I am such an idiot.*

And then I saw it. The smirk. Maybe there was hope for me.

"Well, Shenher," he said, twisting one end of his moustache absently and looking me in the eye. "You probably have a point, there." I nearly fell out of my chair. "However, Corporal Handler is your superior and the rules exist for a reason." He dropped his voice lower and said, "Your answers were perfectly fine—good, even," before returning to his previous volume. "But you'll have to rewrite the exam and get in the 80s to be within range of the class average. Using Corporal Handler's material."

I sighed and nodded.

"I understand."

"Make arrangements with Corporal Handler to rewrite it next week."

"Yes, Corporal." I rose.

"And Shenher?"

"Corporal?"

"I like your style," he whispered, the corners of his mouth curled down.

"Thank you, Corporal." I walked out, feeling better than I had since I began at the JIBC. I didn't care that I had to rewrite the exam. I had stood up, and I had, in a small way, spoken out against something I found wrong. And that felt really good.

I liked Gil Puder's style, too. While Jack Handler was a man I would never respect or emulate, Gil Puder became a mentor to me. Beyond the JIBC, I grew to know him much better over the years. He was seen by many as a renegade, known locally for his pro-legalization views on drugs such as marijuana and his apt assertion—long before it was popular opinion—that the war on drugs was a failure and bred police corruption.

Many police officers quietly respected him for speaking his mind and expressing his opinions in the op-ed pages of local newspapers and publications all over North America. Others within the VPD declared him a quack, especially in the '90s, when so few cops were willing to admit that the war on drugs was a complete failure, much less say it publicly. Rather than support him as a well-spoken member of their team, some well-placed people within the VPD tried to silence Gil, but he persevered. Sadly, he died of cancer in 1999 at the age of forty. It was quick: I'd spoken to him when I'd run into him on the seawall one afternoon and he was dead less than three weeks later.

11

FISH STORIES
(1991–1997)

WITH ONLY FIFTEEN people, my class at the academy was far smaller than the usual twenty-five to thirty. Though predominantly white, the class was almost evenly gender-balanced—truly exceptional in an era when fewer than forty women worked alongside more than a thousand male officers in the VPD.

I became close friends with several of my classmates and shared a basement suite with Ralph, whom I'd gone to school with in Calgary. We'd bumped into each other at the Vancouver running store where I worked while going through the VPD hiring process and, after talking, we discovered we were both on the list for the same recruit class. We each needed a roommate and soon moved into a place together, which became a hangout for a few of our JIBC classmates; the place where we'd study, shoot pool, and play Nintendo after school.

Helen owned the Nintendo box. Early on, she stood out as the smartest person in our class, not only due to her good grades but also to her astute observations of everything and everyone around us. She wasn't given to personal disclosures, so she surprised me by admitting within a few weeks of our friendship that she was a lesbian and the spouse she had mentioned in passing was a woman. Coincidentally, that same week I'd decided to attend my first session of the transgender support group Dr. Watson had told me about at the VGH Gender Dysphoria Clinic, and I shared this with Helen. As our friendship had grown, I'd felt a familiar conflict: lie and present myself as a lesbian or tell her of my true transgender identity? Sensing she was destined to become a lifelong friend, I dared tell her my truth. She responded very supportively, offering to drive me to the group session since I didn't own a car.

The day of the clinic, Helen dropped me off at VGH after school. I entered the meeting room and found twelve people, some standing, talking easily to each other, and others seated, alone. An attractive, fit man in his late twenties or early thirties approached me.

"Hi, I'm Dan. I'm a psychologist and I run the group here." He held out his hand and we shook.

"Hi Dan, I'm Lori."

"Welcome, Lori. Dr. Watson mentioned we might see you. It's great to have you here."

"Thank you."

"Do you want to grab a coffee and take a seat? I think I'll get things started."

I poured myself a coffee and found a seat in the circle of chairs. Dan called everyone to order and we all sat down. He introduced himself and welcomed us.

"Why don't we go around the circle and briefly introduce ourselves, and, if you feel comfortable, tell us a little bit about why you're here today," he said, gesturing to his left. "Why don't you lead us off?" The large, bearded mountain man beside him straightened up and began to speak.

"Hi, I'm Jeff," he said. "I'm here because I'm struggling with the decision about whether to transition to female."

"Welcome, Jeff," Dan said. This continued around the circle, each person expressing a similar struggle. I tried to hide my surprise at some of the people who were so outwardly aligned with their birth-assigned sex in appearance that it seemed unfathomable they could identify as the opposite sex. I worried for them embarking on their transition journeys, but it didn't occur to me that my loved ones likely thought the same about me.

Grief slowly filled the room, like fog pumping silently in through the ventilation system. Person after person repeated a similar, sad, hopeless refrain. Ever the optimist, I questioned whether I belonged there among such obvious suffering. *Surely my problems aren't this bad.* When my turn came, I planned to repeat Jeff's words almost verbatim. *What he said pretty much sums it up.*

"I'm Lori. This is my first time here," I began. "I'm thinking about transitioning to male, but I'm really not sure if I should because my family thinks I'm crazy, and if my employer finds out about me, I have no idea what would happen."

"Welcome, Lori," Dan said. "Those are quite common concerns. I think you'll find a lot of support here for that."

The person beside me was a tired, defeated-looking forty-something person with short grey hair who I would have assumed was a lesbian. After all these years, the memory of her face remains clear because what she said next shaped the course of the next twenty-five years of my life.

"I'm Rona," she began slowly. "I haven't been here in a while." She sighed heavily. "I've been thinking of transitioning since I was young, but I was always too afraid. So, I decided to live my life as lesbian, figured that would be easier." She paused, absently wringing her hands in her lap. "And it was okay for a while. I have a partner, kids, but I find every day it gets tougher and tougher and I can't imagine how I'm gonna live the rest of my life like this," she said, gesturing at her body.

I stopped paying attention before she finished her last sentence, focusing on, "it was okay for a while." I made my decision then and there: I would live my life as a lesbian. Rona's obvious regret and midlife struggle seemed light years away from what I was experiencing in my twenties, the pain in her words lost on me as I grasped at the misconstrued lifeline in her words. *Maybe Rona's miserable, but I don't have to be.* My friend Helen was living as a lesbian and she seemed okay— although she *was* a lesbian. She'd never said she identified as a man, and I doubted that she did. She appeared quite happy as a woman. *I can do this. I'll have relationships with women, but keep my male self under wraps. Maybe I won't lose everything. It's easier than transitioning.*

After the meeting, Helen pulled up and I climbed into her Jeep.

"How'd it go?" she asked.

"Good." She glanced over at me, eyebrows raised, but said nothing. "I'm gonna be a lesbian."

I never returned to the transgender group sessions. The final entry in my Gender Dysphoria Clinic file reads, "Lori informed me she is quite pleased just the way things are in her life and does not think she wants gender reassignment. I will inform Dr. Watson."

I SAT IN the Muffin Break, watching the door nervously, wondering *Is that her?* about each woman who entered. I had answered a personal ad in the local arts newspaper—the one and only I would ever respond to. When Alex, a short, perky redhead, walked into the coffee shop, I knew her immediately from her description. She was cute, very fit, and highly energetic—like Lesbian Gymnast Barbie or the personification of Tigger. I waved my hand slightly from my table and she bounced over to me. I stood to shake her hand and she pulled me into a full body hug for several seconds, grinding her hips into mine.

"Whoa," I said, pulling back from her, wondering if all lesbians greeted each other like that. "Hi."

"Hi! I'm Alex!" *Tiggers are wonderful things!*

"I figured," I replied, gesturing for her to sit down. "Can I get you something?"

"Sure! How about an espresso? Double shot, with a blueberry muffin?" She spoke breathlessly. I found myself scanning her for a knob that would turn her *down*. It was seven in the evening, and I wondered what she might drink to rev up earlier in the day.

"You got it. Be right back." I stood and she winked at me as I walked away. My gut was screaming *danger*, but other parts of me found her attractive and I decided to ride out the date. I returned with our drinks and snacks and was barely seated before she purred, "Ooh, you're much better-looking than your picture."

"I never sent you a picture," I replied, thinking this was part of her strange attempt at flirtation. She laughed and waved a hand dismissively.

"Oh, I must've been thinking of someone else." In my fantasy world of personal ad dating, I imagined everyone to be like me: one and done, in it to win it. I'd assumed that this was her first time, too. I was obviously mistaken. She was a pro and I merely a rookie. She recovered quickly. "I really like the way you look. You're so tall," she cooed.

"Did you get a lot of response to your ad?" I asked.

"Just you!"

"Cool." I refocused. "Tell me about yourself." She reached for the salt and pepper shakers, arranging and rearranging them beside each other, one on top of the other, upside down—spilling both out on the table top. I placed my hands on my lap to resist cleaning it up.

"Well, I'm twenty-one, I work for Brinks as an armored truck driver, I belly dance, I have a Glock nine mil—I have all my permits for it, of course—and I share a basement suite with my friend Callie in East Van, but I'm trying to get into the RCMP..." She paused for a sip of her coffee as I tried to puzzle out the connection between her living situation and the RCMP. "I lift weights and my friends call me EB—guess why?" I raised my eyebrows, shrugging unknowingly. "Energizer Bunny, silly! And I was raised in Saskatchewan but that wasn't my scene, you know, because I like girls—women—so I came here for community college courses. What about you?" She began spacing out Sweet'n Low packets in a little row next to the condiments.

If she had paid any attention to me during her soliloquy, she would have witnessed me almost gasping with relief that

I hadn't told her I was a newly minted VPD constable. They'd warned us about "blue fever"—the term for the overblown attraction some women and men felt for cops—and I wondered if Alex fit the profile.

We shared our coming-out stories as queer people do early on, mine lamentably brief and uninteresting given my very recent membership in the lesbian club, and hers steeped in the daily strife of a gay kid growing up in a strict Christian prairie household. I confided in her that this was my first date with a woman, but I kept my real job under wraps, fearing it could be used against me at some point. I had no solid basis for that fear other than my gut, but I lied and said I was now working from home as a writer.

Somehow, my physical attraction convinced me the two of us were possible. We filled an hour and a half with conversation. I agreed to her offer to drive me home. She parked her early '80s Trans Am in front of my house and turned to me. Emboldened by the recollection that Ralph was away fishing for a few days, I spoke first.

"So," I began. "What have you got going on tomorrow? Are you working?"

"Yeah, not until noon. I'm on the noon-to-eight. We have three shifts, that's my favorite." I realized I wasn't really listening.

"My roommate caught a ton of salmon a few weeks ago; our freezer's full of it," I said. "Do you want to come in and see it? It's pretty cool." I groaned internally. *I sound like the opening line in a bad porn clip. "Wanna see my salmon?"* I needn't have worried.

"Sure!" she said, turning off the ignition and tumbling out of the driver's door.

I let us in and turned on the heat before showing her around the small basement suite, explaining that Ralph was away. I tried to hide my nerves, glancing around to make sure there was no police gear lying around. Neither of us tended to advertise what we did for a living, unlike many other cops we knew. I offered her a Diet Coke and we both stood in the kitchen sipping our drinks.

"Show me the salmon," she said, eying me over the rim of her glass, one eyebrow cocked.

"Oh, yeah, of course." I set my drink down and opened the freezer door. "There it is," I announced, feeling foolish. She stepped toward me, reaching across me as she set her drink on the counter, pressing herself against me while glancing toward the freezer at the piles of fish. I made my move, taking her in my arms and pulling her in to kiss her.

We wound up in my bedroom after fooling around in the kitchen, living room, and all points in between. I lay wide awake as Alex slept, marveling at this new discovery. It wasn't love or anything remotely close to it, but I finally understood all the fuss about sex. Over the next three weeks, we spent most of our time tangled up together, but our relationship wasn't deep and we had very few common interests to discuss.

In the second week I made the mistake of telling her I was a VPD member. She enthusiastically took to calling me her "big cop boyfriend" and her excitement over my career only made me want to break up with her more. Still, every time we met or went out, we'd wind up in bed before I could break the news.

One night, Ralph was away and I invited Alex over, determined to end it once and for all, breaching what I later learned was the cardinal rule of breaking up: don't do it in your own home. Despite my most determined efforts—expressing worry that I was coming down with a cold (combined with fake coughs and sneezes), telling her Ralph could soon be home—we wound up in bed yet again. I was weak. She was fun, uninhibited, and brought out my more masculine side. *We have nothing in common*, I reminded myself.

As we lay there, I started into the most clichéd "it's not you, it's me" speech in history. I managed to avoid suggesting we remain friends, knowing that was exactly the part that wasn't clicking between us. She cried, she thrashed on the bed hysterically, she came on to me, but I finally stood my ground, apologizing repeatedly for hurting her, trying hard to convince her it was for the best.

She stayed clinging to my bed for four hours and I fleetingly considered calling the police. But it would have been *my police* to respond to the 911 call and at that point no one at the VPD knew I liked women. I had no idea what could happen to me or my career if this information got back to the people who'd hired me, the ones I'd shared the names of my past boyfriends with. It was the early 1990s, and I couldn't be certain being a lesbian wasn't an offence I could be fired for. We hadn't covered that in the VPD orientation and I was still on probation.

Finally, I managed to cajole her to leave. As she laced her boots in the doorway, she spoke words that truly frightened me.

"I'm going to call your work and let them know what a jerk you are." Although I'd never told her my fear of being outed at the VPD, she knew exactly how to get to me. I forced myself to breathe calmly.

"Whatever you need to do," I said. "They already know about me, so knock yourself out." I closed the door behind her and collapsed in exhaustion after the long ordeal. Two nights later, while Ralph and I were watching football, the phone rang. I took it into the kitchen.

"Hello?"

"I miss you, I need you," Alex's voice breathed into the phone.

"I'm sorry, I really am, but I think this is for the best. I don't think you should call me anymore," I said gently.

"Can you hear this?" she asked. Before I could answer, I heard the chick-chick of a semiautomatic handgun being racked.

"Alex. What are you doing?" I remembered her showing me the gun at her place and wondering why she needed it at home.

"Does this scare you? How does it feel knowing I'll shoot myself and it will be all your fault?"

"Are you at home? Let me call someone for you, someone you can talk to, okay?" I tried to recall any of her friends I could get in touch with, but aside from her roommate, I knew no one.

"Fuck you," she said, quietly, resignedly. I heard the click of the phone and then only a dial tone on my end.

I sat staring at the phone in my hand for several minutes, both hoping it would never ring again and wishing it would so I'd know she hadn't harmed herself. Ralph didn't know I was seeing anyone; I'd kept it secret from everyone I knew because I never imagined we'd be together more than a few weeks.

I rejoined him in our living room and resumed watching the game. Weeks passed with no word from Alex. Each day I went into work, I'd check the computer for any police service calls to her place, but there were none. I felt terrible for her, but I couldn't make sense of her heartbreak when I considered myself to be deeply unlovable. I wondered if I had underestimated my own power to devastate another person, but it was easier to blame the situation on Alex's instability than take any responsibility for her pain myself. Months after the breakup, I ran into her roommate downtown, and she told me Alex had taken our split very badly at first, but I was relieved to hear she had recovered. It wasn't until years later that I accepted that I had played fast and loose with someone's heart, despite knowing they were fragile.

Unnerved by the entire experience, I turned my energy back toward work and basketball, reasoning that, while I greatly enjoyed the sexual awakening *with* a female partner, I remained dissatisfied with who I was going to bed *as*. I assumed that when it came to dating, Alex hadn't been a typical dating partner, just as Marcus was likely unique among men, but my dream continued to focus on being seen in relationships as the man I was. Making this happen within the lesbian world I was slowly coming to know seemed uncertain at best.

Until I met Helen and Alex, I hadn't known all that many lesbians, and none very well. But I soon met many more in Vancouver. One of my closest friends from back in Calgary, a basketball player named Joyce, offered to connect me with her Canadian Olympic teammate Crystal, the head coach of a Vancouver university varsity women's team. Joyce thought I could meet people to play higher-level basketball with through Crystal, which I was eager to do.

Both Joyce and Crystal identified as heterosexual, and I knew they had boyfriends. But meeting them marked my initiation into a world of athletic women loath to consider themselves lesbians who formed what appeared to be sexless but still complicated and intense "friendships" with other women athletes. The more unambiguously heterosexual athletes steered away from this dynamic, probably less due to prejudice than that they wanted to avoid the theatrics, jealousy, and mean-girl ambiance of the scene. They maintained appropriately respectful friendships with the other women, but stayed away from the drama.

I know my description of this time in the early 1990s comes with an inherent sense of clear distinctions between the sexual orientations, but during this time in history many stuck firmly to the binary of gay and straight. Most kept their sexual orientation private; there were often dire consequences for coming out as gay or lesbian at work or to family. Those few identifying openly as bisexual were met with mistrust and condemnation at worst and accusations of flakiness at best. Many in the gay community exerted pressure on others to announce what they were—to come out, make a commitment, and stay in that lane. Fluidity of sexual orientation, not to mention gender, was an unfamiliar concept treated with suspicion and wariness.

Where the world of heterosexual couples and dating included boundary-setting rules such as not pursuing someone's current partner or dating someone's ex, this lesbian sports world had no guidelines that I could see. Close to half of my 1994 flag football team had slept with each other by the end of our first season and most remained close enough friends to socialize together, even in the aftermath of hooking up with each other's exes. I suspect the women wanted to explore their recently discovered sexual freedom without the rules that bound straight society, but I found it very disconcerting and foreign, even though I participated myself.

Although it wasn't my world, I tried everything to fit in and feel comfortable as a man masquerading as a lesbian. More than a year after my Boxing Day revelation to my parents, I wrote them a letter explaining that I had decided I was probably a lesbian and now had a girlfriend. It did not go over well, and they suggested that I should simply live a celibate life. They had no response when I asked them if *they* could live a celibate life. I proceeded to live as I wished.

Over the next several years, each relationship I entered seemed unnecessarily complex. Although I had some relationships that lasted a year or two, my understanding of what it took to be happy in partnership was sorely lacking and I was usually the one to end things. My personal life was far from ideal, but my work world provided welcome relief.

I walked the beat in Vancouver's gritty Downtown Eastside for more than three years, and then worked on the upscale west side for another. My uniform was like a superhero costume, allowing me to change from mild-mannered, ineffectual lesbian to "manly man" if only in my mind. My military boots brought me close to six feet tall and my bulletproof vest with front-and-back graphite trauma panels—worn under my blue uniform shirt—flattened my chest like a man's. I regained my fit fighting form through weight training, basketball, karate, and running and wore my hair very short in the prototypical lesbian cut of the '90s. I enjoyed that people in the community sometimes took me for a man, at least until I spoke. For those brief, blissful seconds, I felt right.

One night on the Downtown Eastside beat, my partner John and I responded to a call at the Number Five Orange. A beefy bouncer met us at the door of the strip club and provided details about a patron who had been removed for inappropriately touching one of the dancers. He took us upstairs and introduced us to a young woman named Cindy, and left with a sardonic "Good luck, she's a little gooned." The patron had called 911 from a pay phone down the block after his ejection, alleging the dancer had mistreated him. We had no intention of taking the patron's complaint seriously; he mentioned no injuries to himself and clearly made the report in order to retaliate against the club and the woman. We frequently saw gropers like him in these clubs and showed up to support the women and the staff. We just needed a quick statement from her for our report and we would be on our way.

Cindy was indeed drunk. She sat on a stool in front of a makeup mirror and looked John and me up and down, opening and closing her eyes for long periods. "Hellllllo," she slurred. Deciding on me, she leaned in and tipped her head up to look at my face more closely. "You . . . sir . . . are a fox!" She slurred *fox*, making it sound more like "focksh."

John smirked at me and said, "I'm just going to go call radio and let her know we won't be too long. Take her statement and I'll be right back."

"Okay," I replied. It was normal to have poor radio reception inside some of the old buildings downtown.

He strode away, leaving me with Cindy, who was now struggling to stand up. "Why don't you sit back down and we'll talk?" I suggested, pulling the stool up beside her.

"Sherrrr," she said, plopping back onto the stool. We talked for a few minutes and she told me what had happened with the caller, a familiar tale of a patron displeased because a beautiful dancer wasn't paying him enough attention. I took her story down in my notebook before returning it to my chest pocket. As I snapped the pocket closed, Cindy reached for me and rubbed my chest—my trauma plate, actually—with her hand. "You are soooo strong," she slurred as John walked up to us, looking at me curiously. I stood up, embarrassed and amused that she thought I had a chest as tough as graphite.

"What's up?" he asked.

"This is the handsomest policeman on the whole VPD," Cindy declared. "You're... okay," she said, tossing her head at John. "But *he* is a fox!" She winked at me and stood, rose up on her tiptoes, and drew me in to her until her lips were brushing against my ear. She whispered something unintelligible and smiled knowingly.

"Your police*man* is a police*woman*, Cindy. Sorry to disappoint you," John laughed, guiding her away from me and back to her stool. Turning to me, he casually added, "And you have lipstick on your ear, fox." Cindy looked like she might either cry or vomit.

"No. No, no, no." She grabbed my bicep. "This is a man. I am sure of that."

John and I stepped out into the moist night air and walked toward our car.

"So, you're a fox now," he laughed. "Foxy Foxerson!" I gave him a scowl.

"Cut it out," I said half-heartedly, feigning annoyance. Inside, I was thrilled.

12

WOMAN TROUBLE

(1997–2001)

RESIGNED TO LIFE as a woman, I dedicated myself to my career and my social life throughout the '90s. I moved from girlfriend to girlfriend, deeply committed to forging a lesbian life but unable to put a finger on what was missing for me. I predominantly dated police officers and athletes as a result of the circle I surrounded myself with. With a couple of exceptions, my relationships lacked stability and the same level of trust and security I enjoyed with my close, long-term friends, male and female.

I came out within my first year of joining the VPD without fanfare or stress, simply by offhandedly mentioning girlfriends to my partners on my squad during casual conversation. Calling myself gay didn't cause me pain; it wasn't my reality, so I didn't feel vulnerable. My rationale was that if I didn't treat being gay as a big deal, maybe no one else would.

I was successful, and nobody bullied me or treated me with obvious homophobia.

Late in 1997, my basketball and policing worlds collided when I met Carmen, a VPD officer a few years my junior. I'd formed a VPD women's basketball team and when Carmen came to practice, she surprised me with her basketball skills, as I'd only known her as a soccer midfielder.

The passion and intensity of our relationship nearly drowned me; it was so unlike anything I'd ever known in its fire and emotional unhealthiness. Less than one very tumultuous year later, I introduced Carmen to Joyce, my close basketball friend who was still living in Calgary. I had told Joyce about my transgender identity and often confided in her my concerns about Carmen. Their obvious attraction to each other, despite each of them trying in vain to deny it, unnerved me and came out of nowhere, given that Joyce had never expressed any interest in women to me before.

I broke from both of them proactively, certain they were either having an affair already or were soon destined to. They shared an intense relationship, cheating emotionally long before physically. Through friends, I learned that as I distanced myself from our social circle to spare myself any more hurt, they spent more time together and soon became a couple. Not long after, Joyce moved to Vancouver and moved in with Carmen, joined the women's league basketball team Carmen and I played on, and joined Carmen in training in the VPD staff gym where I trained.

Determined to hold on to what joy I had in my life, I had continued playing on our women's league team. One night, I arrived at our game, laced up my shoes, and watched the two of them enter the gym and sit down on our team bench. Carmen and Joyce informed me that Joyce was joining our team and they bent over backward to talk to me, but it felt false and patronizing. I exchanged pleasantries with them—annoyed by the expectation that everyone would remain friendly and social, even after one of us had been stabbed in the back—and trotted out on the court to warm up.

I played the best basketball of my life that night, hitting almost every shot I took, including numerous three-pointers. I stole the ball from the opposition, dished out assists—even to Carmen and Joyce—rebounded, and helped our team win a close game. In the closing minutes, a woman on the other team bumped me hard in midair as I drove to the hoop for a lay-up—a cheap and dangerous move that easily could have injured me. I leapt up off the ground as the ref blew down the play and stepped up to her.

She'd bothered me for years; the kind of out-of-control, bull-in-a-china-shop player who made up for minimal physical skills with dirty play and aggression outside the bounds of acceptable basketball. The women's league refs often let much of this play go, but still she frequently fouled out of games. Ironically, women's basketball was often far dirtier than the men's game—"chippy," as Dad liked to call it. The men banged and bumped in the low post, but the women's game featured grabbing, scratching, and an assortment of other cheap shots usually out of view of the refs.

As I stepped up to her I gave her a hard two-handed shove to her shoulders, causing her to stagger backward. The refs stepped in and whistled me for a technical foul—but as she stared at me, bewildered, I stepped forward to take another shot at her. They rightly ejected me from the game before I could shoot my foul shots. *What the hell is the matter with me?* I turned and walked calmly back to our bench and began to take my shoes off. Carmen moved to sit beside me.

"Are you okay?" she asked. "That wasn't like you." She was right. While an exuberant and animated player, I had never charged or hit anyone before.

"I'm fine." I shoved my shoes into my bag. "She's a hack."

"Yeah, but you've always known that about her," she continued. "You should try to ignore her."

"I hate that I fell for her bait." I shook my head in recollection. "I'm not a violent person. You know that."

"I do know that," she said, smiling at me. I hated that I still felt a tug in my chest as I watched her. "It's what drew me to you in the first place." Comments like that, made in spite of the fact she was living with my former friend, were exactly why I needed to get away from them both. I stood up and swung my bag over my shoulder.

"Right. Thanks." Without another word, I left for the locker room, changed my shirt, and walked out to the parking lot. I never played another game of organized basketball again. What had been my oasis, my safe place, now felt ugly and tainted. If my emotions could be triggered so easily, I needed to step away so I wouldn't hurt anyone in the future.

Being hurt and betrayed by a so-called friend and girl-friend completely shattered me. The pain of loss devastated me deeply, more than anything I'd experienced until that point in my life, and I felt as though Carmen and Joyce had invaded every safe place in my world—work, basketball, social circle—that I loved. Intuitively, I knew my reaction to the situation, while in some ways warranted, represented far more to me than the pain of simply seeing my close friend and my girlfriend cheat on me. *Why does this wound me so deeply?*

On a visceral level, my body ached—not so much from a broken heart but from a broken spirit and the sense of somehow having done myself a deep disservice, the source of which I couldn't divine. Unable to sleep or eat, realizing this had far less to do with Carmen and Joyce and much more to do with me making poor choices in friends and partners, I finally made an appointment with a therapist that fall. Surely, a therapist could help me.

The first person I saw spent most of our first session bitterly retelling her own obviously unresolved partner-leaves-for-best-friend narrative. Discouraged, I sought out a better fit. A couple of months later, I found one. Louise listened as I told her the story and described all the ways I felt stuck in its aftermath. When I finished, she folded her hands in her lap and asked me a question.

"Tell me what drew you to Carmen and Joyce."

"I dunno," I offered. She smiled a little.

"Of course you do. Just think about it and tell me what comes to mind; you might see some similarities, differences," she suggested. I puzzled over this.

"Well, I've known Joyce a lot longer," I began. "She's an amazing athlete, smart, funny. There was never anything sexual between us, none of that drama. I always found her kind of asexual, actually. As far as I always knew, she was straight, until Carmen." I shrugged.

"Good. So: athlete, smart, funny. Sound like anyone you know?"

"Carmen?"

"Try again," she prompted. I sat there, stumped. Then, the light bulb started flickering.

"Me?" I asked, incredulously.

"Bingo. Tell me about Carmen now."

"Well, she isn't as funny and she's smart in a different way from Joyce. Joyce is an actual Rhodes Scholar; so few of us are in that league." I laughed for what felt like the first time in weeks. "Carmen is really strong, fit, an elite-level athlete, a good cook, talks to you like you're the only person in the room."

"Someone people would want to emulate?"

"Oh yeah. I think so."

"You?"

"What?"

"Do you want to emulate Carmen? Emulate Joyce?" I sat there looking at her for several moments, realization slowly creeping over me.

"I want to *be* them, don't I?"

"Do you know why?"

I wished it didn't always come back to my gender identity, but here I was again. I told her about my struggles and the trip to the Gender Dysphoria Clinic. She nodded quietly.

"I just thought maybe if I could be someone more like them, I would feel like I fit, you know?" I said. "I don't ever measure up. I'm not a good enough athlete, a good enough girl, woman, person. The people I wanted to be like rejected me. It's like I just can't ever get to where—what, who—I want to be."

"Can you tell me what it is that's stopping you from transitioning?"

"I don't know."

"You must have an idea."

"I don't want to lose everything and everyone I have."

"You don't know that would happen."

"It's too scary to risk."

We worked together for a few more sessions, talking hypothetically about what I might look for in a new partner. More than six months after the breakup, I still felt certain I was unlovable and best suited to remaining single for the rest of my life. Louise challenged me to write a list of qualities I would want in a new partner. I returned the next session with a list I'd made one night while drunk. Louise studied it for a few moments.

"Okay, we have: smart," she said, making pencil checks beside each item as she named them, "educated, funny, attractive, runner, kind, normal—what do you mean by 'normal'?" she asked, holding her pencil absently while looking up from the list.

"Honestly, just not fucked up." Louise laughed.

"Okay. Not fucked up is a good goal. Where were we?" she continued to the bottom of the list. "A reader, has good friends, a good family, a good job."

"This is pie-in-the-sky stuff," I sniffed.

"What do you mean?"

"This is just the ideal, but I haven't met anyone like this."

"Maybe you're looking in the wrong places."

"Where should I be looking?"

"Try your non-fucked-up friends, I would suggest. They likely know other non-fucked-up women," she smiled.

How will I find someone non-fucked-up when I'm such a disaster?

THE FOLLOWING SPRING, I took a spur-of-the-moment trip alone to Mazatlán, Mexico. Tired of winter and constant reminders of Carmen and Joyce, an escape to warmer climes seemed just the remedy. At LAX, I sat down on an out-of-the-way bench in a large, open waiting area hoping to kill the two-hour layover with a book. I was reading *Muhammad Ali: His Life and Times*, a biography by Thomas Hauser. Shortly after I began reading, I saw someone large in my peripheral vision sit down near me on the padded bench. I didn't look over, my attention captured instead by two black teens—a girl and a boy—walking away from the end of the bench, each impeccably dressed in matching black fur coats and all-black attire, the boy wearing a brightly colored kufi hat and the girl a richly colored African scarf wrapped around her head. They were breathtaking. I watched them walk away, thinking they looked like African royalty, and finally turned my attention back to my book. A deep, resonant voice spoke.

"Quite the man, isn't he?" I looked over at my bench companion for the first time, then blinked in disbelief as I realized this boulder of a man beside me was George Foreman.

"Yes, sir." I replied, setting the book down. "Have you read it?" He laughed—a rich, joyful laugh.

"No, I've heard the whole story from the horse's mouth many times. The man can talk!"

"But you fought each other. Are you friends?"

"He's one of my best friends. Not many people know that."

"It must be nice to share memories with someone who gets what your life has been like."

"It is. It truly is." He paused, then gestured toward my book. "You a boxing fan?" I nodded.

"I grew up watching your fights, you and Ali. And Frazier, Gerry Cooney—back when they really were the main event, you know?"

"Indeed. They truly were." We talked for a while about boxing, his attempts at retirement, and my job as a police officer. He was impressed by it, but I told him it wasn't the best job for marriage and family.

"Were those your kids?" I asked, referring to the striking teens I'd noticed leaving earlier.

"Yes, indeed. Two of them."

"They're beautiful children."

"That they are." He laughed. "A handful, but beautiful all the same. More interested in the arcade than hanging out with their old dad. Do you have children?"

"No, sir." I thought of my shattered lesbian love life. "I doubt that'll happen for me."

"Oh, you're young, yet."

"I don't see it happening," I sighed.

"Man trouble?" I sized him up and decided to be at least partly honest.

"Actually, woman trouble." He laughed again, shaking his head.

"Oh, Lordy! I don't pretend to understand these things, but I do know woman trouble!"

"Really?"

"I was married four times before I met my wife and it stuck."

"Did you ever think about giving up looking for love?" I asked.

"I love women. I knew I just hadn't met the right one, that one day, she'd come along. And she did." He smiled at the memory.

"I don't know…" my voice trailed off.

"You don't seem like a woman with any quit in you. When you're ready, the right one'll come along."

George Foreman's words lingered with me over the next months, but my fear of a new relationship remained strong. My good friend Loretta called me one day. As we chatted, she mentioned a woman she worked with whom she thought I should meet.

"I don't want to meet anyone. I'm staying single forever," I declared.

"Oh, come on. You don't mean that. She's great. Her name's Jennifer, and you'd really like her."

"Nope. Not happening. Thanks for thinking of me, though."

"She's just really tired of men; she thinks she might be a lesbian," she said.

"Oh, God, that's even worse," I groaned.

"Why is that worse?"

"I don't know, but it is," I stammered.

For the next three months, whenever we spoke, Loretta mentioned Jennifer and tried to convince me to meet her. One day, she wore me down to the point where I agreed out of exasperation.

"Fine—if it'll get you off of my back, I'll meet her."

Loretta assured me she had only told Jennifer that I was a good friend of hers, not that she was trying to fix us up. I arranged to meet the two of them at a Granville Street sushi place for dinner followed by a movie one September week-night after work. I arrived first and waited for them in a booth, my eyes on the door and my back to the wall. I saw Loretta step into the restaurant, followed by Jennifer.

Jennifer had long brown hair with natural chestnut high-lights and wore a dark sweater set, leggings, a short-but-not-too-short skirt, black Fluevog boots, and stylish tortoiseshell glasses. Whatever resolve I'd had to stay single evaporated in that instant. *She looks so normal.* But I knew from past experience not to be fooled by appearances. Our eyes met—hers sparkling with a goodness and kindness that pulled me in from across the room—and she smiled at me. I returned the smile, beaming ridiculously. *Why am I smiling like a fool?*

The three of us easily talked and laughed throughout dinner as though we'd all known each other for years. We agreed on seeing *How Stella Got Her Groove Back* and settled into our theater seats, me with M&M's, which I offered to Jennifer and she gratefully accepted—another mark in her favor—as Loretta munched her popcorn on Jennifer's other side, likely feeling like a third nostril.

Jennifer reminded me of my old friends growing up: appropriate, funny, and polite without being stuffy. I felt immediately certain that I could trust her. We made plans to see each other again later that week and after I drove her home that night, I immediately dug the list I'd written up for Louise out of a drawer and confirmed that Jennifer met every requirement I'd been looking for. I wondered if I could ever possibly meet hers.

Thinking that if Jennifer and I were going to make a go of it I couldn't keep secrets, I told her about my gender identity very early on. We were talking one night about how it was we had each come to figure out our sexual orientation, and I explained the truth of my gender identity. If my news surprised her, she didn't let on, listening patiently as I explained the unexplainable. She did ask me one question.

"Do you still want to transition?" My answer, at the time, was honest and represented my most fervent desire.

"No, I'm good now," I replied. "I feel like I'd just be trading one set of problems in for another even bigger set of problems." This had become my go-to statement and a belief I held deep within me, providing me with a sense of safety. When I admitted my struggle, it made me an object of others' compassion, but actually transitioning would surely make me the object of scorn and hatred, I thought.

I wanted those words I spoke to Jennifer and to myself to be true. I hoped I could live a life with her as a female, keeping my transgender struggle manageable, like a chronic health condition that nagged at me all day, every day. I expected that the pull to transition would always torture me, continuing to dance in my vision seductively, temptingly, but ultimately too self-indulgent and terrifying to ever pursue. Reassured that this struggle was behind me, Jennifer moved into my Vancouver condo soon after and we began planning our life together.

Not long before Jennifer moved in, another potentially contentious topic arose between us: having children. I loved kids, but had long ago decided I didn't want any of my own. For me, the concept of physically being pregnant myself removed the plan from the table, but with a busy life and a demanding career, I felt selfishly that I—and maybe a partner—were all I had time to properly care for. I continued to dream of moving to New York one day to write, and kids made that seem even farther out of reach. Jennifer and I were talking about some friends we knew who had children and I posed the question, wanting to find out where she stood before we became any closer.

"Do you want kids?" I asked her.

"Oh, yeah. Definitely. I've always wanted them," she began. "I realized a while back I would even be a single mom if I had to in order to have kids. You?"

I lay there crestfallen, even though I'd known how unlikely it was that she'd feel the same way I did about the issue after getting to know her as I had already. I had a powerful intuition she'd be a great mother. I didn't know how to tell her that children were a nonnegotiable item for me. I took a deep breath.

"I've never imagined my life with my own kids in it—it's just not something I'm all that interested in," I said slowly. "I've always been too wrapped up in my own stuff."

"Do you know why?"

"I don't want to do anything if I can't do it well, I guess," I answered. "It might be a deal breaker for me. Does that worry you?"

"No, not really," she said, smiling. "You might come around. If you don't, we'll figure it out."

Her response seemed to take all the pressure off the topic for me. I lay there dumbfounded, suddenly aware of how small my life's dramas appeared to me in that moment and how thirsty I was for someone else to focus on rather than myself for a change.

"I'll think about it, but I really can't make any promises," I said.

"That's fine."

The more I learned about Jennifer, the more deeply I trusted her. She held my secrets and listened without judgment no matter what I talked to her about. I've often felt deep regret that she met me at the start of a traumatic point in my life that changed me forever.

As my personal life brightened that fateful night in September 1998, my professional life was in jeopardy, but I didn't know it yet. That week I'd been attending the annual Vancouver Police Homicide Conference as part of my job working as a missing persons detective in the Homicide Unit, where I'd been assigned late that July. Each year, I looked forward to the conference, where for a week detectives from around the world presented cases of missing persons, murders, and serial killers. Homicide was my dream assignment and my enthusiasm was uncontainable.

By February 2002, the investigation into Vancouver's missing women that I began in July 1998 would explode into lurid international headlines and Robert Pickton's farm would become home to Canada's largest crime scene in history. For nearly fourteen years, this case would ensnare me, crush my spirit, and leave my career in ruins. My sense of personal failure would nearly kill me.

Jennifer spent precious little time with me as the person I was before this case altered me forever, and I've often regretted the public life I unwittingly drew her—an intensely private person—into. She was the eternally optimistic person who I came home to every day, unaware that I was slowly unraveling, irrevocably darkening. Our home was my respite from the disturbing world of police work, and Jennifer's background—she held a law degree and an MA in social work—allowed her to offer me much-needed perspective.

While by day I collected DNA samples from the families of the missing women and interviewed violent men who preyed on sex workers, in the evenings Jennifer and I planned our commitment ceremony—a Thanksgiving 1999 brunch with fifty of our closest family and friends where we could declare our love and commitment to each other and to our world with joy and hope for the future. Autumn has always been my favorite time of year and our crisp, clear fall day was adorned with orange and yellow leaves. The venue in Vancouver's largest park, Stanley Park, featured a panoramic view of downtown and the sails of Canada Place. We exchanged our vows in front of large windows through which we could see leaves swirling and dancing and, in the distance, waves gently cresting.

I've always been a crier, but rarely out of anger or sadness. Artistic beauty—in music, film, photography, dance, painting, and writing—moves me to gentle tears often and without sadness, only reverence and gratitude. The pain of grief has always emerged from me far differently, the uncontrollable "ugly cry" we all hope to avoid. As I stood in a short black skirt, leggings, and matching cashmere sweater to read my vows to Jennifer, I felt grief rising. She stood beside me in the little black dress she'd borrowed from me, looking radiant and beautiful. *Don't cry, Shenher. Do not cry.*

I tried without success to block out a vision of myself in a dark tux, standing proudly beside Jennifer, but I couldn't stop it. *How can I come to something so right and perfect feeling so wrong?* Fortunately, the words of my vows were powerful enough that nobody seemed alarmed by my tears. I blubbered as I expressed gratitude to Jennifer for all she brought to my life and promised her mother I would take care of her and do everything I could to make her happy. I thanked the room full of our wonderful friends and family who had traveled to be there with us on our special day.

I meant every word and felt no ambiguity in committing to her. *I want to commit to her as the man I am.* I glanced over in the direction of Dad, remembering his words. *Dad, you said it would be all better by the time I got married. It's not gone, it's not over, it's not better. But I'm hoping like hell this exceptional woman will help keep me out of trouble.* I also remembered how he'd refused our invitation weeks earlier to say a few words during the ceremony, telling me he didn't think he "could do that." Still, he was there, and I told myself that was good enough. He warmly welcomed Jennifer and I knew he would grow to love her as his daughter-in-law.

A year later, Jennifer was six months pregnant with our first son, Liam. My earlier fears around having a family of my own had vanished as I'd gotten to know her and I'd slowly come around to the idea. The love and trust I felt for her and the solid team we had become made the idea of expanding our family feel like the most natural thing in the world.

Between planning for a January baby, Jennifer's debilitating nine-month-long morning sickness, and the increasingly dire state of my investigation, those nine months passed quickly, filled with both welcome and unwelcome distraction. Deeply disillusioned, I requested a transfer out of Homicide late in the year. My inability to motivate my superiors and the RCMP to take a serious interest in the investigation of Robert Pickton—later convicted as one of Canada's most prolific serial killers—left me wrecked with burnout. I applied for a couple of different policing jobs and expected to move to a new position in the new year.

That fall I'd been tasked with doing an increasing number of media interviews to speak about the missing women investigation and, while I enjoyed the print and radio spots, the idea of seeing myself on television was far less appealing. I avoided it until I was asked to come on *Gabereau*, a national Canadian talk show hosted by the popular personality and journalist Vicki Gabereau.

I arrived at the CTV Vancouver studios on a cold November morning. I requested minimal makeup, but sat quietly watching in the mirror as the hair and makeup people applied heavy foundation, eyeliner, blush, and lipstick and teased my hair into a helmet. I sucked it up and as I sat across from Vicki in front of the cameras, I used the opportunity to say what I had been expressing publicly with more and more certainty: that I believed Vancouver's missing women had met with foul play. I implored the viewing audience to contact us if they had any information, because I was certain there must be someone who knew something. I met a friend who worked at CTV for sushi afterward and after she'd exclaimed how great I looked, I washed the makeup off my face in the restaurant washroom, hoping to rinse the darkness I felt down the drain.

The show was rerun several times and a month later, Jennifer and I went Christmas shopping in search of a video camera with which to record the baby and were greeted by my big makeup-covered head on the talk show, staring back at us from the hundred or so television screens on display. I turned right around and walked out of the store, a confused Jennifer following me. I told her it made me uncomfortable because I didn't want everyone in the store to notice me, and we waited a few minutes until my portion of the show ended before going back inside. Seeing myself unnerved me completely. I felt as though I looked like a man in drag with all that makeup, nothing like myself, and certainly not at all how I felt on the inside.

13

SITTING ON A PIN
(2001–2003)

WHEN I BEGAN a new position in the Diversity Relations Unit (DRU) I felt refreshed, but still very conflicted about leaving my job investigating Vancouver's missing women. I naively believed that fresh faces and ideas would help reinvigorate those stalled cases.

The soft side of policing had never drawn my interest, but after my deeply disillusioning experience in a failing major crime investigation, I needed a break from the dark side. In DRU, my job was to liaise with minority and marginalized communities within Vancouver and strengthen relationships with people who had historically been ignored or mistreated by police: those who were people of color, Indigenous, LGBTQ, poor, struggling with addictions, and/or living with mental health conditions. The intersections within these marginalized communities and identities fascinated me.

My experience working on the missing women file illumi-
nated for me the many systemic flaws inherent in policing.
In my victims' histories, I saw how easily I could have ended
up on the street as a young trans-identified person. Living
through that life experience granted me a perspective on
sexism and the marginalization of my victims that was both
invaluable and incredibly disheartening. As a visible woman,
I had no agency to change the power structure and stereotypes
holding the investigation back. As an invisible man, I raged
against the unfairness and obviousness of the discrimination
I saw. I became an activist as a result.

My predecessor, as well as DRU sergeant Grant Lesley,
recruited me heavily for the position, and they each portrayed
the section as a progressive haven within the very conservative institution of policing. A few weeks after I'd begun, Grant
invited me to join him at a breakfast meeting hosted by right-
wing public policy think tank the Fraser Institute. Ironically,
my time in uniform at the VPD had spanned less than four
years and for the rest of my career I worked in plain-clothes
positions. In Homicide, I'd worn stylish women's clothing that
tended toward the gender-neutral, kept my hair quite long,
and felt as comfortable as I could expect. In DRU, I sensed a
less formal workplace and I dressed appropriately.

I accompanied Grant to the meeting in neatly pressed, tai-
lored pants and a dark, collared shirt, black belt, and black
shoes; my look could definitely be classified as business casual.
The people Grant introduced me to were dressed similarly, but
he wore a suit coat and tie—one of only a handful of men there
who did. After breakfast, as we were driving back to the office,
Grant cleared his throat.

"I should say, as your supervisor, you need to dress more—how do I say it? Womanly, I suppose." My eyebrow arched, but I said nothing. "Take Beverly Chan, for example—try to emulate her style. That would work for you."

Beverly Chan was an exceedingly stylish and well-turned-out sixty-year-old Chinese Canadian woman who favored saris and long, flowing silk scarves. I was an operational police officer in my early thirties and not given to wearing anything that blew in the breeze.

"You do know Beverly is like thirty years older than me, right?" We'd stopped for a red light and I looked him in the eye. "This isn't an order, is it?"

He became visibly uncomfortable, realizing that perhaps my clothing style was not something he had any authority over. The light changed and he didn't have to meet my angry gaze any longer. He resumed driving down the road.

"Just a friendly tip, nothing more," he said, with a phony air of lightness. "Just trying to help you out. You're an attractive woman, you should flaunt that a little more."

"Right."

Up until then, we had been in sync, sharing a similar vision for the office and my role, but now a red flag waved wildly. I didn't change how I dressed in the following weeks, but I started to notice many other concerning aspects related to how Grant ran the office. When I'd started there, he had encouraged me to assess the unit and make suggestions for how we could improve its function, but the more I saw, the less inclined I was to comment.

My only positive experience in DRU was my new friendship with Rosalyn Shakespeare, a detective and true trailblazer in policing. She was the VPD's first transgender officer and was working in DRU for her last years before retirement. Not only had Roz come out as a woman after more than twenty years as a highly respected police officer, but she went through her physical transition as an active member of the VPD and then proceeded to conduct team training sessions for all VPD members, educating us on what it meant to be a transgender person. This was in the late 1990s—a time when transgender people and issues occupied a place very much on the fringes of society. Her transition caused a big stir in the VPD, especially among the older senior members.

Roz endured a lot of crap, predominantly from her closest male colleagues of similar seniority whom she had once counted as friends. Daily, I heard these guys intentionally call her by her birth name to her face, as well as use derogatory labels like *it* and *that thing* to refer to her. The level of cruelty, disrespect, and dismissal she faced from them, while never showing anything but grace and humility, was heartbreaking to watch. One day, Andy, a senior Homicide detective who was a good friend of mine, came up to my office to take me to lunch. As I was grabbing my wallet, he nodded in the direction of Roz's office and said, "God, I'm sorry you have to work next to that freak." I ignored the comment and we made small talk on our walk to the cafeteria. Once seated, I took a deep breath.

"Why do you have such a hard time with Roz?" I asked. "You guys were partners, friends."

"Oh, he knows—"

"She," I interrupted.

"Oh, fuck—you, too?" He rolled his eyes. "*She*. She knows I'm just taking the piss out of him—her. It's nothing."

"It really hurts her. It makes her feel like you don't acknowledge what she's been through, who she is," I said gently.

"How do you know it hurts her?" He looked at me intently. "She knows how we are with one another; cops take the piss out of each other all day long." I set my sandwich down and watched him for a moment.

"I know it hurts her because I'm like her."

"Oh, what, because now she's a real girl?"

"No. I'm *like* her," I said slowly. "I'm a transgender person, too." His mouth dropped.

"You used to be a *guy*?" His eyes popped, his mouth hung open. I burst out laughing.

"No, fucknut, I mean that I'm like Roz before she transitioned. I'm a man on the inside; I feel like I was supposed to be born a man." I started eating again, surprised at how easy this revelation had been. "I've felt like this my entire life."

"You're shitting me, right?" I shook my head, mouth full. "But you're so beautiful."

"You don't have to be ugly to be transgender."

"Holy fuck."

"Yeah. So, can you try to be a little nicer to her? You wouldn't be a prick like that to me, would you?"

"No, of course not."

"Good. Because you never know, I might transition one day and I expect you would still be my friend, even though you're an asshole."

"Seriously?"

"Yeah. Maybe. I don't know."

"Why don't you?"

"You're seriously asking me that after this fucking conversation?" I grinned.

"I get it. Fair enough." He paused. "But, you should give it some thought. You know, if it would make you happy."

The more I saw Grant's inconsistencies, the more I inwardly questioned his leadership in DRU. His assistant, Barbara—who appeared to be hopelessly in love with him—handled many tasks in the office unsuitable for a civilian police member, and she appeared threatened when I suggested to Grant I relieve her of some of them. The tone in the office became more strained as I asserted myself more.

I lived within walking distance and often came in at six to enjoy the quiet time in the office and get things done. One morning after a week away, Grant stormed into my office, in full uniform and handgun, yelling something about me criticizing his management style and how he'd sue me if I damaged his aspirations for promotion.

My desk faced the wall opposite the door, so I hadn't seen him coming when he entered. He was shorter than I, but towered over me as I sat trapped in my chair, barely able to swivel to face him, unable to rise because his body blocked me. His anger oozed from every pore.

"Grant, I haven't talked to anyone about how you manage the office," I told him truthfully. The only person I'd talked to about the office dysfunction was Jennifer. I suspected Barbara's handiwork was behind this outburst. "Back off," I said through clenched teeth.

He stepped even closer, right arm cocked back, contemplating whether to punch me. I had some karate training and planned on employing a rising block and a good knee strike if he tried it. I prepared for the hit as I spoke again.

"What are you going to do, Grant? Hit me? How do you think that'll impact your promotional chances? But go ahead if you think it'll make you a big man." I prayed he wouldn't test my tough act. I could smell his breath on my face; he was so close I considered kneeing him in the nuts, but didn't want to set in motion a scenario where he might pull his gun out of the holster. Cops could be twitchy that way, especially those with anger management issues.

Just beyond him, I caught sight of two of our female coworkers standing just outside the door, witnessing the entire exchange. They were both very senior police officers—and tough.

"Good morning, Grant," one of them called loudly. This shocked Grant back into reality and he straightened up. I wriggled out of my desk chair, shoved him roughly aside, and strode out of my office. The women asked if I was okay, and I said yes and walked straight down the hall to Human Resources. I wrote a statement, but told them I didn't want to do anything more about it because I knew the way these things went. If I complained formally it would end up hurting my career more than his, but I wanted my statement placed in his personnel file because I suspected that he'd had anger problems before and would again. I later learned from my predecessor that this was true. Then I returned to my office, called a sergeant who was an old friend, and asked him if I could come and work for him in the Financial Crime Unit. He said yes.

My brief experience in DRU made me realize I hadn't dealt with my burnout and disillusionment, and it led me to see dysfunction at every turn at the VPD. I returned to therapy with Louise, hoping to recapture my love for my work. Jennifer stayed home on maternity leave and our home life became a magical respite from all the drama at the VPD. Every time, my conversations with Louise returned to my gender dysphoria, pinpointing it as the issue in my life that caused me the most turmoil. When she would ask me, without ever pushing, what was stopping me from transitioning, I couldn't say anything coherent other than that the thought of losing the life I'd built terrified me. In one of our sessions, she described my problem simply.

"As long as you're sitting on a pin, no matter what else you do, you'll never be free of that pain. You'll always be sitting on that pin."

"I suppose that's true," I said with a wry grin, "but it's *my* pin."

I was in my midthirties and believed I could live with the pin, ignore my crushing wrongness for the rest of my life, reasoning that many people in the world lived under far more difficult circumstances than wishing they could transition to male. I told myself that as far as problems went, this one wasn't real, wasn't life and death. *Live with the pin.* Transitioning felt self-indulgent, as though it would place me at the calm eye of the hurricane while the strong winds of my actions—me changing my own body—would produce devastating results for my young family, our social circle, and my parents and siblings. The possibility that my condition could affect everyone in my world loomed too huge, too impossible to contemplate, so yet again I pressed the lid back down on my pain.

My marriage and family life allowed me to play a somewhat stereotypical male role, although I'd never considered it standard or necessary in a man. In the era I grew up in, few openly discussed the concept of a gender spectrum; it's impossible to say whether, if I'd grown up in a later era, I might have chosen one of the many options of expression that are so much more visible today. I felt most at odds with my physical self and I suspect that this would have been true no matter when I was born.

In our partnership, Jennifer was very clearly a mother and I related to the kids as a father. Jennifer and I aligned with many gender stereotypes—I loved watching and playing sports, maintaining our cars, home repair projects, the Three Stooges, and mafia movies, while Jennifer was a complex, serious-minded feminist who was also a far more nurturing parent, exhibiting many more stereotypically feminine traits than I did. Other lesbian couples we knew seemed to have far more nuanced roles.

Together, we played fairly traditional male/female marriage parts, to the point that we'd sometimes joke that we were like a '50s-era married couple where the husband went off to a job every day and the wife worked hard at home raising the children.

Athletic endeavors continued to help me feel more grounded and connected to my body and I alternated running and lifting weights with my best friend Darwin every day after work. We'd met through an ex-girlfriend of mine whom he used to work with and I'd never told him about my trans identity or thought much about doing so, for reasons I didn't completely understand. He was a professional, confident, attractive gay man and we often speculated that we were siblings who'd been separated at birth. I harbored no doubts that he would support me without judgment; it was me who had a problem telling men that I believed I was one of them. That my admission to Andy had gone well seemed an anomaly to me in a world where guys didn't often open up too much about our inner lives.

The term "penis envy" surfaced in my brain, though I didn't fully understand what it meant. Was I jealous that other men had penises? Was that it? I couldn't say for sure because I'd always felt it was a cosmic error that had caused me to be born without one. Still, I worried that the men in my life would hear my pronouncement and think: *Really? You want this? It's not all it's cracked up to be; there's way more to being a man than the good stuff you see every day. There's way more than the plumbing, the clothes, the unquestioning deference the world showers upon you. It comes with pressure and expectation and crushing stereotypes of how you must be in the world. You can't show weakness, softness, tears. Are you sure you really want that?*

Then, I'd answer back to myself: *I'll take all of it, because none of that is what this is about for me. This is about my most superficial and my deepest sense of myself, the person I see when I look in the mirror and feel when my eyes are closed. That person happens to be male.*

Creating conversations inside my head was a specialty of mine, projecting what I imagined others thought and felt about my gender identity and their own gender expression. The constant back-and-forth and the continual tennis match of pro versus con held me suspended in a state of limbo for years, providing nonstop, exhausting internal arguments for both maintaining my status quo and opening the door to transitioning. Neither course represented a solution; each was merely a mitigation plan to survive my time on earth.

My internal dialogue often presented me with a question: what about all those people in the world living with permanent disabilities and incurable conditions who carry on, knowing their lives and circumstances are not within the norm? I saw myself as someone with a kind of disability, and I longed to be "normal." Just as I couldn't see any joy in my difference, I wrongly assumed—without any exploration—that all those who couldn't walk wished they could, all those who were blind prayed for sight, people who were infertile hoped to create a child, and only when faced with the permanence and irreversibility of their conditions did they come to some sort of acceptance. The sticking point in my own situation lay there, in that sweet spot between "fixable" and not. I vacillated daily, hourly.

There is something you can do.

I could never do this.

People have done this; people do this.

Maybe some people do, but they're not me.

How will you know how good your life can be if you don't try?

Those people end up miserable and alone.

You could do this. You would feel so much better.

I would be a guy in sync with his body, but with no one in his life.

You could live fully and be an example of living courageously.

I could lose everything in my life that I love.

Elective plastic surgery patients had their own place on the flip side of my argument with myself. I felt myself forming judgments when I'd see photos of people—mainly women—who had enlarged their breasts or butts, or sucked out unwanted fat from other places. Seeing my favorite celebrities disappointingly changed by face-lifts and Botox gave rise to feelings of condemnation. *Why? Why would they do that to themselves? How are you any different, wanting to mutilate yourself to shape your body into the man you think you are? How are you any different, trying to conform to some unattainable societal standard of what a man or woman should be or look like? You think these people are flaky, but you want to change your entire body, even your name, to become what you think you should be in your head. Who's the flake here, Shenher? Who's dreaming the impossible dream?*

I stopped seeing Louise for therapy in mid-2001, reasoning that I was fine—once again, I had suppressed my gender angst to a manageable degree. Work, family, and a new part-time job as a technical and story consultant on a Canadian television crime drama series filled my days, creating a hectic buzz that kept these thoughts on the back burner. Writing screenplays and dabbling in fiction fed my creative spirit and I finally began to imagine a life outside of policing for myself.

Then, on February 5, 2002, my world blew apart. Acting on an unrelated tip, police in Port Coquitlam, British Columbia, began searching the farm of Robert Pickton, the man I had long suspected was responsible for Vancouver's missing women. When they discovered evidence belonging to one of the missing women, they called in the RCMP Major Crimes Unit and embarked on the largest crime scene investigation in Canadian history, leading to six murder convictions against Pickton and the discovery of enough evidence to charge him with killing another twenty-one women. He would later brag to an undercover officer of killing forty-nine women, one short of his stated goal of fifty.

This horrifying, but not unexpected, development occurred just as I was beginning to recover my zest for police work. I felt happy at home and was loving my job as parent and partner. I'd been leading a complicated international financial crime investigation, liaising with Interpol officers in Europe as well as investigators with the US Department of Homeland Security, the FBI, and the US Postal Inspection Service, preparing to extradite at least two Canadian citizens to the United States to face charges of defrauding hundreds of senior citizens of millions of dollars in a complex telemarketing scam. This work distracted me from my gender issues, but the Pickton arrest took distraction to a whole new level. The case would hold me in its grip for the next ten years.

In my book *That Lonely Section of Hell: The Botched Investigation of a Serial Killer Who Almost Got Away*, I tell the story of the Pickton case in detail. But in the immediate aftermath of February 5, my mental and physical health deteriorated. Once again, I faced an uphill scramble to find contentment.

14

EXPECTING

(2002–2007)

JENNIFER AND I began to plan for a second child. After much discussion and thought, we decided I would give birth this time. There were two reasons: one was that Jennifer had suffered terribly from morning sickness throughout her entire pregnancy, vomiting multiple times every single day up to and including the day Liam was born. The second reason was that, given our marriage dynamic, we thought it might be good to see life from the other's perspective. The idea of being pregnant unnerved me and I felt ambivalent about the plan, but not entirely opposed. My feeling that I was male was so intense that the notion that my body could even become pregnant seemed, well, inconceivable to me. I had visions of us trying month after unsuccessful month, ending with me throwing up my hands and saying, "See? I knew I wasn't female!"

Jennifer and I talked about the potential negative and positive impacts pregnancy could have on me; she wondered openly whether the experience could bring me more in touch with my femaleness and I felt anything was worth a try. I was a few years older than Jennifer and we decided that rather than waste too much time on me if it wasn't to be, we would change course within a reasonable amount of time and allow Jennifer to have our second child while she was still young enough for us to consider a third someday.

My decision to attempt to bear a child felt bizarre. I suppose it was a combination of resignation, optimism, and a disbelief that I could ever become pregnant that led me to agree to this plan. It seemed like the ultimate leap of faith—daring the universe to call my bluff and prove to me that a mistake hadn't been made in giving me female anatomy. *Maybe this will make me feel like a woman.*

The stress of the Pickton farm search took a toll on me physically as well as mentally. After a number of unsuccessful months and another negative pregnancy test in April, we considered giving up and bringing Jennifer in to bat. I decided to give it one more try. I booked time off of work for a few weeks on stress leave to see if that might help. I felt like I'd put in a good effort and Jennifer told me she'd had enough of a break from the morning sickness that she felt willing to give it another go. Both of us accepted whatever came next. And sure enough, one morning in May, I held up that pregnancy test—lucky number seven—and it showed positive.

I stared at the little white stick for a full minute in our upstairs washroom before coming downstairs to show it to Jennifer.

"You're not going to believe this," I said, as I walked into the kitchen, stick held out to her. It was me who didn't believe it.

"Oh, my God!" she exclaimed, hugging me tight before stepping back to look at me. "How do you feel?"

"I can't believe it's real. That my body can do this." I paused. "Am I up for this?"

"Of course you are." She hugged me again. "And I'll be right here beside you."

I experienced pregnancy like a newcomer to a foreign land, marveling at the small changes inside and outside my body. Unlike poor Jennifer, I had almost no morning sickness, but I did experience several unusual health issues that doctors could not explain, which reinforced my continued belief that I couldn't actually be female or pregnant. Determined not to let pregnancy unduly impact my fitness, I exercised every day as before, running until the twenty-eight-week mark and cycling to work until week thirty-two, when Jennifer begged me to drive and avoid injuring myself or the baby.

Because I was used to doing many things alone, during gestation the baby was an unexpectedly ideal companion, distracting me from a workplace where colleagues peppered me with questions and comments about the ongoing search of the Pickton farm and my involvement in the case. Details of each new murder victim's DNA found at the crime scene emerged every few weeks, rekindling media and police interest in the search over and over again, and I kept my sights firmly fixed on the year of maternity leave I planned on taking when the baby arrived. Secretly, I dreamed I would find a way to never return to the VPD when my leave ended.

One year almost to the day after the farm search began,

Jennifer drove me to BC Women's Hospital for a planned C-section, scheduled weeks before due to a known complication. I felt grateful to not have to endure labor; I harbored no dewy-eyed dreams of childbirth and had been worried that the experience might be the last, most unfathomable glimpse into womanhood that would push me over the edge into insanity. The bun was ready. I'd taken one for the team. *Let's get him out of there and get on with the fun part.*

Just the day before, Jennifer and our friends—many of whom we'd met through an informal moms' group our midwives had convened when Liam was born—threw us a baby shower, complete with my mom in attendance, who had flown out from Calgary to help us out after the birth. While the entire pregnancy had been surreal, the shower topped it all. The incongruity of sitting there, opening gifts for a new mother and baby, while I felt like a stranger in a body that now had a baby bump the size of a small basketball, hit me hard. *This is so weird.* I felt as though I was looking down on myself from the ceiling, watching this *woman* playing me in my life—grossly miscast, but playing the role as always. The entire pregnancy had felt that way.

I lay back in the hospital bed as the nurse inserted an IV into my hand, savoring my last precious moments of rest, aware of how much work a baby would be. Soon I was in the operating room, Jen beside me in a gown, a small fabric wall obstructing my view of my lower half, and the procedure began.

Forty minutes later, I stared with wonder at our new son, this incredible little person who came out of *me*. Never had I felt more profoundly jarred by the difference between my physical reality and my psychological one. Until that moment, my pregnancy had been an act, a charade, a gag where I expected someone to jump out of nowhere and tell me I'd been punked. Instead, a doctor handed me little Barry and announced, "Ta-da!" The magic trick was complete. Our son was healthy and perfect. *Somehow, you made an amazing baby, man.* Despite all of my gender angst, helping to create all three of our beautiful children remains my greatest accomplishment.

Throughout my year at home with our little boys, I tried to avoid news of the Pickton investigation and take pleasure in our idyllic home life, but I continued to experience graphic nightmares and surges of anger. I returned to therapy again, hoping for some relief—and this time, Louise diagnosed me with post-traumatic stress disorder (PTSD), the result of working on the missing women investigation and witnessing its tragic outcome. We touched on my gender dysphoria, more as an aside than a main symptom, and I tried a number of different therapies in a quest to feel better. With so many distractions and a busy family, I still felt confident I could rise above all of these challenges and emerge happy and healthy.

The summer of 2004 seriously challenged that belief as I struggled both personally and professionally. It shouldn't have come as a surprise, given his long history of smoking, but Dad was diagnosed with non-Hodgkin's lymphoma, news that left me staggering like a boxer after too many body blows. He'd seemed immortal, a steadfast presence I'd just assumed would always be there. The fact that his cancer was a slow-progressing type gave me little comfort. In the early weeks after his diagnosis, he nearly died during a surgery to remove one of his kidneys, and his recovery afterward was slow. Although he eventually stabilized and returned to a healthy life, he endured several scares over the next twelve years and my new awareness of his mortality shook my entire foundation.

The summer after Dad was diagnosed, a VPD sergeant and good friend took me out for coffee to tell me of a job opening in his office. It sounded like a great fit for me and I immediately applied. The Threat Assessment Unit turned out to be the best policing job I'd ever had, and it extended my flagging career for another nine years. On the face of it, the position entailed researching potential protests and large, outdoor public gatherings in Vancouver and advising my superiors on how to properly police these events. It gave me a chance to educate my colleagues on issues important to activists and oppressed peoples taking to the streets to be heard. My worldview as a closeted marginalized person made me empathic to people the police could not or did not want to understand and this job allowed me to effectively present their positions and influence how we policed them.

It took me many years to see that my overarching objective was to ensure that no one died or became injured through police incompetence or misunderstanding. I feared a repeat of all that had gone wrong in the missing women investigation and saw it as my duty to prevent such a debacle happening again. I attacked my job with a zeal I hadn't felt in years, logging hours and hours of overtime attending protests and conducting surveillance, my BlackBerry always at my side, even during evenings, weekends, and vacations.

In those five years leading up to Vancouver hosting the heavily-protested 2010 Winter Olympic Games, my partner and my supervisors welcomed my commitment to the job and making sure the VPD was never caught off guard. I made everyone look good and myself feel indispensable. My commitment to my job became increasingly obsessive.

It seemed to take more and more effort to distract myself from my gender dysphoria with each passing year, but the prospect of transitioning without ruining my life seemed impossible. Jennifer felt ready for pregnancy again, so we decided to have one more child, and our daughter Lizzy brought me even more light and love I wasn't sure I deserved. Jennifer was able to take maternity leave and I threw myself even deeper into my work. The more I built up the things I valued—family, career, a solid circle of friends—the more trapped by all of it I felt. If I'd had nothing to lose, I would have lost nothing by transitioning, but as the stakes grew higher, so, too, did my discomfort with my gender.

One day, my research at work inadvertently led me to discover that the VGH Gender Dysphoria Clinic no longer existed; it had been replaced by a small, decentralized transgender care team overseen by one of the province's healthcare authorities and run out of a downtown Vancouver public health clinic. I discovered that a local transgender man named Lukas Walther was available for consultation and counseling at the clinic.

The prospect of discussing and perhaps pursuing transition filled me with that familiar mixture of hope and terror. That dormant excitement arose in me again, and I made myself an appointment to talk with Lukas and explore my options.

Lukas greeted me in the small lobby of the clinic office and led me into a private interview room. He was a middle-aged bald man with a short greying beard and a wiry, muscular build, and I never would have guessed he wasn't assigned male at birth had I not known. There was nothing unusual or noteworthy about his voice or appearance other than his small stature; at five feet nine, I towered over him.

I felt reassured by his reserved, understated demeanor— he was a serious person here to discuss serious issues. I don't know what I expected; certainly not some raving lunatic or zealot, hoping to convert as many people to Team Trans as possible, but my own internalized stereotypes about transgender people haunted me and would continue to for many years. The fact was, while I knew several trans women, I had never, to my knowledge, met a transgender man before. I quickly dismissed Shirley in my mind, but just as quickly questioned why he wouldn't count. All of my beliefs about gender and who was allowed to call themselves what suddenly loomed large in front of me. *How can you judge and label these people when you are one of them?* I realized that if I held such notions about whether an internal sense of one's gender was legitimate, the rest of the world likely had even harsher ideas.

Watching Lukas in jeans, plaid flannel shirt, shaved head, and facial hair, so comfortable in his own skin, I felt pure jealousy: of his bravery, of his self-knowledge, of his ability to help others navigate this road with more ease and support than he had likely ever been given. He began by telling me a little bit about himself; his was an increasingly familiar narrative of struggling to find his way as a lesbian on Vancouver's east side. I sensed he had been a far more political lesbian than I, and he acknowledged that he had lost professional opportunities and faced scrutiny for his outward appearance and more radical lifestyle. Again, I felt a surge of jealousy at his courage as I desperately clung to my privilege.

Still, I knew I had nothing to prove to him or to myself. His pragmatic style seemed to say, *This is more or less what you can look forward to, take it or leave it; it's no skin off my nose if you transition or not.* He asked me what he could do to help me and I told him my own story.

"So, you've been trying to manage this a long time." He exhaled as he said it. "Normally, or I should say, often, I send people away to try different things like dressing more in line with how they feel, or getting a haircut, or expressing themselves and their gender differently—something manageable that helps them get through the day." He paused. "But it seems you've tried all that and you're quite sure of what you want."

"Does it?" I asked, knowing what I wanted but terrified of wanting it. The familiar euphoria at talking seriously about transitioning had returned, but the uncertainty lurked nearby.

"How does the idea of transitioning make you feel?"

"Absolutely fucking terrified, but excited."

"Terrified of the physical pain? Surgeries? Hormonal changes? Or the changes to your life?"

"I couldn't care less about the physical pain; if it were just that, I'd do it tomorrow," I laughed ruefully.

"Who do you see yourself as, as you grow older? Male?"

"Yup."

"How does the thought of not transitioning feel to you?" I sighed, realizing before even speaking just how that felt.

"Depressing. Like my life will be one long stretch of drudgery until I finally die."

"Yikes."

"Yeah." We sat quietly for a few beats. "Tell me what the process looks like. What would I have to do?"

"Well, the rules are changing quite rapidly, but as of now, you first have to see an assessor—she's a private psychologist contracted by the province. I'll give you her name and a referral from me. Before you can get any surgery or hormones, you have to have her assessment that you are a good candidate for transition.

"Then you're required to live for a full year as male; use a male name, present as male, the whole deal. Some people fudge that a little, maybe say they have when they haven't done it that long, but I'd advise against that. It's worthwhile to see what you're getting into."

"But won't that be unrealistic, since I'll still look like a woman to a large extent? I'll still sound like one, for sure. It seems like the worst part would be calling myself a man when I still look like a woman." *This sounds an awful lot like how it is for me right now.*

"Well, the theory is that if you're committed and sure that you need to do this, then you're willing to deal with that discomfort to get where you need to be. We'd want you to be sure so there's no regret after transition." He leaned forward in his chair. "The fact is, for us, as trans men, it's far easier to pass once we're on hormones and we don't often have to deal with such awful transphobia and social awkwardness, not the way trans women do.

"Many trans women go their whole lives enduring people calling them 'sir,' teasing them, misgendering them. You're lucky," he continued, gesturing to me. "You have good size, slim hips, broad shoulders; you won't have any trouble passing when the time comes and you're big enough that people probably won't try to mess with you." I took in his assessment of my physical self, on the one hand relieved, on the other, reminded of the way horse owners spoke of their animals as having good size. *How many hands high am I?*

"Once you've done all that, to get surgery and hormones you'll need that assessment, as well as a second one from a psychologist or your family doctor."

We discussed smaller details, then shook hands. Lukas wished me luck. On the short walk to my car, my feeling of elation quickly evaporated into familiar fear and resignation that transitioning was just too huge to contemplate. I returned home and told Jennifer about our conversation. I shared my struggle with her but I didn't let her know just how much I longed to transition. And she didn't press me for more information on my feelings about it—we were both too afraid of the answer.

A few weeks later, I stepped into the comfortable, bookshelf-lined Gastown office of Dr. Melady Preece, the psychologist specializing in assessing emotional readiness for hormones and surgery in transgender people in BC. She had a quirky air, long blonde hair, horn-rimmed glasses, and an aging surfer-girl vibe that I found amusing. I told her of my past assessment at VGH and this seemed to elevate me in her eyes. I'd clearly been around the transgender block. Her intellect was obvious as soon as we began to talk. Her comprehensive assessment took two hours. I completed the written tests she gave me, and she then asked for a few minutes to have a look at them. Finally, she spoke.

"Well, then. Why haven't you transitioned?" I felt taken aback by her blunt manner.

"Uh, as I told you, I'm really afraid I'll lose everything if I do."

"I've had many, many people sitting right there where you are and they have done surprisingly well. What is it you're waiting for?"

"I, uh, well..." I stammered.

"Everything I've seen of you and you've told me indicates this is very clear for you. You are not someone on the fence about this in your mind, are you?"

"No, I suppose not."

"I'll write you your letter, for hormones and surgery. You can decide how much of either you want. I'll suggest that your VGH assessment should satisfy the two-doctor requirement because I don't think there's any ambiguity for you other than the fact that transitioning is very hard."

"There's one other thing I'm worried about," I said, suddenly aware of another issue that had been lurking in the back of my mind for the past couple of years.

"Yes?"

"I've been involved in a big police investigation, and I fully expect it's going to go to a public inquiry. The idea of transitioning and being on display is too much for me. I can't do it."

"Yes, I can see why that would be. When is that happening?"

"I don't know, but someday, once the trial is over, I guess. No one has called for one, but there will be one. There *should* be. I'll be on the stand as long as anyone, likely several days."

"So, you don't even know if there will be an inquiry?" I felt my face flush hot. *She thinks I'm being ridiculous.*

"No, I don't. But there will be, I just feel it."

"So, you could transition and be all done before it even happens?"

"I suppose," I agreed. "But, then I'm still 'that cop chick who became a dude' in the media and in the inquiry. It's really distasteful to me."

"I see." She stood up. I joined her, shell-shocked at the speed with which this had all transpired, though I didn't know what I had expected. That she would tell me I wasn't transgender? That she felt I could be magically cured of this? *I know she's right, but I'm not ready for this.* "Well, what do you want to do, then?"

I paused near the door, chest tight, heart pounding. "Thank you. I need to think." I walked out, then raced through the hallway and down the winding staircase. Out on the street, I stopped, taking in huge gulps of air, trying to catch my breath. *I can't do this. I can't do this.*

On a dark November evening a few days later, a colleague shot himself in the detectives' lounge of the VPD downtown headquarters. He and I weren't extremely close, but I'd liked and respected him and his work immensely and we shared many close mutual friends in the Major Crimes Unit. We were all devastated by his suicide. Because I was suffering from PTSD that I barely understood or accepted, let alone treated, I suspected that the cumulative trauma of policing could have been at the root of my colleague's desperate act. His death made me wonder if suicide might be an option for me, but I quickly dismissed the idea. I knew my growing depression hadn't beaten me and that I possessed a resilience some didn't. I knew that even with my challenges, there was a chance tomorrow would be a better day than today. I resolved to keep living as female, but try harder to ignore the pressures of keeping to gender norms.

Feeling depression closing in around me, I made an appointment to get a haircut the following week. I sat in my hairdresser's chair and told her what I wanted. A lesbian who'd been cutting my hair for many years, Inge had a cool and sporty androgynous style that I often wished I could rock as well as she did. At earlier appointments, I'd asked her to cut my hair like Johnny Depp's long man-bob, often bringing a photo. She'd always thought I was half-joking, but I'd always been deadly serious. Still, she went along with it.

"Short? Really?" she asked, incredulous. "Like *really* short?"

"Yeah, like yours." I gestured to her short, messy cut with a certainty I didn't feel.

She started in with the scissors and I watched with detachment as my long brown waves fell to the floor. I felt both liberated and scared. When she was done, I stared at myself in the mirror as she swiveled the chair around, holding a hand mirror so I could see it from all angles. It was a nice hairstyle, objectively, but all I saw looking back at me was a strong-featured woman with short hair—maybe a butch lesbian, perhaps a stern German intellectual too entrenched in philosophical studies to worry about such trivialities as fashion and hairstyle. Long hair had softened my masculine features and provided camouflage. Now uncovered and unmasked, I could only see how wrong everything about me—my hair, my body, my face, my entire presentation—looked through my eyes.

"Great, it looks great," I lied, paying Inge and hurrying out of her shop. I threw myself into my work in preparation for a week away from home on training.

My partner Matthew and I attended a weeklong Internet threat assessment research training course at an RCMP facility two hours east of Vancouver. The campus was comfortable and well-appointed with a large gym, expansive grounds, a cafeteria serving nutritious food, and a licensed lounge with a huge TV for watching sports.

I tried to ease my depression by spending each evening with Matthew in the lounge watching hockey games over progressively more pitchers of beer. My thoughts grew darker each day, and it seemed as though the other people on the course were avoiding me; I wondered if it was because of my haircut. I feigned higher spirits than I felt during my nightly calls to Jennifer so I wouldn't alarm her. Finally, on Thursday night, drunk for the fourth time, I knew I had to make a change and get off this dangerous path of depression and hopelessness. I informed Jennifer, casually, that I thought I should quit drinking. As always, she gently supported me.

I resolved to face my troubles sober.

15

THE CHANGE
(2008–2014)

BETWEEN THREE BUSY children, home renovations, my increasingly demanding job collecting and analyzing security intelligence for the Olympic Games, the constant drip of news from the Pickton investigation and court case, and my efforts to distract myself from my gender disconnect, it felt like I had very little energy for things I used to manage easily. Although my PTSD symptoms had subsided to some degree, the unrelenting nature of the Pickton case kept me in a constant state of high anxiety, affecting my mental and physical health. Immersing myself in work helped to keep my mind occupied; I was even considering competing for promotion to sergeant.

Downtime was my enemy, but in the spring of 2010, I could no longer avoid it. I needed ankle reconstruction surgery, the result of years of basketball-induced ankle sprains and a couple of previously undiagnosed broken bones from running. I'd postponed the surgery until after the Olympic and Paralympic Games concluded, but the week after the final flame was extinguished, I went under the knife to fix my foot.

The surgery was successful, but having so little to do during my recovery felt torturous. I read voraciously but had few outlets for physical movement; I was required to wait several weeks to begin physical therapy, and did rehab work lying on my back in my basement gym. Resigned, I set my sights on enjoying my home time, attacking a new stack of books, and hanging out with Roxy, the new labradoodle puppy we'd picked up the week before my operation, who was destined to become this man's best friend.

Two of the books I read during this time made a profound impact on me. The first was academic Aaron Devor's *FTM: Female-to-Male Transsexuals in Society*, a groundbreaking sociological study of forty-five self-identified transgender men. A trans man himself, Devor skillfully and compassionately explores every aspect of these men's lives before and after transition and I learned a great deal from it. The second book was Leslie Feinberg's *Stone Butch Blues*, a novel that the author described at one point as a "thinly disguised autobiography" about Feinberg's own experiences as a working class gender nonconforming person within the lesbian community in 1970s New York State. Where Devor's heartening book encouraged me, Feinberg's depressing, dark novel documented every fear—real or imagined—I had about transitioning. I turned to the Harry Potter books for escape, reading the entire series, feeling more of a kinship with Harry's struggles.

Watching Jennifer tackle all the tasks at home with such good humor while I was incapacitated caused me to reflect on my own role in our family. I was constantly stressed, always working even while at home, and I saw myself as resentful, cranky, entitled, always trying to prove myself, unable to enjoy our family, and bitter about my lot in life. While there were some aspects of my job I found rewarding, the police culture wore on me; it had never fit me well. During my downtime I began to explore potential new careers I might pursue when I was finally free of the Pickton investigation.

Later that summer, as my recovery progressed, the provincial government finally announced the inquiry I had both dreaded and demanded into BC's missing women investigation. My increasing anxiety levels threw me deeper into workaholic mania.

Dogged for years by insomnia, night sweats, and nightmares, I began to notice fatigue, memory lapses, loss of libido, allergies, itchy skin, tingling extremities, and an occasional electric shock sensation in my neck similar to an elastic band snapping. Google search results detailed the many wild and unsettling symptoms of menopause, and I realized with a jolt that I was going through "the change," as Mom called it. Just when I'd thought I'd been dealing better, though not *well*, with my femaleness, perimenopause (the early stages leading up to menopause) hit me with crushing force.

Since I was in my midforties, I supposed it made sense, but for someone who'd rarely paid attention to women's health issues or closely identified with the physical experience of women, this final proof that I would not only live but also age as female hit me hard. Menstruation, ovulation, regular cervical examinations, breast exams—throughout my life, all of these female health-care rituals had felt like trips to strange planets I wasn't intended to inhabit. I felt certain the women in the waiting rooms were eyeing me, wondering what I could possibly be doing there. *What does he need with a bra, anyway?* I found small comfort in the possibility that perhaps some of my physical ailments were the result of aging and not entirely the stress of awaiting public scrutiny of my failed investigation.

I made it through the nineteen months leading up to my testimony at the Missing Women Commission of Inquiry, but the entire experience left me shattered, disillusioned, and despondent. I resisted a powerful desire to drink, longing for that hit of relief that came with the first sip. As more of a binge drinker, sobriety hadn't been too difficult for me with a young family and a partner who wasn't a big drinker, but I found myself thinking *just one drink wouldn't hurt; it might take the edge off* and I knew I had to resist.

The inquiry itself was a farce, a disrespectful poke in the eye to Vancouver's missing and murdered women, their loved ones, and the lawyers trying to represent them. Seeing my photo plastered over the front pages of Vancouver area and national newspapers, television, and websites rattled me; my efforts to improve my tired, makeup-less appearance by wearing custom-made suits didn't help me in my goal to appear "normal," as usual. I'd resolved not to watch TV or go online, but my image was everywhere: newsstands, the grocery checkout aisle, and on increasingly ubiquitous big screens all around the city.

Since that first meeting with Dr. Preece, I'd held my problems closer and closer to my chest, speaking of them only to my new therapist, Dr. Joanne MacKinnon, whom I sought out a month after giving my final testimony in the spring of 2012. Louise had retired, and I was lucky to discover Dr. MacKinnon. Our twice-weekly sessions that year focused on my policing trauma and enabled me to drag myself into work each day, but I hadn't yet raised the issue of my gender identity with her. By the time the commissioner released his final report in late 2012, the inquiry's failings were obvious and my obsession with them obscured my vision completely, leaving me unable to address my other problem.

It wasn't until Dr. MacKinnon and I worked through some of those things that I could begin to see that the pin I'd been sitting on all these years was now the size of a railroad spike. In May 2013, I was referred by a colleague to a residential group therapy course called the Veterans Transition Program (VTP), dedicated to helping military officers and first responders with debilitating PTSD to transition out of their professions and into new lives. Dr. Matt Graham, one of the psychologists leading the group and responsible for intake, called me at home one night to discuss my suitability for an upcoming VTP session.

My depression was reaching a desperate stage and I felt this program was a last chance to stop my spiraling PTSD. My work with Dr. MacKinnon was progressing, but as long as I remained in policing, it felt like placing a Band-Aid on a machete wound. I had been off work for a couple of weeks on stress leave and I knew that I needed something more intensive than our twice-weekly sessions. Dr. Graham and I chatted easily for several minutes, getting to know one another a little.

"I have to say, I'm afraid this program coming up is a men's group," he said. "We have had women in the men's group once or twice, but we found it wasn't ideal for either the men or the women. Neither group felt completely free or safe to disclose their issues, so we're not that keen to have any more mixed groups." My heart dropped. In that moment, I made a fateful decision.

"I don't know if this helps—" I paused. "But I identify as a transgender man and I would be far more comfortable in a men's group. I know you have to consider the other men, too, but all I can tell you is that from my end, that would be my preference." I realized I no longer cared about keeping my secret; all I wanted was to stop the pain.

"Okay. Thank you for sharing that with me. That's very interesting." He seemed genuinely empathic and concerned. "Can you tell me a little more about that, if you're comfortable?"

In an almost clinical monotone, I told him the basics of my experiences dealing with gender dysphoria.

"That's got to be a tough slog for you," he said when I finished. "I'm sorry you've had to suffer with this."

"I've managed okay to this point, but it's getting harder." There was a long silence.

"Look, I'm not sure what to tell you right now. My gut thinks this could work, but let me talk to my partner on this group, Dr. Mike Dadson. I can't make any promises, but I will get back to you within a couple of days, okay?"

To my surprise, Matt and Mike welcomed me into the upcoming VTP. "I have a strong feeling this is the right decision," Matt said, when he called me back to invite me to join the group. At the end of the ten-day program and every time I've run into

Matt since, he has made a point of telling me how glad he is that he trusted his instincts to include me. I'm very glad, too.

I came out to my group as transgender on the first day—four other men plus two military paraprofessionals and Drs. Matt and Mike. Sitting there, listening as each man introduced himself and told of how he came to be there, I knew I could no longer hold my gender history separate from my life's other challenges and the damaging, soul-destroying career choices I'd made that had landed me where I was that day.

I briefly told the story of myself in kindergarten, thanked them for including me, and asked that they—if they could— treat me like one of the guys, because I truly believed that I was. I warned them that this issue would likely form part of what I discussed in our ten days together. I watched the men as I spoke, unable to determine their reactions to this unusual disclosure, but as we went around the circle for feedback, their support of me was unequivocal, vocal, and palpable. This group of military men embraced me—literally and figuratively—and would become instrumental in my recovery.

The pinnacle of each participant's ten days was a therapeutic enactment of an incident central to their own trauma. The rest of the group would step in as role-play participants, playing various parts to act out the scene, so that the man whose experience we were recreating would not have to put himself in a place of past trauma and could rather stand aside, supported by Matt and Mike, watching a stand-in for himself go through the event. The enactments could be historically accurate or an amalgamation of events designed by the participant and the treatment team to maximize their impact. I chose the latter for mine.

We decided to recreate a scenario from when I was age four or five where I felt I'd done a disservice to myself as the young boy I knew myself to be. We could effectively change the outcome so that I could embrace and protect that little guy, rather than banish him to the fringes of my life by alternately ignoring him or berating him for existing. I had to open myself up to the process and withhold any judgment. Matt and Mike created an atmosphere where we all felt free to be vulnerable, and I took the plunge alongside this battle-hardened group of soldiers.

I was able to hear the reassuring words I'd always longed to hear as that young boy: that I was okay, that I could be loved, that being myself didn't have to mean being inherently wrong. The youngest guy in our group, a soldier of twenty-two, played the role of me, and I am eternally grateful to him and the others for putting their all into it. It's difficult to describe the power of this exercise, but I felt a visceral shift in myself as we enacted it. My compassion for myself burst to the surface and has remained there ever since.

All my poor coping choices emerged in stark clarity after this exercise. One of the guys in the group observed that I seemed to retreat from success at every point in my life when success appeared imminent, and I knew he was right. I realized that I'd habitually failed to stand up for that little boy throughout my life—by fearing to express myself through writing, by allowing my fear and pain to stop me from playing and coaching basketball, by choosing police work as a profession—pressing him to the margins every time he tried to assert his need to be heard and to flourish. *My need to flourish.* I'd tried to separate him from me, but *he was me.*

Armed with my new self-awareness, I returned to Dr. MacKinnon to process these developments. My suspicions validated, I trusted my gut and the reassurances of the men in my group that I'd given all I could to policing. It was time for me to stop harming myself. I knew I couldn't return to the VPD. It was then that my therapy started to pay dividends and we were able to more effectively work through my policing traumas.

I took a medical leave from work, hoping to regain my health to the point where I might consider future work but accepting it would not be in policing. The emotional work was arduous; I saw Dr. MacKinnon twice weekly, as well as an occupational therapist once each week for exposure therapy. The combination of this therapy with the last twenty-plus years of policing and the breakthroughs I'd achieved through the VTP group exhausted me, and I slept more than ten hours a night for much of the first year and a half as I recovered at home. I took long walks with Roxy and renewed my love of running now that my ankle was fully healed.

Still, I dreamed I could push the increasingly intrusive desire to transition aside the same way I'd managed to for so many years. I hoped that expressing more of myself through clothing choices and open dialogue with Dr. MacKinnon would be enough. In those years, these two life issues—gender dysphoria and PTSD—were parallel streams flowing down the same mountainside, not touching or converging, despite the awareness the VTP group had awakened in me. I'd married for love, brought children into the world to create a loving family, and slowly came to realize that I'd built this life, this safe haven, all to keep myself out of trouble. *Can it keep us safe forever, can it protect all of us from the wrongness of me, from the awfulness of the world, from this thing I fear I won't be able to stop myself from doing?*

One afternoon I sat chatting with our nine-year-old daughter Lizzy in her bedroom. I had begun to ruminate about celebrating my fiftieth birthday the following year, and Lizzy was calculating how old I might be when the time came for her own anticipated milestone: getting married. She didn't know who the groom would be—or bride, as she informed me, explaining she wasn't sure which it might be—she just planned to kiss this as-yet-undiscovered person on their wedding day, not before, and only very seldom after. The conversation then moved on to wedding attire.

"I want you to wear a dress to my wedding," Lizzy stated. "Mama will be wearing one." In one of those parenting moments where you debate whether to go along with the dream or insert some reality, I decided on reality.

"Well, I was thinking I'd like to wear a suit," I ventured. "That's a little more my style." She scrunched up her face and shook her head.

"Oh, no. You need to wear a dress. It's a special occasion," she said, her tone laced with disappointment.

"How about a nice tux?" She shook her head vigorously. I chose a tactical retreat rather than face my Waterloo.

"Okay, we can figure it out closer to the time. It isn't like you've booked the caterer, yet, right?" I laughed lightheartedly. She smiled at the joke.

"I guess you don't need to go buy your dress yet," she said somberly.

"Cool, thanks," I said, as Jennifer entered the room looking at us quizzically. I gave her one of those worried, we-have-to-do-something-about-this looks, but left it at that.

My conversation with Lizzy poured cold water on any simmering plans to transition, illuminating the degree to which I feared that it would screw up our children. I'd always believed that education and open dialogue could conquer anything in parenting, but I now felt deeply worried they would not take it well. Lizzy was a highly emotionally intelligent child, thoughtful, compassionate, and empathic far beyond her years. That she stuck so steadfastly to her wish for me to wear a dress shocked me, leading me scurrying back into the closet, certain I could never transition. Rather than do the sensible thing and talk with Jennifer about it, I remained stuck in my own misery, resolved to a life of incongruity.

I've often made decisions based on intuition, and those few choices I've regretted were the result of ignoring that little voice. I've always known our kids to be three good, kind, sensitive, and infinitely loving human beings, qualities I attributed—and still do—almost completely to Jennifer's love and skill as a mother and her dedication to nurturing their development. I wasn't around much during my workaholic phase when they were really young. Even so, we forged a connection and as they grew older, it never seemed as though their interest in hanging out with us waned at all. Sure, we reached the point where they stopped holding our hands to cross the street, but I feel so lucky our kids never hit a period where they rolled their eyes at our every word or didn't want to spend time with us.

As I contemplated physically transitioning, I thought of the damage friends had endured due to their parents' actions: emotional or literal abandonment, suicide, alcoholism, drug abuse, infidelity, divorce. If I transitioned, would I be setting our children up for the same sorry adulthoods of endless therapy, toxic relationships, and unmet potential? *Could I do this to them? Would "this" sentence them to all of that?*

I decided to trust our kids. Sick of a lifetime of vacillation, I slowly began to open up to them about my lifelong struggle. They were two young teens and one preteen—it seemed the worst possible time in their short, fragile lives to live through the transition of a parent. That very reality felt like an added safeguard against me actually doing anything, and I opened up the discussion as a small step, rationalizing that it was a compromise instead of completely blowing their lives apart.

Jennifer and I had both enjoyed safe, secure, stable upbringings and we shared many details of our family lives and our own youths with our kids, unvarnished and real. We wanted them to understand the complexity of family. We each had experienced periods of great loneliness as teens and we wanted our kids to know that we were there to support them, no matter what challenges they encountered, especially in adolescence.

The tone of these conversations would feel familiar for any parent of teens or preteens. I explained the difference between sexual orientation and gender identity, relating them to myself and the life I'd lived, to which they each on different occasions responded with some variation or another of "well, duh." I was able to point to transgender characters recently cast in some of our favorite television shows and presented in young adult novels the kids were reading to help start the conversation.

A young person in our social circle had begun a male-to-female transition in her early teens, which further opened the door to new insights and wholehearted acceptance from my children. Still, I told my stories of struggling with knowing I was "different" with a certain air of detachment, explaining to the kids that transition was something "that some people decide to do to deal with being different." It wasn't until one of them very casually asked, "why don't you transition?" that I began to think they might emerge not only okay, but unburdened—that their lives might remain intact. The realization dawned on me slowly over several months. *Our kids are pretty amazing people and they really do love me.*

Suddenly, it seemed, I noticed that transgender stories were being reported on in the news and transgender characters were appearing on television dramas like *Orange Is the New Black* and *Transparent*, some played by trans actors. Laverne Cox's portrayal of Sophia Burset in *Orange Is the New Black* struck me as groundbreaking, well before Cox—a transgender woman herself—was featured on the May 2014 cover of *Time* magazine heralding the "transgender tipping point." These new trans characters weren't shallow and undeveloped; they were regular people who formed part of a larger narrative, a greater story arc that didn't seek to exploit them as freaks, twisted serial killers, or the butt of jokes, as had been the trend in mass media for so long. Seeing trans people on television or learning more about trans celebrities wasn't the attraction for me; watching trans stories move from the fringes of society to mainstream visibility was. Seeing trans and gender nonconforming people's stories daily online and bursting into the collective consciousness on the street and in coffee shop conversation blew open the doors of my closet. I felt safety in those numbers and wondered how much regret I'd feel later in life if I didn't build up my courage and start to fully live.

As has always been my way when processing big decisions, I became withdrawn and insular during the year before my fiftieth birthday. When I imagined myself as an elderly person, every picture my mind conjured was of me as an old man, not an old woman. I didn't make a bucket list for the second half of my life because I knew it would contain only one entry: stop being afraid and live your life. While I had previously pushed my desire to transition down and suppressed it through the coping mechanisms I'd employed throughout my life, many of my methods had ceased to work and I could not stop thinking about transitioning. *Should I? Shouldn't I?* was replaced with *How? When? Am I prepared? Can I convince Jennifer and the kids to join me on this journey?*

These questions kept me up every night, and when I did finally fall asleep, I would awaken with a start—heart pounding—and my racing mind wouldn't allow me to fall back asleep for hours. One night, as I anxiously paced the halls of our home in the hours just after midnight, I stepped into the boys' room, breathing in every scent, sight, and sound. I stood there, watching their little chests rise and fall as they slept. Barry moaned loudly a few times, as he often did. Liam uttered a string of gibberish before rolling over. I ached with the familiarity of them. *Will I have to throw this all away once I make my decision?*

Some weeks, out of pure fatigue, I'd consciously force the idea out of my head, telling myself I was not going to transition, to stop thinking about it and envision a future life as a woman. I could push it aside for a few hours—far less than the day or two I could manage in my younger years—but I couldn't visualize a female future and the thoughts would eventually burst forth again, rushing in with such force that I couldn't resist them.

One fearful week, I'd lapsed back into thinking I could avoid transitioning, which made me tense and cranky. Jennifer and I were dressing for the wedding of some friends and, as usual, I agonized over what to wear. Finally, I chose a collared shirt and one of the custom suits I'd had made for the inquiry. When Jennifer saw my choice, she wrinkled up her nose and suggested I wear something else, selecting a black turtleneck. Resigned, I put it on with black pants; the monochromatic chic worked, but still I felt dejected. I had taken to wearing a chest binder—a tight heavy elastic undergarment that completely flattened my chest—but even that failed to make me feel more congruent. As we mingled during the cocktail portion of the reception, a striking, younger straight couple we knew well joined us. As we caught up with them, I stared spellbound at the man's vintage black suit and coral shirt. *Why am I not wearing a suit?* That moment was pivotal. The prospect of transition had shifted from an "if" to a "when"; I could no longer stop it.

It was never about cool suits, or hair, or liking sports and cars. It was never about a fear of ambiguity or a preference for all things "male" over all things "female." It was never about seeking an escape from the second-class citizenry experienced by women in the world. My experiences moving through the world as female had been resoundingly positive. My deepest sense of self was indisputably male. It wouldn't be until I felt that first dose of testosterone—with its powerful sense of *rightness*—course through my body that I would know what had been missing, like a safe finally clicking open after the right combination of numbers was entered.

I longed to adopt more outward symbols of manliness: facial hair, clothing styled for men, my man's body built by a lifetime of physical activity. For all the variability among every type of man there is, I just knew I was one, that in a binary world, I fit into the male box far more surely than the female one. Neither was lesser or greater than the other.

It just is. I just am. I'm a man.

16

LORIMER
(2014–2015)

AS MUCH AS I worried about the impact of my transitioning on the people in my life, I knew the only relationship that truly and inextricably relied on my gender was the one I had with Jennifer. Over the years, I'd occasionally—unconsciously and unfairly—made her into a bogeyman in my mind, a personification of an obstacle on my quest to bring myself into alignment. I regretted that I didn't share my thoughts with her more completely all those years, that I didn't tell her how all-encompassing my desire to transition was every single day of our lives together. Whenever I'd had a problem, she'd been my rock, my closest confidante, my counselor—it was ridiculous that I wouldn't go to her to figure this out. That she loved me—the unlovable—seemed unreal to me and I was so afraid of losing her that I minimized the extent of my problem as much as I could. In seeking to convince myself that I could hold off on transitioning for a lifetime, I led her to believe it, too, and even my early disclosure to her years ago wasn't enough to prepare her for the shock of our looming, new reality.

During this period, I found myself writing much of my transgender story into the first draft of my first book, because experiencing my doomed investigation as a man disguised as a woman increased the outrage I felt at the injustices of that case. As I worked on that book, my awareness that I, the protagonist in my story, was bound by chains more unyielding than those of professional failure came into sharper focus. I felt I had to face the risks; I could only be free if I confronted, and revealed, the secret that I had felt burdened with my entire life. In many ways, it seemed natural and most honest to reveal this part of myself in the book. However, when I looked at the book as a tribute to the missing and murdered women and a true-crime depiction, I knew it wasn't the time or place.

I still hadn't firmly decided when to begin physically transitioning, nor had I told my publisher any more about my identity other than what could be deduced from the first draft. I came to the conclusion that I didn't want to detract or distract from the important narrative of the story of my failed police investigation by adding my gender dysphoria to the mix.

Still, writing while keeping a whole part of who I was under wraps wore on me and made it clear that my decision to transition was the right one. The book felt like one more shackle restraining me from expressing my true identity. Daily, I seemed to hear of someone new who had transitioned.

Nearly ten years after my panicked departure from Dr. Preece's office, Dr. MacKinnon wrote a letter for me, addressed to my family doctor, explaining that I was transgender. I contacted Dr. Gail Knudson, the provincial health authority's doctor who administered transgender care, and she advised me of what I needed to do before I could be prescribed hormones or qualify for any surgeries. The first stop was a trip back to see Dr. Preece for another assessment, since it had been so long since we'd last spoken.

Dr. Preece's office hadn't changed. I sat down and threw my arms up in resignation.

"Okay. I'm ready to do this thing," I announced.

"Congratulations," she said, smiling. "Tell me how you arrived at this decision." We talked about my process, how my family was handling the idea, and I told her what specialists and surgeons I wanted to see. As I was preparing to leave, I paused at the door.

"You know, Doctor, you scared the crap out of me the last time I was here," I said, smiling.

"Really? Tell me why." She seemed genuinely concerned.

"I don't know. You made transitioning seem so simple, so easy, as though there was nothing to think about other than doing it," I explained. "I've always felt it was a more complicated issue than that." She watched me, nodding.

"It is a complex issue," she agreed. "I pushed you a little because you were so clearly suffering. And now, you know for sure that you're ready."

I understood. I thanked her again and left.

My family doctor referred me to Dr. Marshall Dahl, a Vancouver endocrinologist trained in prescribing hormones for transgender people. I began to explore and make plans for surgery, hoping my busy schedule in the upcoming year would allow for ample recovery time but determined to make the time, regardless.

I tried to include Jennifer in the making of my plans, but I'd left little room for negotiation. Jennifer had hoped I might only have chest surgery but not take hormones, because those changes would be audible and visible. Still, when she'd implored me to "just transition inside your own head" and told me that she felt my decision was based on my concern for how strangers saw me, not the people who cared about me, I felt terrible but I couldn't grant her request. If I had shared my struggle more honestly with her over the years, she would have known I was at the end of my rope.

There was no doubt Jennifer was angry with me, but there was never a moment when I didn't know she loved me. She was always reading about parenting and it was through her study of the work of American MD and psychologist Leonard Sax around the innate differences between the sexes that she came to understand one's developing gender as a spiritual longing, a need for guidance from and connection with suitable gender role models. She had an epiphany where she understood what I had missed out on in my own upbringing as a trans kid craving that connection with the world around me. She not only forgave me; she embraced our new reality. I'm the luckiest, most grateful man in the world to have her. The seeming hypocrisy of taking vows, promising to do everything I could to make her happy, and then turning her life upside down did not escape me when I decided to transition. I worried far less for the kids. I knew they'd be okay; they were unfazed when we told them, to such an extent that we'd had to lay out some hypothetical negative scenarios they might encounter to ensure they had a realistic idea of how cruel people could be. One of them said, "Good, we'll be normal now," after years of being a two-mom family, and we all had a good laugh as we reminded him we would never really be "normal" but that we understood what he meant.

That August, we took a family vacation to Salt Spring Island with my parents, and Jennifer and I strategized over how to tell them during the trip. I steeled myself for the conversation, on edge with expectation, ever-watchful for a good time to broach the subject.

We booked two small cottages on a property at the island's south end; Mom and Dad's a tiny deckhouse literally hanging over the water, ours situated at the top of the property's steep embankment near the road. As soon as we arrived we realized my mother, who, at eighty, had mobility issues, would never be able to walk up or down the precarious incline. I felt mildly surprised when my father shied away from the hike as well, telling me he was still "a little out of puff" from a recent hospital stay for a lung issue. But our gracious hosts ferried my folks up and down the hill in their 4x4, and they were able to come and go to our cabin and leave the property whenever they wanted.

Mom and Dad wanted to hit golf balls, so Liam, Barry, and I took them to the local golf club on a hot, sunny afternoon. Mom took a rest on a bench nearby after hitting a few balls, and I joined her in the shade.

"Gosh, Barry looks just like your dad, doesn't he?" she commented. I watched the two of them for a few moments, the uncanny resemblance obvious.

"They're like clones of each other," I laughed. "Barry's really good at math, too."

"He's shy like your dad, too."

"Yeah."

"And that Liam is such an athlete; he's a natural golfer."

"He's one of those people who just tries something once and he's good at it," I said. "Do you know he's never hit a golf ball before?"

"My word, that is something." She sighed. "You know, this is somewhere I could have seen us living, your dad and I."

"Really?" I wasn't entirely surprised, because the island is a very beautiful place, but it's also very progressive, with a large LGBTQ community, and the population predominantly supports Green Party candidates. "It's pretty different from Calgary, but I could see you guys really liking the artistic community here."

"I saw a lot of posters in the town for concerts and readings."

"True," I agreed. "You could still move here, you know."

"Oh, I think that time has passed us by. We're a little old to move now, and your dad needs to be near his doctors."

Despite living with cancer, Dad approached life robustly, with only the occasional hospital admission and no need for chemotherapy. He and two retired engineer friends built life-size playhouses together for several years, beautiful two-story structures complete with electricity, which they raffled off for charity twice a year. He walked for miles, golfed, lifted weights, gardened, cooked, and climbed up on ladders far too often for all of our comfort. When he left us one Salt Spring morning to return to his car before we'd completed the short walk to a lavender festival, I knew something was wrong.

He'd promised Lizzy a trip to the Salt Spring hardware store that afternoon to look for items to furnish the fairy garden she was building back at home. I wasn't sure he was up for it.

"Dad, we can try for the hardware store another day. You look like you could use a rest," I suggested after lunch.

"No, no, I promised Lizzy and the boys we'd look at some things at the hardware store. It's quite a place, you know." He'd been in a couple of days earlier and could not stop talking about the selection and variety for such a small-town store. "And I want to get you one of those miracle cloths I was telling you about."

"Okay, if you're sure you're up to it." I knew he was exhausted, but Mom gave me a look that said there would be no telling him what to do.

Once at the hardware store, he patiently strolled through the aisles and engaged the clerk for help finding particular items on Lizzy's highly specialized list, but I could see him fatiguing fast. He bought gifts for all of us, then rushed down to the cabin for a nap as soon as we got home. We had to rouse him for dinner a few hours later and he was too tired to join us at the local movie theater for a showing of *Inside Out* that evening.

That he was the first adult in our family to get cancer seemed a testament to his commitment to us and taking one for the team. A smoker for nearly forty years, he subjected all of us to fumes during the years when no one understood how harmful such exposure was. Even when he was diagnosed with cancer in 2004 at the age of sixty-six, he was reluctant to acknowledge that his smoking was the cause, reminding us of all the furniture finishing and painting he had done without a mask and the farm work around asbestos and fertilizer without a respirator.

Looking back, I feel guilty for giving him such a tough time about smoking; I didn't understand addiction and how hard quitting was. He tried to quit unsuccessfully many times before enrolling in Calgary's Tom Baker Cancer Centre smoking cessation program and stopping for good some fifteen years before his own diagnosis. I now see his anger at us for pressuring him to stop smoking not as him insisting on his right to this pleasure, but as guilt and fear that he had unwittingly exposed us all to potential harm. I remember him breaking the news to me right after he learned he'd lost his own brother Andrew to liver cancer at the age of forty, his voice quavering, fighting back tears. In shock, I responded, "Are you kidding?" He was not. He was not someone who took cancer lightly.

Cancer took my dad seriously, too.

Dad's obviously deteriorating health made it clear that the Salt Spring visit was not the time or place to tell my parents about my transition. I knew I'd have to raise it with them in September once they were back home in Calgary, either on the phone or via a letter. I'd now loaded that month with a book release, the start of gender transition, a huge disclosure to my parents, and the small matter of commencing a master's program in the study of professional communications. I welcomed the forward movement, but it seemed an ironic set of circumstances for someone who wanted to stop using distraction to avoid living an authentic life.

Salt Spring turned out to be the last time Dad and Mom ventured beyond Calgary together. While I was living the best year of my life, my father's was ending. I handwrote a short letter recounting my failed efforts to live as a woman and telling them of my transition plans, disappointed in some ways not to talk face-to-face but relieved in others because I felt unsure as to how they might respond. I nervously dropped the envelope through the mail slot, reminded of how badly this conversation had gone twenty-five years before. It felt like a lifetime ago. A few short days later, I received a letter addressed to me in Mom's neat, distinctive cursive. I felt like I was sixteen again, sitting in their basement, waiting to hear how they planned to send me away.

I read Mom's careful script, professing her and Dad's love for and pride in me—and above all, their support for our family and my transition. She confessed to a moment in the past where she had written a letter but never sent it in which she questioned her own ability and willingness to support Jennifer and me as soon-to-be lesbian parents—and admitted how wrong she had been. She wrote of not being able to imagine the deep loss to her life that not knowing our wonderful kids would have been. Reading her admission, I felt connected to her and grateful that she would share something she wasn't proud of.

I slumped over in our front entrance with relief, not realizing until that moment how much I'd hoped they would respond this way. I called them immediately. We spoke for a long time, the three of us on the phone. They asked respectful and astute questions and I patiently answered them. Finally, when we'd moved on to other topics such as Dad's treatments, Mom sighed and said with a laugh, "There you go. Your father's losing all his hair and you'll be getting more!" I could never have dreamed she would react with such equanimity and grace.

My publisher scheduled my book's release for early September 2015 and I planned to begin taking testosterone on September 1, estimating that I would have some time before the effects became noticeable. Jennifer worried that because I already appeared quite masculine, change would be immediate, but her fears were unrealized and the process was frustratingly slow for me. I had experimented first, trying testosterone once that August. I hadn't expected to feel an immediate effect with the first dose, but instantaneously my groin area came alive to such a degree that it felt like someone had taken a cattle prod to my nonexistent cojones. A deep tangible relief flooded my entire body and mind—my anxiety disappeared. I wondered if it was psychosomatic, but it felt real.

After an excerpt of the book was featured in the Saturday edition of *The Globe and Mail*, I began a busy round of interviews on television, radio, and in print. I wondered if my voice would crack during my interview with Anna Maria Tremonti, host of CBC Radio's *The Current*, which I was scheduled for that first week of September. In reality, the only thing that began after that first dose was the waiting: for each new whisker to grow on my chin, for my voice to deepen, for my outside shape to slowly morph into the man I'd always known I was on the inside. My body had to catch up, but I basked in the immense relief that, for all intents and purposes, I was already there.

My only regret in transitioning is that I didn't do it sooner. Even before that first dose of testosterone, I knew I would not be one of the very few trans people—I have yet to meet one—who experience regret. When I administered the first dose, I felt a tangible rush of integration and relief, a rightness I can't adequately explain. It felt like the tumblers of a complicated locking mechanism sliding effortlessly into place with a satisfying click. I'd dreamt of the day I'd transition for my entire life and nothing had ever felt so right for me.

Occasionally, I've tried to imagine what it would feel like to have maintained a female appearance and my mind can't even form the picture. No one has ever asked me if I regret transitioning; my answer would be a spontaneous belly laugh followed by a resounding "no." It isn't that I have any disdain for my female form, an ill-fitting outfit I wore for decades, but quite the opposite. I feel deep compassion for my earlier self, who was in pain—much of it remains very much alive and a portion of the totality of who I am. I'm the same person, now living in the right body.

Within a couple of weeks of returning from Salt Spring, my parents received news that Dad's cancer had progressed, meaning he would need a rigorous course of chemotherapy to slow tumor growth and hormone treatments for his prostate, where the cancer had spread. As I began injecting myself with testosterone, my father was forced to inject drugs that suppressed androgens (the group of sex hormones that include testosterone), which had many side effects, including some feminizing effects. He faced all of this with his characteristically good humor, telling me one day on the phone that he "was going in a female direction" while I was heading in the other.

Dad's chemo and androgen suppression treatments improved his prostate test results, something the doctors told us was their objective, and they were pleased. The tumors—one near his remaining kidney and a couple of others along his spine—seemed to be slowing in growth, if not shrinking. He wasn't in pain and reported that his side effects were minimal, but the early treatments sapped his energy and took his hair, and he slept much of the week after each month's chemo. We talked frequently and he maintained his humor and optimism.

"We heard you on *The Current*," he said one mid-September morning. "You sounded very good."

"Thanks, Dad. How are you feeling?"

"Oh, well, you know. A bit like a pin cushion these days, with all the needles and tests and things."

"Are you still getting the belly shots?" I asked, referring to the androgen suppression treatments.

"Yes, but they're hoping I'm almost done with those. I have these big bruises, like your mom's been poking me," he said, laughing his *hey-hey-hey* laugh, and I smiled.

"Yeah, she's tough, isn't she?"

"She sure is. Keeps me in line." *Hey-hey-hey.*

Our chats followed this pattern most days. He wasn't much of a phone talker. Many times, I'd call home and Mom would get on the extension and we'd try to have a three-way conversation, but, as the quiet one, Dad always seemed the odd man out, a thoughtful speaker who didn't talk over anyone. Eventually, when I started to realize he wasn't going to be around forever, I'd call more often so I'd have a chance to talk with him privately.

"How are Jennifer and the kids?"

"Good, they're out at VanDusen Garden, running around in the leaves before the rains come back."

"How are they making out with your... the *changes*? Your transition?"

"Well, the kids are doing great; it's like they don't really notice or care. I gave them a lot of warning, so they've had a lot of time to adjust. Jennifer's having a harder time, which I can understand. I think it affects her far more than anyone else."

"You make sure you take good care of her. Don't mess that up. She's been so good for you."

"I know," I said. "I won't."

"I might go up and do the gutters this afternoon if I get time."

"Oh, jeez, Dad. Are you sure you're up for that?" I thought of how I felt climbing the ladder to change light bulbs on the outside of my house, and I was almost thirty years younger. Much had changed since we both scrambled across roofs together in the summers.

"Oh, it isn't much. Couple steps on a ladder, I can't see paying someone for that."

"Remember last time you took a lungful of gutter dust?" He'd used his leaf blower to blast them clean.

Hey-hey-hey.

"Your old man had them thinking he had lung cancer!" *Hey-hey-hey.*

"I know, right? Be careful. Wait until Mom's home if you're going up."

"We'll see."

We hung up shortly after, and I cursed myself for not telling Dad that I was changing my name. Of all the elements surrounding a gender transition, changing one's name always struck me as profoundly unnerving. Perhaps in the same way most people accept their assigned sex as immutable, even if less than preferable on some days, I'd never loved my given names, but I had accepted them as undisputedly mine. Just as I might wish I were taller or blonder or my head was larger, envisioning a different name seemed frivolous and a ridiculous waste of time. I'd known a couple of people over the years who had changed their names for reasons known only to them and it had struck me as flaky and unstable, yet who was I, a person about to undergo a wholesale revision of my entire body, to cast judgment on them?

My name represented my history, the label under which I'd traveled through life, conducted myself, *lived*. After talking with friends and Dr. MacKinnon—all of whom suggested that Lori could easily be a man's name; indeed, there were some male Loris and Lauries out there—I considered leaving my name the same, not because I loved it, but because it was *mine*. But there remained the not-so-small problem that my legal name was Lorraine Suzanne and there was no mistaking what gender those belonged to when I lay my birth certificate or passport on the counter at the airport.

I worried about those interactions with border agents or police, those situations where you presented ID to people who held your fate in their hands—folks you couldn't always rely upon to be decent and balanced. I knew firsthand the danger of misplaced power in the hands of mean-spirited bullies.

And so I embarked on the search for a new name, a far less depressing prospect than settling on "Renée" all those years ago. Sure, there were names I'd always liked, and those of people I admired, but, as with selecting baby names, many of those same names had bad associations or negative connotations—they might be the name of someone's deadbeat ex-husband, a murderous television character, or rhyme with a body part. I considered Thompson as a first name, as it was Mom's family name and that of one of my favorite writers, Hunter S., and Jennifer helped me resist this warped and whimsical choice. After fifty years of approaching my gender with the utmost seriousness, this opportunity to recreate myself seemed an ideal way to remove those shackles of dark, despairing life-and-death choices and have some fun with the whole business.

I settled on Lorimer Sebastian Shenher; *Lorimer* as an homage to Jennifer's Scottish heritage and my love of all things Scottish, and *Sebastian* as a nod to my maternal grandmother's French family, who emigrated to Canada well over a hundred and fifty years ago. The name Lorimer demonstrated an obvious link to Lori/Lorraine, and the chance to reclaim the name Sebastian after my French class disappointment all those years ago loomed large. It would have been my choice as my new first name had I not wanted to preserve some aspect of Lori. My timing was good: Alberta and British Columbia both had recently begun allowing transgender people to change their gender marker—M or F—on birth certificates and driver's licenses without requiring surgery, so I worked through the arduous process of obtaining new identification using my new legal name and gender marker by late 2015, though I didn't share publicly that I had done so until the following spring.

I experienced transition as universally positive, and I couldn't ignore the high degree of privilege I enjoyed throughout the process as someone who could afford the cost. Changing my name and various pieces of ID was an expensive process after all the different fees for things including a new passport, birth certificate, and driver's license, as well as changing land titles, wills, and medical services—the cost was close to a thousand dollars. It wasn't lost on me that many people can't afford this most basic necessity when they transition.

I felt such relief to finally be free of my self-imposed con-
straints that I often ignored it if strangers mistakenly called
me "ma'am," "she," or "her" in those in-between days as my
looks slowly changed. However, when family members made
the occasional slip-up, I'd correct them quickly, often with
some irritation. Realizing how unfair this was to them—the
people who'd supported me the most—I tried to understand
why I was reacting this way. I concluded that it was because
it felt intentional, when in truth it wasn't; afterward, they
would apologize profusely in embarrassment. The people in
my life were getting used to a new reality—names, pronouns,
and all—just as I was. I knew the difference between an honest
mistake and deliberately misgendering a trans person as a way
of refusing to accept that person's identity, and I knew what
my loved ones were doing wasn't the latter. I reminded myself
of the humor with which I first approached transitioning and
resolved to show more grace, despite my frustration.

17

CHILD'S POSE
(2015)

———

I STOOD IN the sparsely furnished tenth-floor hallway, clad only in a surgical gown, paper robe, and slippers. I pressed the down button for the elevator and in less than a minute the silver doors opened and I stepped inside, joining two women and one man. I glanced downward, amused and elated by my attire and why I was wearing it. I felt aware of the others eyeing me with curiosity and perhaps even caution, wondering how this building they worked in could house a surgical facility without them knowing it, which added to my mirth.

The women exited on different floors, leaving the man to ride with me to the lobby. As we descended, he glanced over at me and asked, "You having a good day?" I thought about the events unfolding in my life and could only answer in the affirmative.

"I'm having a *very* good day, thanks. You?" I felt the Ativan the nurse had given me minutes earlier kicking in.

"Really good, thanks for asking." He smiled, gesturing to me to step out ahead of him into the lobby. I waved without turning around.

"Have a good one," I called, walking into the small pharmacy as I reached into a chest pocket in my gown for the piece of paper the nurse had given me minutes earlier upstairs. I passed it to the pharmacist, who asked me a couple of questions about any allergies to medications, told me it shouldn't be more than ten minutes, then excused himself to prepare my prescription.

I padded back out across the lobby in my paper slippers, admiring the unusual November sunshine, shivering a little each time the sliding doors opened and the cool breeze blew on my bare lower legs. People glanced at me occasionally, but to the seasoned downtown crowd, a tall, pale, fiftyish white lady pacing an office building lobby in a hospital gown wasn't the weirdest thing they'd likely see in their day. I could have taken a seat, but despite my calm exterior, I wouldn't have been able to sit still for my excitement.

Lady.

I patted the chest pocket unconsciously to make sure my bank card was still there, allowing my hand to linger a moment on the top of my small breast. *How strange it is to know these will be gone in a matter of hours. Were they ever really mine, or were they just appendages in my mistaken custody? Could we find their rightful owner? They seem a shame to waste.* Yet they had not been wasted. To my astonishment, they had nurtured my baby son for months and I'd marveled at the functionality and utility of their design. If I removed my robe, several lines—courtesy of the surgeon's black marker—would have been revealed, the roadmap for a procedure I'd waited my entire life for. *How many ways have I tried to find comfort without taking this radical step? How much struggle has been enough to prove I tried my best?* Relief and acceptance flooded through me.

Finally.

I recalled how the private clinic's flustered nurse had apologized profusely when she realized that she had forgotten to give me the prescription for painkillers before I'd undressed to be prepped, first offering to go downstairs to the pharmacy for me, then reconsidering after realizing the phone might ring. I assured her I couldn't care less if I went down in my gown. Surprised but relieved, she thanked me for being understanding, again apologizing for not giving me the script when I first arrived for my appointment. She couldn't have understood that nothing could ruin this day for me.

I'd always wanted top surgery. Many trans men opt for no surgery at all or undergo this one—the most popular—and decide that's as far as they wish to go. As I sat there waiting for my painkillers, I hadn't decided how far I would take my medical transition. Generally speaking, genital surgery for trans men is far more difficult than genital surgery for trans women, because it involves unique and very complicated challenges for surgeons, such as lengthening a urethra. There are many different procedures trans men can undergo and the field is rapidly changing.

"Shenher? Lorimer Shenher?" I rushed back inside from the lobby, wondering how many times he'd called me. I stepped up to the counter and paid before boarding the elevator again for the tenth floor. Within twenty minutes, I lay stretched out on the operating table, arms attached to long, skinny extensions, *a little like Jesus on the cross*, I thought ruefully, never entirely able to leave the deep imprint of my Catholic upbringing behind me.

"You ready, brother?" I recognized the eyes of Dr. Cameron Bowman, the surgeon behind the mask hovering over me, and smiled at him. "We've got some work to do."

"*So* ready," I replied. He nodded, patting my shoulder.

"Just breathe normally and count backward from ten, okay?" the anesthesiologist beside him coached, gently placing a mask over my face. "We'll see you when you wake up."

"Ten, nine..." I was out.

IN THE WEEKS leading up to my surgery, interviews for the book and a three-week out-of-town residency for a master's degree in communications had occupied most of my time. I spoke with my parents several times a week, learning the latest in Dad's cancer treatment, but a nagging sense of guilt plagued me, an awareness that my life was finally beginning while his showed disturbing signs of an earlier-than-desired ending. I told myself I would go to Calgary to see him as soon as things settled down with school and the book promotion, but in truth, Calgary was hard for me.

Every time I'd returned since leaving Calgary that Boxing Day, the sense that the motions of my youth had all been acts of extreme effort and disingenuous fakery infected every moment. Just as the rolling foothills, the vast sky, and the Rocky Mountains resided in my very DNA, so too did the deep melancholy that came with knowing that my home wasn't there. It never had been. After all the years in Vancouver, when I looked back at my life in Alberta, it seemed that repression, forced conformity, and sadness cloaked all of my memories. I seldom visited, and when I did that familiar darkness propelled me in reverse through the years, right back to twenty-three, eighteen, fourteen, twelve, eight, four—those achingly lonely years I'd been unable to forget.

"Hey Dad," I croaked, calling the day after my surgery.

"Hey, Lori. How was your surgery?" Dad asked.

"Good; how are you doing? You had your chemo this week, didn't you?"

"Yes, I did. I'm feeling pretty punk, I have to say, but a little better than last month."

"That's good. Have you been sleeping a lot?"

"Yes, quite a bit—in fact, I may head back to bed soon; I was up a while today and I think I tired myself out a little."

"Don't let me keep you," I urged.

"I have a few minutes in the tank. Your mom shaved my head today."

"No way! Was that weird? You've never been without hair, have you?"

"Not since I was a newborn, I don't think so." He laughed, his *hey-hey-hey* a little weaker than the last time we'd talked a couple of days before. "It had to be done. I was shedding all over the place."

"Wow. Did Mom do a good job?"

"You know, she really did."

"Better than those haircuts she gave us when we were kids?"

"Quite possibly better." *Hey-hey-hey.* "So, how are you feeling? Pretty sore?"

"Yeah, this isn't for wimps. These tubes hurt whenever I roll over, but I can't complain, since I asked for it," I laughed. He joined me. *Hey-hey-hey.* "Makes me feel like a bit of a shmoe thinking of all those poor women who have radical mastectomies and then chemo or radiation right afterward. I don't feel like I have much cause to complain."

"Well, elective or not, the pain's the same. I hope you'll feel better soon."

"Thanks, Dad." He sounded tired. "You want to hit the sack?"

"Yeah, I think so. We'll talk soon. Love you, Lori. I'll put your mom on."

"I love you, too, Dad. Have a good sleep."

Mom and I talked for a few minutes about Dad's side effects before we moved on to our other favorite topic—politics—and discussed the impending start of the 2016 US presidential primaries, marveling at the seemingly ludicrous prospect of a campaign to elect Donald Trump. I remember coming home from school every day in the early '70s to find Mom glued to the TV, watching every moment of the Watergate hearings. I felt glad that she had this to keep her busy while Dad slept.

"I think I may come for a few days in January," I told her after we'd exhausted all things Trump.

"Oh, that would be lovely; we'd be glad to have you here."

"Is there a good time?"

"Your dad has his chemo the last week, and some appointments with the specialists you could come to with us."

"Sure, that would be good."

"And maybe you could take him to his chemo? I'd love a little break," she said. "I could putter around the condo myself for a change."

"Of course."

The day after that phone conversation, I felt a pain high up in my left leg. I'd been given warnings about blood clots after surgery many times, but had never experienced one. Uncertain, I called Dr. Bowman late that Friday afternoon and he advised me to go to the ER. I quickly assessed my status: top half male after a recent mastectomy, bottom half still female, my overall gender presentation ambiguous after only three months on hormones. Still, I couldn't leave this potential medical emergency unaddressed. Jennifer and the kids were out, so I drove myself to Burnaby General Hospital and checked in at the ER desk, simply telling the clerk that I'd had recent surgery and I was concerned I might have a blood clot.

With a level of uncaring possessed only by the newly post-op or the very drunk, I sat, un-showered, in my sweatpants and baggy jacket waiting to be examined. Finally, they called my name—still Lorraine, since the change wasn't yet complete on my medical card—and I followed a nurse to an exam bed. She pulled the curtain behind us and I sat down on the bed. A tall, soft-spoken, maternal woman of about fifty, she introduced herself and asked what had brought me there.

"Well, I had some surgery and I'm worried I might have a DVT," I said, ridiculously reasoning that using the acronym for a clot—deep vein thrombosis—might make her respect me a little more.

"I see. Can you show me where your pain is?" I pointed to my thigh and she palpated it for a few moments, asking me questions about the pain and how long I'd had it. "When was your surgery?"

"Tuesday," I answered, preparing myself for what I knew was coming.

"What did you have done?"

"A mastectomy and chest contouring." It was actually called *male chest contouring* but I was hoping to leave that out.

"Are you currently receiving chemotherapy?" she looked at me with sympathy.

"No. I should tell you, I'm a transgender man. This surgery was an elective procedure and I'm otherwise healthy." I was surprised I felt no shame or embarrassment at this disclosure, only relief. She smiled.

"This is probably the last place you want to be this week, huh?" she asked, as she touched my shoulder for a moment. I laughed a little.

"Exactly."

"Alright, let's get the doctor to have a look; we'll take some blood and see what's going on, okay?" I nodded. "It shouldn't be too long." I thanked her and she disappeared behind the curtain.

The blood work came back inconclusive, the numbers apparently right on the borderline of indicating clotting, leading the doctor to advise me to drink lots of fluids, keep moving as much as possible, and return if it got worse. He was extremely professional and kind, advising that if I could avoid the blood clot protocol, it would be far better for me in the long term. I returned home and had no further problems with my leg. The experience was as positive as it could possibly have been and renewed my hope that being a trans man in the world didn't have to be awful.

My recovery seemed to take an eternity in comparison to the surgeries I'd had in my younger years, but by Christmas I'd returned to my normal physical activities. I had avoided my hot yoga classes for more than eight months, tired of the side-long glances and complaints to the front desk from women in the locker room who—somewhat rightly—worried that I was a man in the wrong place. I'd endured those tense locker-room silences all of my life, whipping my shirt off quickly so others would see I had female anatomy, sometimes striking up a conversation with someone so that my voice would be heard as sounding much the same as theirs, but I wasn't the same and never had been. Women's washrooms and locker rooms always loomed as fraught territory and, though no one ever confronted me directly or with any hostility, I saw the raised eyebrows among the girlfriends and overheard the comments when I walked out. *Oh my God, I thought that was a guy for a sec! Too funny! Call security, I think there's a man in the ladies'. This one.*

Now, I was ready to return to the yoga studio. I changed in the men's locker room without incident and stood toward the back of the class to practice, sweating shirtless the entire ninety minutes, the same as all the other men, unsure and uncaring if anyone even noticed me, my hairless teenaged boy body, or my fresh scars.

THE LAST SNOW-COVERED peaks of the Rockies loomed spectacularly on this bright, sunny January day, a stark contrast to the dark, oppressive sky and dense ferns of the Vancouver rain forest I'd flown out of that morning—each landscape beautiful in its own right, but indisputably antithetical. Calgary's borders seemed to have stretched, even in the couple of months since I'd last flown in, a sprawling mini-metropolis that struck me as randomly popping out of the flat, unappealing landscape; only the Bow and Elbow Rivers made it seem a sensible location for a town.

Dad pulled the car up from the cell phone waiting area and he and Mom climbed out to greet me. Mom hugged me first, looking healthy and less tired than I'd expected. As Dad embraced me, I rubbed his bald head and hugged his thin frame. I felt my throat choke a little; I often experienced this when I hugged him and I could never understand why. It wasn't a new phenomenon or a response to his cancer—I'd fought back emotion whenever we'd embraced for years. Clearing my throat, I stepped away and took a good look at them. He looked far shorter than his six-foot height, his face pale and gaunt.

"Do you want to drive?" Dad asked, tossing me the keys before I could respond.

"Sure!" I tried to hide my relief as I climbed into their Honda Accord. The last few times I'd driven with them, their nervousness overwhelmed all three of us. The Calgary rush-hour traffic was far denser than I remembered as we crossed the downtown core to their home on the city's west side. Our conversation was easy and light, save for Mom's occasional panicked interjections of "you have to merge soon!" and "get over as soon as you can, you need to be in the other lane to make the turn!" While generally sound advice, I suspected that her worry over freeway driving in a busy city sprang from a deeper anxiety felt by them both, imagining a future where Mom would make this drive alone.

I had to concentrate to ensure I didn't drive to our old family home out of habit; the pull of that familiar route remained strong. A couple of years earlier when Dad was still in relatively good health, they had downsized from their large rancher to a two-bedroom condo overlooking the city on the edge of a golf course, where many of their friends from the old neighborhood had moved. The old house was the one I'd come home from the hospital to as a newborn, and aside from that year in Indiana it was the only home we'd known as kids growing up. Dad had kept it in tip-top shape, but they'd known the time was coming when their ability to manage the upkeep would fade and they hadn't wanted to leave us kids with the huge job of going through all of their things when they were gone or incapacitated.

I unpacked my suitcase and walked out of my parents' spare room to find Mom in the kitchen preparing dinner. The condo was open and spacious and I couldn't immediately see where Dad had gone.

"Can I help?" I asked, sitting in front of her on a stool at the island.

"You can make a salad. I'm not doing much, just heating up some of your dad's spaghetti sauce; he's been freezing all kinds of food for me even though he isn't eating much." I took some vegetables from the fridge and began tearing lettuce.

"Where is he?"

"He's gone to lie down for a bit. He's feeling quite tired. He usually takes a nap every day and he missed it this afternoon."

"Isn't he usually pretty good a couple of weeks after treatment?"

"I'm noticing he takes longer and longer to recover after the chemo each month," she said, passing me a salad bowl. "I think it's cumulative."

"Right," I said, swallowing a thick knot of worry in my chest.

Dad groggily padded out of the bedroom a couple of hours later and Mom made him a bowl of soup; he wasn't feeling hungry enough for spaghetti. We discussed our plan for the next morning: a trip to the cancer center for appointments with his oncologist and his care team to go over his most recent blood work and discuss his chemo scheduled for the day after. He went back to bed soon afterward.

I was in an awkward in-between stage of transition. When I met new people, some made a quick assessment and referred to me as "sir" and "he" and "him," while others were led less by my clothing, men's hairstyle, and demeanor and more by my still-deepening voice. To add to the confusion, my hair was salt-and-pepper grey, so while I looked my age of fifty-one in many ways, my voice and smooth skin indicated someone far younger. Self-assessment is difficult for me, as I would imagine it is for many transgender people, given that my exterior failed to match my interior sense of myself for so long. However, the level of relief and rightness I had felt since beginning hormones far eclipsed the very small level of self-consciousness I now experienced.

When Mom began introducing me to Dad's care team as their daughter, Lori, the funny glances and second looks began. Sure, I'd come out to my parents as transgender and there had been many discussions about the ins and outs of my treatment and goals, but since we rarely spent time together in person, a discussion of how to refer to me and introduce me had never happened. I suppose I was waiting for the time when I would appear so unquestionably male that it would feel natural for people in my life to make the change to my new pronouns and name. Maybe I'd also hoped they would just know to refer to me as male without me having to ask.

In fairness, at the beginning of my transition, adopting a new name felt so strange that I told everyone that while I'd taken Lorimer, I was fine if they wanted to continue to call me Lori. I told the kids they could keep calling me Mommy—Jennifer was Mama—if they preferred, but they thought it might be too easy to slip up in public and call out, "Mommy, look at this!" to me on the ferry or at the mall, so we settled on Lorm for me at home because they found Lorimer too formal and only suitable for the occasional Scottish-accented exclamation to get my attention.

Dad's nurses and doctors explained the status of his prostate and blood counts—they were reasonably pleased with both. I knew quite a bit about the blood system and asked several questions about the relationship between his counts and some of the side effects he was experiencing—swollen lower legs and feet, fatigue, extremely tender fingernail and toenail beds—and they answered them in detail. Given how tough Dad was, I knew if he complained about sore fingernails and toenails they had to hurt a lot. We left with new prescriptions and returned home to rest up for his chemo treatment the next day.

Exhausted, Dad went to bed and Mom and I watched TV. I took a deep breath.

"Mom, have you had a chance to tell your friends about me yet? I know this won't be our biggest concern, but I worry we're going to be going to Dad's funeral someday and you'll have enough to cope with. It might be awkward that people aren't going to know what the deal is with me."

"Actually, I have. I've told Mary, Carmel, Audrey, and Elaine," she announced proudly.

"How did it go?"

"Once I worked up the nerve, pretty well; they were very supportive and understanding."

"Were you surprised? I know you were worried in the fall that your friends might judge you."

"I really wasn't all that surprised, they're all quite tuned in to these things now, and Elaine knows a lot as a nurse. They were very nice about it."

I felt that familiar mix of happiness and dejection over all the years I'd wasted worrying about how everyone else would deal with my transition, only to realize it wasn't so difficult.

I heard noises in the kitchen early the following morning and came out of my room to find Dad at the stove.

"Do you still eat oatmeal?" he asked.

"You bet," I answered, touched that he'd made it for me. "Are you having some?"

"No, I'm not that hungry," he said, spooning a sizeable dollop into a bowl and passing it to me.

"You have to eat."

"I'll have a coffee and some toast. If I eat too much before the chemo, I feel nauseous right away."

"Okay."

We chatted over the newspaper together, just the two of us, as we had so many mornings when I was in high school. Dad's appointment was early, so we hustled down to the car and enjoyed the short snow-free drive in bright Calgary sunshine.

We sat in the busy waiting room of the cancer center, watching as predominantly middle-aged adults waited for their treatment times. Most people were accompanied by a partner or loved one.

"It's really great you could come with me today," Dad commented. "Your mom needed a break. She finds it hard to be here, but she won't let me come by myself."

"How are you doing?" We'd talked all about his condition over the past two days and I knew he was worried about her.

"I know a lot of it right now's from the chemo, but I've been slowing down for the past year or so. This might be it for me." I nodded slowly. There seemed little point in trying to argue with him or tell him how to feel.

"Are you getting tired?"

"No, I'm okay, it's early."

"I mean, generally. Of all of this stuff. Do you have a sense of what might be enough or what that might look like when you realize it?" He took a moment before answering.

"I am tired, but I'm not quite ready to be done with it. Here's the thing: this thing isn't going away. It's what will kill me, so when I start to feel like too much of a burden to your mom, I know that will be it for me."

We heard Dad's name called and followed the nurse into the large treatment room, where many of the staff greeted him by name. She led Dad to a padded armchair and placed a warmed blanket over his legs and midsection as I sat down beside him. Only thin curtains separated each of the treatment chairs. Dad cracked a few of his famously dorky jokes as he familiarized me with the functions of many of the items around us. The nurse inserted an IV and set up the tree to administer the drip through which the chemotherapy drugs would enter his system. Satisfied with her work, she interrupted us.

"Okay, Joseph, you know the drill. Push the call button if you need us or your friend here can let us know. I'll be back to check on you in a bit." She closed the curtain halfway and left us.

"That's funny she called you my 'friend,'" Dad laughed.

"No one knows quite what to make of me, I guess." I shrugged.

"So, how is it going? Your transition."

"Good. You know, as weird as it is, I just feel so much better."

We sat there for a while, me watching his medication drip into his arm, Dad leaning back in his chair, eyes closed. He looked up after a few minutes. "Here's the thing about being a good man: you take care of your family. It isn't complicated. You do that, you'll be fine," he said, watching his IV. "That's all you need to worry about." I let this sink in, surprised by his words and their impact. Surprised by the comfort they gave me.

"There is one other thing I need to talk to you about," I said after a couple of minutes. "I'd like it if you and Mom could start introducing me as your son—as Lorimer—since Lori seems odd, especially right now when I'm kind of in the middle."

"I think I can do that, but I have to say, your mom is having a very hard time with it all. She's trying, but it's hard for us, still."

"I understand. She seems like she's really trying."

"She is."

"Part of it is that I'm starting to be seen visibly as male, and when you refer to me as 'she' or introduce me as your daughter, people are confused. In some situations, that may end up being unsafe for me, if I encounter someone who reacts with anger or violence," I explained. "Maybe you could talk to her, let her know that part of it?"

"I'd never thought of that. Of course, it makes perfect sense. I worry so much you'll run into someone who wants to hurt you because of this."

"I've been really lucky, but I know it happens." I noticed a man and woman about Dad's age waving at us, trying to get Dad's attention from across the room. "Do you know them?" I asked. Dad squinted, then smiled and waved with his free arm.

"Oh, yes. That's Patrick Burns and his wife, Alma. Pat taught for me at St. Cyril's. He has cancer, too—some type of lung cancer, I can't remember exactly. He's on a similar chemo schedule to mine, we see them in here every month."

"Oh."

"He's almost fifteen years younger than I am, can you believe it?" Dad whispered. The man's haggard face bore heavy wrinkles and his hair was entirely grey. Dad's hair had become almost all white in the past few years, but he looked far younger than Pat.

"No way."

"He was an even heavier smoker than me; I don't think he's ever quit, even now," he said, shaking his head. "I hope you inherit my full head of hair. Could you go bald now that you're on hormones?"

"It's a possibility. Lots of trans guys do, but I'm hoping not." I ran my hand through my thick hair. Pat and Alma approached our cubicle.

"Knock, knock!" Pat called out as he and Alma stepped inside the curtain.

"Come in, come in," Dad laughed.

"And who is this handsome fellow, Joe? One of the grand-kids, I presume?" Pat said, extending his hand. "Pat Burns." Embarrassed, I stood and we shook.

"This is, uh, my middle son, Lori—uh, Lorimer—this is Pat and Alma Burns," Dad announced. My heart swelled with pride for my dad. That this seventy-eight-year-old devout Roman Catholic could open his mind and heart to me as his son moved me deeply. Alma stood silently appraising me and shook my hand when I offered it.

"Pleased to meet you both," I said.

"Good Lord, Joe, how do you have a son so *young*?"

"Good genes, I guess," Dad laughed. *Hey-hey-hey.* "Or maybe the young mistress I keep on the side."

Pat laughed. "Joe, you're the last guy I'd ever see with a mistress." Turning to me, he said, "Your dad's a solid guy." I nodded in agreement. "You're not the lawyer from Edmonton?"

"No sir. I'm the cop from Vancouver."

"Of course, of course," Pat said. Alma wasn't buying it; I could see quite clearly she thought something wasn't quite right about me.

They remained standing since there were no other chairs and we chatted for a few minutes about the length of my visit and their respective treatments. Alma didn't speak, restrict-ing her movements to eyeing me with suspicion the entire time. They soon left as Pat became tired as the effects of his chemo began to take hold and he begged off to get home to his couch.

"Thank you," I uttered quietly after they'd left.

"Practice, that's all I need," he smiled. "I'll talk to your mom."

Dad slept the following day, giving me an opportunity to meet my sister Katherine for a long lunch at the University of Calgary, where she worked as a human resources professional. We compared notes on Mom and Dad and I updated her on what Dad's care team had to say. We shared stories of our families and were laughing about something her daughter—my twelve-year-old niece—had said when Katherine fixed her gaze on me, a strange look on her face.

"What?" I asked.

"You look great and it pisses me off," she laughed.

"What do you mean?" I asked, confused.

"You always had better breasts than mine and now they're gone. I get why you had to do it, but ..." her voice trailed off.

"You wish we could've figured out a transplant?" I finished.

"Yes! Exactly!" She smiled. "Seriously, I'm so happy for you, I really am."

I HUGGED MY parents at the door to the airport departures level a few days later, that familiar emotion welling up inside me as Dad spoke into my ear, "I'm really glad you came." I nodded as I let go of him, unable to speak.

After a moment, I told them, "Thanks for everything." Mom and I hugged. I gave a small wave, hoisted my bag over my shoulder, and walked away.

I would never see my father alive again.

18

THIS IS WHO
YOU ARE NOW
(2016)

DURING MY BUSY late winter and early spring presenting at writers' festivals and media events, I spoke with Dad often, and I began discussing tentative plans to spend another week with my parents. I made a point of telling Dad as many funny anecdotes as I could of my adventures, after he told me they helped him tolerate the side effects from his treatment that still plagued him despite the doctors' decision to stop his chemotherapy after the session I had attended with him. Their rationale was that the side effects had begun to overshadow the benefits, and the chemo had accomplished what they had hoped it would.

My own physical metamorphosis continued and I noticed my increasing awareness of the accompanying emotional and psychological changes. As my body aligned itself, I began to map out just what kind of man I wanted to be. My personality remained very much the same. I changed in small ways that I attributed to testosterone and an overall lessening of anxiety; I spoke less, listened more, felt less misunderstood, expressed my desires more clearly, stood up for myself and others more—and generally cared far less what people thought or said about me. I also noticed all the ways I'd internalized how others saw me when I moved through the world as female. This crystalized into a new kind of dissonance I'd previously been unaware of, separate from my own gender dysphoria.

At the same time as I'd gone through life knowing I was male inside, I knew that others saw me as female, and I carried both visions of me in my mind, like two constantly debating, competing voices. It had been like living with a sort of gender interpreter on board for my entire life. Many psychologists talk of our internal critic or that negative inside voice feeding us messages of our weaknesses and frailties, telling us not to bother trying anything because we will surely fail. In addition to that voice, I had another one parroting back the words I imagined others thought about my gender—truly a trippy situation. In public settings, I often found myself talking back to that voice, reminding it I was done with the self-doubt.

I look good in my suit.
People probably think you look like a boy playing dress-up.
My muscles are getting pretty big.
People are probably wondering why you're lifting so light.
My voice sounds much deeper these days.
People probably think you sound like a Smurf.

Each time one of these interactions began to take shape in my mind, I'd pinch myself as a prompt to stop and counter the thoughts with a powerful reminder that I didn't have to obsess about these things any more. It took some time, but eventually I was able to stop.

On April 7, 2016, I presented at New York's Lincoln Center as part of a panel for the Women in the World Summit, curated by Tina Brown and sponsored by the *New York Times*. I was there to discuss Canada's crisis of missing and murdered Indigenous women and girls.

I called Dad from my hotel during the break in the afternoon's events, knowing he would appreciate hearing about my experiences among the other presenters and high-profile guests.

"It's too bad your mother isn't here to hear this," he said when I'd finished. Mom was out buying groceries.

"You can tell her when she gets back. I have to get ready to go out again, we have an awards banquet thing tonight at the UN—otherwise I would've called tonight."

"*The* UN?" he asked.

"Yeah."

"That's quite a trip. I hope you're writing it all down."

"I am. You know me." I smiled to myself. "You'll be proud to know I had spinach and couscous in my teeth for a good part of lunch."

Hey-hey-hey. "I always hated lunch meetings; they put good food in front of you and then expect you to talk."

"How are you feeling?"

"Oh, you know. Pretty tired; I'm napping a lot."

"Hang in there," I urged him. "I should probably get going.

Oh, and if you're up, watch *The National*—I was interviewed for tonight's show."

"Oh, we'll watch or make sure we tape it, then. Thanks for letting us know."

"Talk to you soon, Dad. I love you."

"We love you, too, Lori. Lorimer." *Hey-hey-hey.*

The conference participants buzzed with anticipation the next day for the closing speaker: Meryl Streep. Everyone who had presented gathered backstage as the production assistants instructed us where to stand; we would all pose onstage for the final photo, with Meryl in the middle. After she gave her rousing speech she joined us as we milled about backstage. Many of the women spoke with her and posed for selfies. I stood chatting with Michele Pineault—the mother of Stephanie Lane, one of the victims in my investigation, with whom I'd been on the panel and who was a huge fan of Meryl Streep. Michele stepped up to Meryl, introduced herself, told her a little of her story, and soon they were posing for a selfie right in front of me. Meryl was generous and attentive and put her arm around Michele's shoulder for the photo. I felt so happy for Michele, whose life had had so much misery in it.

I don't know what possessed me, but I was suddenly struck by the notion that my parents would want a photo of me and Meryl, even though I wasn't a selfie person. I greatly admired and respected her film work and activism, but I had never felt a desperate need to interact with celebrities—certainly not to hero worship them or to collect souvenirs from them. I'd lived an oddly Forrest Gumpian life in that I had met many public figures, but I'd never asked for a photo with anyone. I approached her as she said goodbye to Michele and said,

"Ms. Streep, my parents would love it if I sent them a photo of us. Would you mind?"

At first, I thought she hadn't heard me. She barely glanced my way. Then, as she turned in another direction, I heard her say something to the effect of, "I wouldn't want to disappoint your *parents*," as she and her assistant stepped away through the crowd. I was steamrollered by humiliation and shame as I suddenly realized who she'd seen when she'd looked at me.

She was there to support and empower women like her, women who'd spent a lifetime sidestepping entitled men, powerful men, violent men. She saw *a man*. In a suit and tie. Fifty years old, short hair, tallish. Maybe even *pretending* the photo was for his *parents*. In a roomful of women. At a feminist event. *For women.*

This is who you are now. This is what people see when they look at you. Finally, your outsides match your insides and you need to start acting appropriately. You need to own that and understand what women see when they look at you, no matter how much of a supporter of women you are. They won't know that you lived some version of their reality for fifty years. You need to prove it every single day by the kind of man you are. You may be an ally, but you never belonged—and you don't belong now.

I desperately wished I could take back those ten seconds, not because I cared what she thought of me, but because *I cared what I thought of me.*

For the group photo, I stood hidden in the back row, only my grey-suited arm and half my face visible. I was feeling so mortified that I almost stayed backstage, but I didn't want to make a fuss, envisioning some production assistant helpfully pushing me out there, thinking I was just resisting because I was shy.

Afterward, I immediately met my good friend Sandy Garossino in the lobby, who had traveled to New York from Vancouver to attend the conference as my plus one. Sandy had accepted the news of my transition easily and wholeheartedly, expressing sadness only at what she wistfully referred to as losing me from "Team Estrogen," as I retreated from charter to honorary member. I was too ashamed to even tell her of my failed interaction with Meryl Streep. We walked through Central Park to the Upper East Side and spent the rest of the afternoon in the Guggenheim, mesmerized by compelling works of art while I contemplated my future as a wannabe good man.

After I returned from the summit in the middle of April, Dad's health deteriorated rapidly and without explanation and I debated whether to go to Calgary sooner than my planned visit the second week of May. Every time I called, Dad was sleeping and Mom and I didn't want to wake him. He called me twice, but our chats were brief because he was so fatigued. I was scheduled to attend the BC Book Prizes awards dinner at the end of the month because my book had been nominated, and I called my parents a few days before to discuss whether I should attend or travel to Calgary instead. Mom said she didn't imagine there was any need for me to come before May, but we couldn't know for certain. Dad came on the line after.

"Don't miss your dinner for me," he said weakly.

"Yeah, but I don't have to go if you need me."

"Your mom's taking good care of me. I'll see you when you come visit."

The dinner was a unique experience and although my book had been nominated for six different national awards that year, it wasn't selected as the winner of any. The recognitions were an honor, but I had no investment in winning; the chance to spend an enjoyable evening with my editor and the good friends who accompanied us was more meaningful to me. Still, I couldn't stop thinking of Dad.

The following Friday, as I was booking a flight for Calgary, Katherine called me. When I answered, she simply said, "He's gone." Then she told me the story of that morning: Dad had suffered a stroke in bed. Mom had been worried about his condition and had called an ambulance before the stroke, and while Katherine and the EMS attendants were there with her, Dad passed away, seemingly without pain.

I believe Dad knew he was done. A few days earlier, at Dad's request, Mom had called a priest over to administer the last rites, the Catholic sacrament intended to prepare a dying person's soul for death and beyond. Dad and Mom had talked earlier in the month about moving him to long-term care when a bed became available, but I don't think he'd believed he'd live that long. I thought of our conversation during his chemo appointment, how he never wanted to be a bother, especially to Mom. He was tired and had no fight left. He chose to drift away painlessly in his bed, making as little fuss as possible.

You take care of your family.

19

THE FATHER, THE SON
(May 2016)

———

AS I FLEW into Calgary, sporadic and random visions of my father swirled around me, a poignant tornado of memory of a life at once achingly long and breathtakingly brief.

I'm not ready to be here without him.

I'd always felt reassured, knowing he was on this earth somewhere with me, even during all those years we lived miles apart. All I'd ever wanted was for him to guide me, to teach me. And now he was gone. And I had so much left to learn.

I stayed with Mom at the condo, just the two of us, as family and friends gathered in town in advance of the funeral, each of us glad for the calm while Katherine prepared for Jennifer and the kids to fill her house in a few days. I'd booked a one-way ticket, unsure of how Mom would be and what she might need me to do in the coming days or weeks. Her comfort level with the computer was low and Dad had handled almost all the condo chores, from igniting the fireplace pilot light to organizing the storage locker for easy access to their golf clubs. I thought about how she'd been two years older than him, a fact that gave her great pleasure; she'd often tell friends and family how she'd bagged a younger man as Dad sat back, smiling shyly.

As a devout, lifelong Catholic, Dad wished to have a full funeral Mass at St. James, the church our family had attended for more than forty years. St. James had been Dad's church, where he'd served for years as a lay minister and each of us kids had been given our various sacraments as we grew up. By Tuesday we learned the funeral could be that Friday—the thirteenth—and we quickly set about making arrangements.

I'd grown distant from the church in my late teens, much to Dad's sadness. It was only as an adult that I found the courage to stop attending Mass; as a child, if I had ever said, "I'm not going to Mass this week," I would have been met with, "Are you sick?" for that was the only acceptable excuse other than travel, which apparently was treated as a special exception. Dad presented a good argument, reasonable and calm as always, when we would talk about my lapse in faith. I never had the heart to tell him that it couldn't accurately be called a lapse since I'd never bought into Christianity from the start.

"Dad, I just don't feel anything," I told him one day when I was about twenty.

"But you go to Mass to be with other people," he'd explain.

"But what if *they* aren't feeling it, either? Then we're all just sitting there, a bunch of lost souls."

"You go there to be closer to God, if even for an hour out of your week."

"I feel way closer to God on my long Sunday run than I do sitting in church with a bunch of hypocrites, Dad." As a marathon runner, I could spend an hour or two running around the reservoir, lost in my own thoughts and appreciation of nature. Surely, that could be my religion.

"What do you mean, hypocrites?" he asked, with curiosity, not rancor.

"I see what we all do during the week, the way we treat people, each other, then we all come back here and act like we're so good and devout."

"Did you ever think that maybe the others need *you* at church? Need your faith to help them be stronger?" I laughed out loud.

"Me? I don't think so." I thought about what the church would think of me or do with me if they ever knew my secret—if they found out I was the lost little sheep that I knew myself to be as a transgender person. "I don't think my being there does anything for anyone."

"It helps me," he said quietly.

"Oh."

After that, I still ran on Sundays instead of going to church, but I made a point of sitting with Dad at the kitchen table, talking about his faith and his view of religion when we were alone in the house. I took several religious studies courses at university and we'd debate the merits and downfalls of different world religions over coffee. His faith was so strong, never showy, and I respected that a great deal.

Mom exuded a calm that I'm sure masked pure exhaustion during the week leading up to the funeral. She had barely slept that last month as Dad deteriorated, worrying about him falling if he got up in the night. She began to sleep better, but their king-size bed developed a squeak the first week without him in it balancing her weight, a metaphor neither of us acknowledged aloud but I sensed we were both aware of. I firmed up her side of the bed frame with a four-by-four block of wood that seemed to fix the problem, and she slept well for the first time in months. I saw Mom not as the intimidating force of will I knew growing up, but rather as an elderly, bereaved widow, lost without Dad. She seemed happy to let me take over many of the arrangements: notify people, check in with banks and insurance companies, deal with the funeral home, write the obituary, and arrange for us to see Dad one last time before he was cremated. I threw myself into these tasks, grateful for something to do, and Friday arrived in a blur.

Katherine hosted our relatives for a buffet dinner the night before the funeral, a wake of sorts that brought together many of Dad's Calgary and Saskatchewan kin—including my uncle, one of Dad's two remaining siblings of seven. Dad's twin sister Josephine had passed away the year before he did. Close friends of my parents and family—all of whom I'd known since I was born—filled the house with stories and more than a few tears.

I'd wanted my dad to live for many more years because I loved him dearly, but I'd also selfishly hoped to postpone the awkwardness of coming out to so many people—many of whom I hadn't seen for decades and likely never would again—at his funeral. Grateful that I'd moved beyond those in-between days where I'd felt more labradoodle than male or female, I steeled myself for the weirdness I expected from some of my older, rural cousins, aunts, and uncles—the ones I'd often referred to as the "Conservative Party of Canada wing" of the family—who had little or no exposure to LGBTQ people. I avoided talking about myself as much as possible, preferring to focus on asking them questions about their memories of Dad and listening to stories of him I hadn't heard before. In the time-honored Shenher tradition of elephant avoidance, dating back to the days of my grandmother's observations of my gender incongruence, no one mentioned my changed appearance.

I recognized I now resided firmly in the "no more fucks to give" stage of transitioning and my only real concern was for my family and honoring Dad. The vast majority of my cousins were very kind to me and we reminisced fondly about Dad and our summer adventures on our uncles' farms as teenagers. The worst reaction I received was being ignored by one couple. My aunts and uncles were polite to me, if not entirely comfortable, and the two days around the funeral passed without incident.

On Friday morning, Jake, Katherine, and I gathered with our families at Mom's condo. There was an expectant feeling in the air as my siblings and I prepared our own parts of the eulogy. Over breakfast that morning, Mom and I shared that all we both really wanted was to get this day over with; we were each worn out by the emotion of the week.

The fourteen of us inspected each other as we prepared to walk out to the limo. Jake approached me, each of us in a navy suit. He silently reached for my tie and tightened and straightened it with a crisp tug and a final pat, surprising me and causing my throat to catch with emotion. It was just the kind of thing Dad would've done. I gave him a nod and we rallied the gang to send Dad off.

Father Mike greeted Mom as we walked into the church's large meeting hall before the service and Mom introduced Katherine and me as a committee of church ladies busily laid out sandwiches and dessert for after the service. A short, bald, rotund French Canadian of about sixty, Father Mike both resembled and sounded like the love child of Nathan Lane and Truman Capote. He eyed me quizzically for a moment, repeating my name several times, as if trying to place me. "Lori, Lori, Lori," he nodded, as he held my hand in his. Turning to my mother, he said, "He is your grandson, *non?*"

"No, this is my son, Father," Mom said firmly. I fought to contain my smile; I was so proud of my mom. He frowned, unable to process the contradictions of a baby-faced, slim, fit, greying man in a navy suit with a mature voice—I hadn't grown any facial hair yet.

"He is so young," he gushed, still clutching my hand in his sweaty mitt. He forced himself to stop staring at me.

"I must get ready for Mass," he said, and kissed Mom on the cheek and scurried away.

I hadn't been in a Catholic church in well over twenty years. I was very familiar with the Church's stance on LGBTQ people and its declaration that our children were illegitimate; this, coupled with the abysmal way the Church had handled sexual assault cases where priests had abused children, young staff, and parishioners—male and female—had dealt a final blow to my almost nonexistent faith in my early twenties. There had never been a place for me in the Catholic Church, and I remembered that suddenly. The Church had never bothered to *know* queer Catholics, and I'd been no exception.

My siblings and I stood around the lectern, and Katherine took her turn first. After she finished speaking, I stepped to the mic and peered out over the rows of pews. I realized that in all the years of attending Sunday Mass, plus confession, funerals, weddings, and Holy Thursday and Good Friday services, I'd never addressed the congregation, never stood looking out from that vantage point. Later, we would agree there were over three hundred people—friends, family, fellow teachers, and so many students whose lives he'd touched—there to honor Dad, whom everyone knew simply as "Joe." The pews were filled with people sniffing back tears, each lost in their own unique memories of him.

I cleared my throat and spoke, my voice loud, steady, clear—a voice that failed to waver throughout the entire story I told. I began with this:

"My father was the best man I will ever know."

20

LIFE AS A MAN

(2016–2018)

MY FIRST TWO years of transitioning played out like a second puberty, but instead of angst and depression, this one was defined by excitement—over physical changes such as facial hair, a deepening voice, and increased musculature—and newfound confidence.

All teens believe that no one before them has experienced what they're experiencing; that they alone see, feel, and agonize over the world with a depth of loneliness and pathos no one can possibly understand. It wasn't until I transitioned that I realized I had been stuck in the tortured mind-set of a sixteen-year-old boy for much of my life, and living with PTSD hadn't helped. I had been volatile, quick-tempered, and triggered by every incident I perceived as unfair during my first adolescence; it marked a point when the rainstorm first broke, soaking me in resignation to a reality that I was female and there was nothing I could do to change it. As a preadolescent, I had not yet experienced hopelessness. Through puberty and beyond, I lived it.

My mind began to take a different shape as I entered the third year of my transition. I felt the beginnings of a maturation—not just physical, but emotional, social, intellectual. I'd always been a joker, as quick with a self-deprecating quip as I was to dole out a dig in jest directed at someone else. I suspect people found me funny, but I could never be sure. People laughed and commented on my sense of humor, but the more astute likely sniffed out insecurity and an unconscious desire to keep the conversation on a superficial level. My policing career prevented me from growing away from this habit and though I was far from the worst offender, I stewed in my work's sitcom-laugh-track atmosphere, honing my craft.

Police officers are notoriously hard on each other and tease colleagues mercilessly—perversely, they work even harder at it the more they like or admire their target. While female police officers face sexual assault and harassment, male police officers endure never-ending hypermasculine taunting and the way they've been socialized to never show weakness makes it impossible for them to ask their tormenters to cut it out. Each day working with a police squad is accompanied by a three-beat drum track playing continuously in the background to emphasize the jokes. *Ba-dum-tss! Ba-dum-tss! Ba-dum-tss!* All. Day. Long. Right after you hear someone assign the blessing, "he's a good cop," you'll hear the benediction: "he's hilarious." The humor is lowbrow and uncomplicated; those who excel at it are revered.

I had failed to move beyond that dissatisfied teen boy until now. I knew how to turn the mind-set off and on; when I found myself in more mature crowds or situations I was able to act appropriately, but anxiety or nervousness often brought out the quips and pushed my deeper thoughts or observations into the background. When I found myself in conflicts, my feeling of being unfairly treated raged to the surface, sucking all reason and wisdom from my position. This was especially apparent in my marriage and it was Jennifer who first observed that I behaved like a sixteen-year-old boy during arguments with her—just what every guy wants to hear from his wife.

Just as I had after my doomed interaction with Meryl Streep, I sensed my behavior around women needed to change. No longer could I get away with the comments or language that might have been witty coming from another female. I have always been too quick with advice for others—intended to help, but likely perceived as controlling or overly corrective. Early in my transition, I realized this habit now came across as "mansplaining"—that condescending male habit of telling women what something is or how to do it when said women are fully aware already, thank you very much. I come from a long line of interrupters. As a female, my ways didn't seem offensive, but as a man, I've had to check myself and my urge to talk over others or jump in with my point and I constantly have to remind myself that the words of others are every bit as—or more—valid than my own. It has surprised me to notice that as a visible man, my words do seem to matter to others more; I'm invited to weigh in publicly more, and my opinion is sought out more often. The contrast is striking and only serves to illuminate all the ways women's views are suppressed or ignored in our world.

As a visible man, I felt I needed to up my appropriateness game, especially with women. Female friends have said they think I may be overly critical of myself. They notice more of a change in themselves than in me; one said she found herself more prone to interpreting me differently as a man and suggested she may actually be watching for behavior she never would have considered problematic before. Another has said she now finds me more attentive and a better listener, but also prone to moments of impatience, which I can certainly see. I do feel I've grown more reserved in my interactions, but I'd like to think I've remained openhearted and share as much as I always have.

I'm continually finding my way and I still sometimes forget I'm an older middle-aged man, not that teenaged boy. In the first, frenetic, scandal-driven weeks of the #MeToo movement of fall 2017, I was finishing up at my massage therapist's office when the administrative assistant—a very attractive, friendly, twenty-something woman who books my weekly appointments—called out to me, asking if I wanted to book another appointment. I had been thinking I had several advance appointments already booked and could hold off a week, but when I glanced over and saw it was she who'd called to me, I paused and said, "Well, maybe if it gives me the chance to talk with you," with a smile. I thought I was being charming and cute—until I saw the look of disappointment flash across her face. *I've made her uncomfortable.* I felt no better than a cat-caller on the street. I had become part of the problem.

"I'm so sorry," I said, as I walked to her desk. "I only said that because you're so pleasant to talk with and you always help me get a good appointment time. Please accept my apology."

"Oh, it's fine, Lorimer," she said, flushed, "Really."

"Well, I don't think it is and I am truly sorry. It won't happen again," I said, opening my phone calendar. "How about something around the twentieth?" I realized I was still covering new territory after a half century of watching how men went through the world. Modeling the good examples of male behavior that I'd witnessed over a lifetime and tossing out the bad should have been obvious and easy, but it actually required awareness and effort.

I notice small changes in my life now that I'm walking through the world as a man, but my observations are unscientific, based strictly on anecdotal information from my own experiences and those of my female friends. I give lone women a wider berth when I pass them on my morning run in the forest, careful not to come too close or startle them if I'm coming up from behind. Often, when our paths cross, women won't say hello or meet my gaze and I suspect it's for safety; they likely don't want to engage with a strange man when they're alone and vulnerable. At first, I'd say hello as I had always done, but when I saw that many women appeared uncomfortable or frightened, I stopped. If I'm walking the dog after dark, I'll cross to the other side of the street rather than come up on a woman from behind. Perhaps this is paternalistic, but I was once someone who should have been afraid.

Before I transitioned, even as a teen and young adult, I'd walk alone in the dark at night, run through all sorts of very isolated and dark places by myself, forgetting that to a human predator, I was a female, no matter how I felt in my head. Sure, I had police and martial arts training, but it's a miracle no one ever attacked or threatened me as I ran in wooded areas in the early morning or late evening; most women runners I know have at least one story of a tense or harassing encounter, but I have none, presumably because of good luck, a taller build, and an androgynous look in my running gear and hat.

I find that people now call me "sir" all the time on the phone and in service and professional situations—far more often than I was ever called "ma'am." This one is more difficult to unpack. Women in my life generally hate being called "ma'am," so people may hesitate to say it. But my gender was also sometimes questionable at first glance and people may have chosen not to call me anything for fear of getting it wrong. However, I still feel an indisputable difference in how I am treated by strangers. As an over-fifty white man, I can say with certainty that people treat me with far greater respect as a visible male than they ever did when I was visibly female.

To bastardize the notorious Donald Rumsfeld-ism, I could never have known all the unknowns I didn't know before, but I sure know them now that I know them. I find the difference in the way I'm treated unnerving at best, unacceptable and sad at worst. A female friend recently dejectedly suggested that I should just accept the way the world is and enjoy this new privilege, but that feels disingenuous and so disrespectful of the experiences of women all over the world.

I can't take pleasure in this "respect" knowing that not everyone enjoys such preferential treatment. Just as I have my entire life, I point out injustice whenever and wherever I have the opportunity to. If every man called out sexism when he saw it and stood up to violence against women, it would end. It doesn't need to be a direct or physical challenge; often a well-placed "c'mon, man" is all it takes to alert badly behaving men that the male audience they're misguidedly trying to prove themselves to isn't impressed.

As a kid, I internalized every message intended for boys and young men, even though no one was looking for me to behave like one. I knew who and what I was; those messages meant for girls were confusing and somewhat lost on me while those intended for boys loomed as an unattainable standard. Looking back, I can see now that these behavioral blueprints were destined to leave all men—cisgender as well as transgender—miserable and filled with shame and inadequacy.

Although I rage at the world a little less now than I did before transitioning, I am deeply dismayed at the attitudes of some politicians, religious extremists, and trans-exclusionary radical feminists who deny the legitimacy of the existence of trans and gender nonconforming folks. The progress that LGBTQ people have enjoyed in recent years has suffered from a significant right-wing backlash, accompanied by higher numbers of murders of transgender people—predominantly trans women of color—and assaults against many in the LGBTQ community in North America and around the world.

The religious far right has led a push for anti-LGBTQ legislation in the US, hand in hand with the Trump administration's rollbacks of Obama-era protections in areas such as military service, marriage equality, and basic human rights protections. Canada's Bill C-16, which extends the Canadian Human Rights Act to include protections for gender identity and expression, passed successfully in 2017, but not without significant opposition from Conservative members of Parliament such as Marilyn Gladu, the member for Sarnia-Lambton, Ontario, who expressed concern that "there are many people in this country who do not believe that a transgendered [sic] lifestyle is God's plan or that it is medically beneficial." Trans-exclusionary radical feminists joined with conservatives to testify against Bill C-16, odd bedfellows who share the beliefs that "trans women aren't real women" and that trans bodies and lives aren't legitimate or worthy of protection.

I'm not a women's studies scholar, and many of these terms and philosophies are fluid and ever-changing, but my beliefs align with what I've come to know as third-wave feminism, which focuses on diversity, civil rights, inclusion, and intersectionality of gender, color, race, and class. The writing on this wave of feminism by Kimberlé Williams Crenshaw and Rebecca Walker led me to believe it is a compassionate philosophy that accommodates different experiences of gender, including those of trans women. This framework differs significantly from the one used by self-styled "gender-critical feminists," known more widely as trans-exclusionary radical feminists, or TERFs, who believe that only "women-born women," or cisgender women, can call themselves women and be included in women-only spaces—that only women who have been born, socialized, and lived their entire lives as women can know the true female experience of oppression and misogyny.

Trans-exclusionary radical feminists believe that transgender women—assigned male at birth and presumably raised with all the privilege and experience of males in society before transitioning—cannot possibly identify with what it means to be female in a misogynist society, and this forms their grounds for excluding trans women from "women-born-women only" spaces. While I accept their right to their own opinions, the cruelty and hatred of trans-exclusionary radical feminists is simply incompatible with empathy and compassion.

I strive to live with empathy and compassion myself. I try to begin at home, striving to be an attentive partner to Jennifer and a nonjudgmental parent to our children, but I know I will always be flawed and far from perfect. My experience as a transgender man is not the definitive one; there is diversity within every marginalized group and all individuals carry their own unique history. I see my new life as an opportunity to coach and teach in new ways, including my role as a parent to three amazing kids.

I feel incredibly fortunate to say that I made it through, that I am blessed with a beautiful family and an amazing life. I did my best with the tools I had. I've managed to regain everything I thought I had lost—writing, relationships with family, my love of basketball, and a bright future. My parents did the best they could in an era when few were aware that there could be transgender children in the world. My hope is that parents in this new world of information and resources can guide and support their children who may be struggling—whatever their issue—to reach their fullest potential, without shame, without judgment, and with boundless unconditional love.

EPILOGUE

SO MANY YEARS have passed since that last full-court women's league basketball game. After that night, I walked away from basketball, preferring the occasional clandestine shooting session alone, late at night or in the early morning hours in the VPD gymnasium downtown, savoring a purity where it was just me, the ball, and the court. If anyone ever walked in—which was rare—I promptly left, preferring to safeguard those moments of solitude, alone with my game.

One recent summer's evening, I began to search online, looking for an over-fifty men's basketball league or drop-in session. I found nothing but an Osteofit for seniors class. I vowed to keep looking as the kids called me to come out and play with them.

I squinted into the setting sun that silhouetted the basketball hoop, casting a long shadow across the outdoor court. My teen sons and I were joined by two other boys in a pickup game against another adult and four teens, and the pace was fierce. My daughter prefers to create quirky passing games that we play together one-on-one, so she happily watched from the sidelines, despite our exhortations to join in. Jennifer relished a blissfully quiet hour or two with the house to herself.

I felt buoyant sprinting up and down the court; I passed to my boys, set picks for them, encouraged them to fight through screens on defense. The other man and I took it easy on the kids, although at twenty years younger than me, he was far more of a threat.

Playing with my family beside me, I see a future for all of us. This game brings me joy again, now that I have finally found my place within it.

This. This is enough, making the most of the gifts I have, forging on.

ACKNOWLEDGMENTS

IF I HAD known all the wonderful ways my world would open up, I would have found a way to transition when I first learned it was possible all those many years ago. Leaving policing, writing my first book, transitioning, completing a graduate degree—each of these events has expanded my world and introduced me to incredible people and experiences.

One of those people is Sandy Garossino, who I like to think of as my fairy god-sister. Sandy has quietly and not-so-quietly championed me and my work since we met in 2015 and she moderated my first book launch. She has introduced me to worlds that would not have been open to me without her and her equally generous partner, Ravi Sidhoo. I'm so grateful for the experiences I have had through them and their many contacts and for those opportunities that I'm not even aware came through their benevolence. I'm proud to call them my friends.

I'm deeply grateful to Angel and Paul Murphy, the dedicated young couple behind the terrific Words on the Water Campbell River Writers' Festival. At the 2016 festival, I read an early draft of my stories of standing in the kindergarten washroom line and bra shopping with my mom. The crowd and my fellow writers—Wayne Grady, Eve Joseph, Grant Lawrence, Tracey Lindberg, Lucia Misch, Timothy Taylor, and John Vaillant—generously offered me their feedback and encouragement. This book arose from their mentorship that weekend.

I don't feel I could have written this book without standing on the shoulders of so many transgender writers, activists, and allies and their important work. The work of Ali Blythe, Jennifer Finney Boylan, Ivan Coyote, Aaron Devor, Aydian Dowling, Leslie Feinberg, Jamison Green, Christine Jorgensen, Janet Mock, Parker Molloy, Jan Morris, Renée Richards, Julia Serano, Vivek Shraya, Rae Spoon, and so many others has educated me, moved me to laughter and tears, and helped me feel so much less alone. Their courage became mine; the hope they give others saves lives.

To my wonderful classmates, instructors, and the staff at Royal Roads University who made those early days of graduate studies—which coincided with the start of my transition—so easy for me, I thank you. My time there was truly life changing in so many ways.

To all of my medical practitioners—Dr. Cameron Bowman, Dr. Marshall Dahl, Dr. Alison MacInnes, Dr. Joanne MacKinnon, Dr. Gail Knudson, Dr. Melady Preece, Dr. Oliver Robinow, and Dr. Ralph Strother—who have helped me connect with my physical self; I hope you know your work is life-saving for so many people.

Deep gratitude to Michael Levine, Damon D'Oliveira, Jen Richards, and Clement Virgo, whose efforts to bring these stories to life beyond the page continue. Rob Sanders, Nancy

Flight, Andrea Damiani, Jennifer Gauthier, Lara LeMoal, Nayeli Jimenez, Will Brown, Josh Oliveira, Stefania Alexandru, and all the hardworking people at Greystone Books have been so patient with me to make my books possible. A special thank-you to Alice Fleerackers, who has fielded the good, bad, and truly bizarre of requests for my time, and to her successor Megan Jones, who now conducts that circus. Big thanks to Alex Kapitan, intrepid copy editor who helped me avoid the many landmines one can step on when navigating the fields of gender and sex. And to my editor Jennifer Croll, thank you for your patience, your keen eye, and your humor throughout this process. You have made it as painless as possible and I'm grateful to you.

Writing a memoir is a tricky business, often hardest on those closest to the author. To my mother, brother, and sister, thank you for your love and patience with a process where I examined our upbringing under a microscope. To every one of my old friends, I'm so honored to not have lost a single one of you in this process, and to the many new ones I've made on this journey: thank you.

I'm continually astounded by and grateful to my partner Jennifer, who models kindness, love, and a search for meaning every day. I'm so grateful for our three beautiful children and for their acceptance of my drive to tell deeply personal stories in the hope it may help others who struggle. I could not feel prouder of them all. Their love sustains me.